Living Values Education Activities for Children Ages 8–14, Book 1

DEVELOPED AND WRITTEN BY

Diane G. Tillman

WITH ADDITIONAL ACTIVITIES AND STORIES FROM

Batool Arjomand
Pilar Quera Colomina
Lamia El-Dajani
Linda Heppenstall
Sabine Levy
Ruth Liddle
John McConnel
Marcia Maria Lins de Medeiros
Ioanna Vasileiadou
Peter Williams
and other educators around the world

www.livingvalues.net

Tillman, Diane G.
   Living Values Education Activities for Children Ages 8–14, Book 1 / developed and written by Diane G. Tillman with additional stories and activities from Batool Arjomand . . . [et al].
   Includes bibliographical references
   ISBN: 9781731023407

Copyright © 2000–2018 Association for Living Values Education International

This is an update and expansion of the 2001 original book, *Living Values Activities for Children Ages 8–14*, published by Health Communications, Inc. The expanded version has two volumes, Book 1 and Book 2, and is published independently by the Association for Living Values Education International (ALIVE), a non-profit Swiss Association, through Kindle Direct Publishing.

ALIVE Address: Rue Adrien-Lachenal 20, 1207 Genève, Switzerland
For information about professional development workshops and LVE generally, please visit ALIVE's website at www.livingvalues.net.

The development and advancement of Living Values Education is overseen by the **Association for Living Values Education International** (ALIVE), a non-profit-making association of organizations around the world concerned with values education. ALIVE groups together national bodies promoting the use of the Living Values Education Approach and is an independent organization that does not have any particular or exclusive religious, political or national affiliation or interest. The development and implementation of Living Values Education has been supported over the years by a number of organizations, including UNESCO, governmental bodies, foundations, community groups and individuals. LVE continues to be part of the global movement for a culture of peace following the United Nations International Decade for a Culture of Peace and Non-violence for the Children of the World.

All rights reserved. This book is a resource for values-based educational purposes. No part of this publication may be reproduced, including reproduction within other materials, without prior written permission of the publisher.

Graphic design of cover by David Warrick Jones
Cover image of globe with children purchased from Shutterstock
Inside artwork by I Wayan Agus Aristana, Media Productions, Karuna Bali Foundation, Ubud, Bali
Former editors: Carol Gill and Allison Janse

Living Values Education Activities for Children Ages 8–14, Book 1

CONTENTS

A note from the author	1

Setting the Context 3

The Need for Values and Values Education	3
LVE's Purpose and Aims	4
The Living Values Education Approach	5
LVE Resource Materials	7
The Living Values Education Series	8
Materials for Young People At Risk	10
Living Green Values	13
LVE Distance for Adults, Families and Study Groups	13
Extend and Variety of Use … and some of LVE's partners in different countries	14
History of Living Values Education	16
Results — Reports, Evaluations and Research	18
A Few Observations and Stories	18
Evaluations and Research Results	22
Results in a Refugee Camp and with Street Children	26
Results with LVE's Drug Rehabilitation Program	27

Exploring and Developing Values 29

Teaching Values	29
The Developing Values Schematic — The LVE Method	30
Values-based Atmosphere	32
Components of Living Values Education Activities Units	36
Bringing in the Values of Your Culture	42
Making Values Education a Practical Reality	42
Implementation Details	44

Living Values Education Activities for Children Ages 8–14, Book 1

Incorporating Values into the Existing Curriculum	46
Share Your Values Creations with the World!	48

Values Units . . .

*Peace I . Respect I . Love and Caring . Tolerance . Honesty . Happiness
Responsibility . Simplicity and Caring for our Earth and Her Oceans*

Unit One: Peace I — 50

Reflection Points		51
Goals and Objectives		52
Peace I Lesson 1	Imagining a Peaceful World	54
Peace I Lesson 2	Mind Mapping Peace and Peacelessness	56
Peace I Lesson 3	If We Were All Peaceful	57
Relax/Focus	Physical Relaxation Exercise	57
Peace I Lesson 4	Baking a Peace Cake	58
Peace I Lesson 5	A Special Place	59
Relax/Focus	Peace Relaxation Exercise	60
Peace I Lesson 6	Increasing Peace at School	60
Peace I Lesson 7	Bullying No More — Creating Assertive and Benevolent-Assertive Responses	62
Note to Educator	Conflict Resolution Process	67
Peace I Lesson 8	Introducing Conflict Resolution	69
Rap Song	Cool Off	71
Peace I Lesson 9	Conflict Resolution Continues: What We Like and Don't Like — Under the Anger	72
Relax/Focus	Peaceful Star Relaxation/Focusing Exercise	73
Peace I Lesson 10	Listening as Part of Conflict Resolution	73
Options	A Peace Circle and/or a Peace Club	75
Peace I Lesson 11	Conflict Resolution — Peers as Mediators	76
Peace I Lesson 12	Bullying No More — Peer Intervention	77
Peace I Lesson 13	Creating Verbal Stories — Growing Peace or Conflict	80
Peace I Lesson 14	Collaborative Painting	81

Additional Peace Lessons and Activities

Peace I Lesson 15	For Ages 8 and 9: Dove Game	82

Unit Two: Respect I — 85

Reflection Points		86
Goals and Objectives		87
Respect I Lesson 1	Respect, Disrespect and Qualities	88
Respect I Lesson 2	Feeling Disrespected — and My Advice about How People Should Treat Others	91
Relax/Focus	Flowers of Respect Relaxation/Focusing Exercise	93
Respect I Lesson 3	Talking to Myself and the "It's okay to make a mistake" Rule	94
Respect I Lesson 4	Colors of Respect and Disrespect — and Mobiles	95
Respect I Lesson 5	The Colors of Respect — Princes and Princesses	97
Relax/Focus	Star of Respect Relaxation/Focusing Exercise	98
Respect I Lesson 6	The Colors of Respect — and Discrimination	98
Respect I Lesson 7	The Colors of Respect and Disrespect — Creative Expression	100
Respect I Lesson 8	What stories about respect would you like to share?	100
Respect I Lesson 9	Greetings of the World	101
Respect I Lesson 10	Conflict Resolution and Listening with Respect	101
Respect I Lesson 11	Strategies to Stop Conflict	102
Respect I Lesson 11B	For Ages 11 to 14: Bullying No More — The Art of Distraction	104
Respect I Lesson 11C	For Ages 11 to 14: Bullying No More — Keeping Your Head in the Face of Danger	106
Respect I Lesson 12	Different Ways of Giving Respect	108
Respect I Lesson 13	Our Qualities	109

Additional Respect Lessons

Respect I Lesson 13	Paint a Picture with a Friend in Another Country	109
Respect I Lesson 14	Health — Respect is Taking Care of Your Body	110

Unit Three: Love and Caring — 112

Reflection Points		113
Goals and Objectives		114
Song	Someday	115
Love Lesson 1	Imagining a Loving World	116
Love Lesson 2	Story — The Four Thrones	117

Story	The Four Thrones	117
Love Lesson 3	Mind Mapping a Loving World and a Non-Loving World	119
Relax/Focus	Sending Love Relaxation/Focusing Exercise	120
Love Lesson 4	Stories about Caring	121
Love Lesson 5	Words of the Heart	122
Love Lesson 6	Drug Prevention: Selling Drugs — Caring or Selfishness?	123
Story	Joe Got Fooled	123
Love Lesson 7	I Am Lovable and Capable	126
Relax/Focus	I am Lovable and Capable Relaxation Exercise	127
Love Lesson 8	Kindness to the Self	128
Love Lesson 9	Love is Understanding	129
Love Lesson 10	Conflict Resolution and the Effect of a Caring Attitude	130
Love Lesson 11	Love is Caring, Love is Kindness	130
Love Lesson 12	A Trustworthy Friend	132
Love Lesson 13	Creating a Story	133
Love Lesson 14	A Mural	134

Additional Love and Caring Lessons

Love Lesson 15	Project	134
Love Lesson 16	Show and Tell	135
Love Lesson 17	Kinds of Love	135
Love Lesson 18	Drug Prevention: Drug Sellers Pretend to Be Nice at First	136
Story	Drug Sellers Use Kids Like Slaves	136

Unit Four: Tolerance 140

Reflection Points		142
Goals and Objectives		142
Tolerance Lesson 1	Divisive or Inclusive?	144
Story	The Shorties and the Tallies	144
Tolerance Lesson 2	Real Stories	147
Tolerance Lesson 3	Moving Like You	148
Tolerance Lessons 4 - 8	A Rainbow of Cultures	148
Note to Educator	Cultivating a Spirit of Tolerance	151

Tolerance Lesson 9	A Collage of Tolerance, A Map of Intolerance	151
Tolerance Lesson 10	Discrimination	152
Tolerance Lesson 11	A Pretend Immigration	153
Tolerance Lesson 12	Disarming Prejudice	154
Tolerance Lesson 13	The Key	156
Tolerance Lesson 14	Tolerating Difficulties	156

Additional Tolerance Lessons and Activities

Tolerance Lesson 15	An Ending Note	158
Tolerance Lesson 16	Walking in Your Shoes	158

Unit Five: Honesty   160

Reflection Points		161
Goals and Objectives		162
Honesty Lesson 1	Honesty and Trust	163
Story	The Emperor and the Flower Seeds	164
Honesty Lesson 2	Thinking about Corruption — Reflecting on Integrity	167
Honesty Lesson 3	Mind Mapping Honesty and Dishonesty	168
Honesty Lesson 4	An Honest Heart Benefits Many	169
Honesty Lesson 5	For Ages 12 to 14: Corruption Versus Honesty	170
Honesty Lesson 6	Lying Versus One Minute of Courage	171
Honesty Lesson 7	Films About Honesty	173
Honesty Lesson 8	Trust	173
Honesty Lesson 9	Pressure to be Dishonest	175
Story	The Miner and the Prince	175
Honesty Lesson 10	Lost and Found — and Consequence Maps	177
Honesty Lesson 11	In the Guise of Honesty	179
Honesty Lesson 12	Honesty and Friendship	180

Unit Six: Happiness   181

Reflection Points		182
Goals and Objectives		182
Happiness Lesson 1	Happiness	184
Happiness Lesson 2	Giving Happiness and Unhappiness	185
Happiness Lesson 3	Words that Give Happiness and Pegasusses	188
Reflective Story	Pegasusses	189

Living Values Education Activities for Children Ages 8–14, Book 1

Happiness Lesson 4	Happiness is Sharing	190
Happiness Lesson 5	The Opposite of Happiness: Sadness and Depression	191
Relax/Focus	Taking Care of Me When I Feel Sad Relaxation/Focusing Exercise	193
Happiness Lesson 6	Encouraging or Discouraging Self-Talk	194
Happiness Lesson 7	Three Wishes	196
Happiness Lesson 8	Happiness at Home	197
Happiness Lesson 9	Quality	199
Happiness Lesson 10	Including and Excluding	199
Happiness Lesson 11	A Happiness Tree or a Giving Tree	200
Happiness Lesson 12	The Three Rings — Keeping Balance	201
Happiness Lesson 13	Enact Happiness	202

Additional Happiness Lessons and Activities

Happiness Lesson 14	More Secrets of Happiness	202
Community Project	Happiness Walk	203

Unit Seven: Responsibility 204

Reflection Points		205
Goals and Objectives		206
Responsibility Lesson 1	Trust Walk — and Advice	207
Responsibility Lesson 2	Mind Mapping Responsibility and Irresponsibility	208
Responsibility Lesson 3	For Ages 8 and 9: Mini Plays of "Right" and "Wrong" Ways of Doing Things	209
Responsibility Lesson 3	For Ages 10 to 14: Responsibility Is "Walking My Talk"	209
Responsibility Lesson 4	I Want Responsibility's Partner Value to Be . . .	211
Responsibility Lesson 5	Responsibilities in the Home	212
Responsibility Lesson 6	Sharing Tasks	214
Responsibility Lesson 7	The Right to Education—and My Responsibility	215
Responsibility Lesson 8	Global Responsibility and Making a Positive Difference	217
Responsibility Lesson 9	My Responsibilities	218
Responsibility Lesson 10	Taking Responsibility Makes Me a Good Friend	219
Responsibility Lesson 11	A Play	220
Responsibility Lesson 12	I Believe	221

Living Values Education Activities for Children Ages 8–14, Book 1

Additional Responsibility Lessons and Activities

Responsibility Lesson 13	A Program	221
Responsibility Lesson 14	For Ages 11 to 14: Rickshaw Girl	221
Responsibility Lesson 15	For Ages 12 to 14: Would I like to be more committed?	222
Responsibility Activity	Community Project	222
Responsibility Activity	Civic Functioning for Ages 13 and 14	223

Unit Eight: Simplicity and Caring for the Earth and Her Oceans 224

Reflection Points		226
Goals and Objectives		226
Simplicity Lesson 1	Simple Art	228
Simplicity Lesson 2	Learning from Indigenous Cultures	228
Simplicity Lesson 3	A Nature Walk	230
Simplicity Lesson 4	Simple Things in Life That Mean So Much	231
Simplicity Lesson 5	The Ocean	232
Story	Out in the Dinghy	232
Simplicity Lesson 6	How Trash Effects Marine Animals	237
Story	Circling the Seagull	237
Simplicity Lesson 7	Ocean Gyres	242
Story	Toxic Plastic Soup	242
Relax/Focus Exercise	Sending Peace to the Earth Exercise	246
Simplicity Lesson 8	The Ocean's Dead Zones	246
Story	We Can Make a Difference	247
Simplicity Lesson 9	One Thing Effects Many Things — Systems Thinking	251
Story	To the City Council!	251
Simplicity Lesson 10	The Exchange Between Trees and Humans	255
Story	Trees, Oxygen and Hope	256
Simplicity Lesson 11	Growing Organic and Being Vegetarian Effects the Earth and Ocean	259
Story	An Organic Garden	259
Simplicity Lesson 12	Reducing Our Carbon Footprint	262
Story	Carbon Footprints	263
Simplicity Lesson 13	What's one thing I can do to help the Earth?	267

Story	Living Green Values	267
Simplicity Lesson 14	Advertisements Try to Get You to Believe . . .	270
Simplicity Lesson 15	Freedom from Desires	272
Simplicity Lesson 16	Enjoying Simple Things	273
Simplicity Lesson 17	A Play	273

Additional Simplicity and Caring for the Earth and Her Oceans Lessons & Activities

Simplicity Lesson 18	The Precious Present	274
Simplicity Activity	Simplicity Challenge — Declutter	274

Appendix 276

Item 1: All Values	Mind Mapping	276
Item 2: Peace	Conflict Resolution Steps	278
Item 3: Respect	Story, Lilly the Leopard	279
Item 4: Respect	Story, Pillars of the Earth	281
Item 5: Respect	Story, Crazy Like a Fox	283
Item 6: Respect	Story for Ages 11 to 14: Samosas and Peace in the Face of Danger	286
Item 7: Happiness	Story, The Heart School	287
Item 8: Responsibility	Story, TC Wants a Dog	294
Item 9: All Values	Relaxation/Focusing Exercises	296
	Physical Relaxation/Focusing Exercise	296
	Peace Relaxation/Focusing Exercise	296
	Peaceful Star Relaxation/Focusing Exercise	297
	Flowers of Respect Relaxation/Focusing Exercise	297
	Star of Respect Relaxation/Focusing Exercise	298
	Sending Love Relaxation/Focusing Exercise	298
	I am Lovable and Capable Relaxation Exercise	298
	Taking Care of Me When I Feel Sad Relaxation Exercise	299
	Sending Peace to the Earth Relaxation Exercise	300

Cited Books and Songs 301

Acknowledgments 305

About the Author 307

Living Values Education Activities for Children Ages 8–14, Book 1

A note from the author

I have had the privilege of being involved with Living Values Education (LVE) for 22 years, writing educational resource books and traveling around the world to conduct workshops and seminars — at UNESCO, schools, universities, retreat centers and refugee camps. When I initially became involved with LVE, I focused on developing a program that would help all young people explore and develop values. I wanted to develop something that would involve and inspire marginalized youth and also act to challenge privileged youth to look beyond their usual circles. I was yet to deeply understand the importance of values or values education. Twenty-two years later, I now see the world through a values lens. I am honored to be part of the global LVE family as we continue to co-create LVE.

I've often felt devastated, as I'm sure you have, when reading of violence and atrocities toward children and adults, the continuing plight of women and children in many parts of our world, the misery of refugees, and the horrors of violence in so many countries around the globe. I believe nurturing and educating hearts and minds is an essential component in creating a sensible peaceful world of wellbeing for all.

A lack of basic education leaves young people incredibly vulnerable, apt to be taken advantage of and usually condemned to a life of poverty. They are susceptible to believing whatever those in authority tell them. For example, if you were a young person without an education and a powerful soldier handed you a rifle and offered wellbeing for you and your family if you killed…. Yet, in developed countries where there are functional education systems, thousands of young people have traveled to join radical groups. Many of these young people are marginalized and want to belong to a larger "family", to be in a place where their courage and qualities are admired. The first instance decries the lack of basic education, the second the lack of providing safe nurturing, supportive environments and educating hearts. The importance of Education for All and the development of a values-based learning environment as an integral part of values education cannot be overstated.

If we were to expand this view outward, we could ask how humanity became embroiled in a state of seemingly continuous violence. What are the anti-values that create violence and war? What are the values, attitudes and communication skills that create peace, equality, dignity, belonging and wellbeing for all? What do we want in our world?

What young people learn is later woven into the fabric of society. When education has positive values at its heart, and the resulting expression of them as its aim, we will create a better world for all. Values such as peace, love, respect, honesty, cooperation and freedom are the sustaining force of human society and progress.

Thank you for joining the Living Values Education family to help make a positive difference for children, educators, families, communities, and the world.

Diane G. Tillman

SETTING THE CONTEXT

Living Values Education is a global endeavor dedicated to nurturing and educating hearts as well as minds. LVE provides an approach, and tools, to help people connect with their own values and live them. During professional development workshops, educators are engaged in a process to empower them to create a caring values-based atmosphere in which young people are loved, valued, respected, understood and safe. Educators are asked to facilitate values activities about peace, respect, love and caring, tolerance, honesty, happiness, responsibility, simplicity, caring for the Earth and Her Oceans, cooperation, humility, compassion, freedom and unity to engage students in exploring and choosing their own personal values while developing intrapersonal and interpersonal skills to "live" those values. The sixteen values units in the updated Living Values Education Activities books include other related universal values such as kindness, fairness, determination, integrity, appreciation, diversity, gratitude, inclusion and social justice. Students soon become co-creators of a culture of peace and respect. A values-based learning community fosters positive relationships and quality education.

The Need for Values and Values Education

The values of peace, love, respect, honesty, cooperation and freedom create a social fabric of harmony and wellbeing. What would you like schools to be like? What would you like the world to be like? Reflect for a moment on the school or world you would like….

Children and youth grow toward their potential in quality learning environments with a culture of peace and respect. Relatively few young people have such a values-based learning atmosphere. A culture of judging, blaming and disrespect is often closer to the norm and is frequently mixed with varying levels of bullying, discrimination, social problems and violence.

The challenge of helping children and youth acquire values is no longer as simple as it was decades ago when being a good role model and relating moral stories was usually sufficient. Violent movies and video games glorify violence and desensitize youth to the effect of such actions. Youth see people who display greed, arrogance and negative behavior rewarded with admiration and status. Young people are increasingly affected by bullying, social problems, violence and a lack of respect for each other and the world around them. Social media often negatively impacts teens who are already emotionally vulnerable. Cyberbullying and sexting have been linked to the increase in the suicide rate of pre-teens and teens. Marginalized and troubled young people rarely achieve their potential without quality education. Feelings of inadequacy, hurt and anger often spiral downward and meanness, bullying, drug use, drop-out rates, crime and suicide increase.

As educators, facilitators and parents, there are many things we can do to reserve this downward trend and create wellbeing … for young people and our world. As Aristotle said, "Educating the mind without educating the heart is no education at all."

LVE's Purpose and Aims

The purpose and aims of Living Values Education were created by twenty educators from around the world when they gathered at UNICEF's headquarters in New York in August of 1996. The purpose remains unchanged. The aims have been slightly augmented as has our experience and understanding since that time.

LVE's purpose is to provide guiding principles and tools for the development of the whole person, recognizing that the individual is comprised of physical, intellectual, emotional, and spiritual dimensions.

The aims are:
- To help individuals think about and reflect on different values and the practical implications of expressing them in relation to themselves, others, the community, and the world at large;
- To deepen knowledge, understanding, motivation, and responsibility with regard to making positive personal and social choices;
- To invite and inspire individuals to explore, experience, express and choose their own personal, social, moral, and spiritual values and be aware of practical methods for developing and deepening them; and
- To encourage and support educators and caregivers to look at education as providing students with a philosophy of living, thereby facilitating their overall

growth, development, and choices so they may integrate themselves into the community with respect, confidence, and purpose.

The Living Values Education Approach

After ten years of implementing Living Values Education, a team of LVE leaders around the world gathered together to describe what they felt LVE was … and had become.

Vision Statement

Living Values Education is a way of conceptualizing education that promotes the development of values-based learning communities and places the search for meaning and purpose at the heart of education. LVE emphasizes the worth and integrity of each person involved in the provision of education, in the home, school and community. In fostering quality education, LVE supports the overall development of the individual and a culture of positive values in each society and throughout the world, believing that education is a purposeful activity designed to help humanity flourish.

Core Principles

Living Values Education is based on the following core principles:

On the learning and teaching environment

1. When positive values and the search for meaning and purpose are placed at the heart of learning and teaching, education itself is valued.
2. Learning is especially enhanced when occurring within a values-based learning community, where values are imparted through quality teaching, and learners discern the consequences, for themselves, others and the world at large, of actions that are and are not based on values.
3. In making a values-based learning environment possible, educators not only require appropriate quality teacher education and ongoing professional development, they also need to be valued, nurtured and cared for within the learning community.
4. Within the values-based learning community, positive relationships develop out of the care that all involved have for each other.

On the teaching of values

5. The development of a values-based learning environment is an integral part of values education, not an optional extra.
6. Values education is not only a subject on the curriculum. Primarily it is pedagogy; an educational philosophy and practice that inspires and develops positive values in the classroom. Values-based teaching and guided reflection support the process of learning as a meaning-making process, contributing to the development of critical thinking, imagination, understanding, self-awareness, intrapersonal and interpersonal skills and consideration of others.
7. Effective values educators are aware of their own thoughts, feelings, attitudes and behavior and sensitive to the impact these have on others.
8. A first step in values education is for teachers to develop a clear and accurate perception of their own attitudes, behavior and emotional literacy as an aid to living their own values. They may then help themselves and encourage others to draw on the best of their own personal, cultural and social qualities, heritage and traditions.

On the nature of persons within the world and the discourse of education

9. Central to the Living Values Education concept of education is a view of persons as thinking, feeling, valuing whole human beings, culturally diverse and yet belonging to one world family. Education must therefore concern itself with the intellectual, emotional, spiritual and physical wellbeing of the individual.
10. The discourse of education, of thinking, feeling and valuing, is both analytic and poetic. Establishing a dialogue about values within the context of a values-based learning community facilitates an interpersonal, cross-cultural exchange on the importance and means of imparting values in education.

Structure

The development and advancement of Living Values Education is overseen by the **Association for Living Values Education International** (ALIVE), a non-profit-making association of organizations around the world concerned with values education. ALIVE groups together national bodies promoting the use of the Living Values Education Approach and is an independent organization that does not have any particular or exclusive religious, political or national affiliation or interest. The development and implementation of Living Values Education has been supported over the years by a number of organizations, including UNESCO, governmental bodies, foundations, community groups and individuals. LVE continues to be part of the global movement for a culture of peace following the United Nations International Decade for a Culture of Peace and Non-violence for the Children of the World.

ALIVE is registered as an association in Switzerland. In some countries national Living Values Education associations have been formed, usually comprised of educators, education officials, and representatives of organizations and agencies involved with student or parent education.

Activities

In pursuing its mission and implementing its core principles, the Association for Living Values Education International and its Associates and Focal Points for LVE provide:

1. *Professional development courses, seminars and workshops* for teachers and others involved in the provision of education.

2. *Classroom teaching material and other educational resources*, in particular the original award-winning series of five resource books containing practical values activities and a range of methods for use by educators, facilitators, parents and caregivers to help children and young adults explore and develop widely-shared human values. This series of books, now updated and expanded, plus Living Green Values and an additional 11 values-education resources for young people at risk, are specified in the following LVE Resource Materials section. The approach and lesson content are experiential, participatory and flexible, allowing — and encouraging — the materials to be adapted and supplemented according to varying cultural, social and other circumstances.

3. *Consultation to government bodies, organizations, schools, teachers and parents* on the creation of values-based learning environments and the teaching of values.

4. *An extensive website*, www.livingvalues.net, with materials available for downloading free of charge, including songs, posters and a distance program for adults, families and study groups.

LVE Resource Materials

Designed to address the whole child/person, Living Values Education Activities engage young people in exploring, experiencing and expressing values so they can find those that resonant in their heart, and build the social and emotional skills which enable them to live those values. The approach is child-centered, flexible and interactive; adults are asked to act as facilitators. The approach is non-prescriptive and allows materials and strategies to be introduced according to the circumstances and interests of the users and the needs of students.

The Living Values Education Series

The Living Values Education series, a set of five books first published in April of 2001 by Health Communications, Inc. (HCI), was awarded the 2002 Teachers' Choice Award, an award sponsored by *Learning* magazine, a national publication for teachers and educators in the USA. Materials from the books, and in some cases up to all five of the books, were published in a dozen languages.

The original Living Values Education Series
- *Living Values Activities for Children Ages 3–7*
- *Living Values Activities for Children Ages 8–14*
- *Living Values Activities for Young Adults*
- *Living Values Parent Groups: A Facilitator Guide*
- *LVEP Educator Training Guide*

In 2018, the Association for Living Values Education International began updating this initial set of five books. Building on the original material, updated information, an expansion of activities and additional values units were added. Because of the amount of added content, the Living Values Education Activities books are published by ALIVE as two volumes, Book 1 and Book 2. ALIVE's intent in separating from HCI, our esteemed publisher, was to make these educational resources more accessible to educators in all continents by offering the series not only as regular books but as eBooks and free downloadable units.

The updated and expanded Living Values Education Series
- *Living Values Education Activities for Children Ages 3–7, Book 1*

- *Living Values Education Activities for Children Ages 3–7, Book 2*
- *Living Values Education Activities for Children Ages 8–14, Book 1*
- *Living Values Education Activities for Children Ages 8–14, Book 2*
- *Living Values Education Activities for Young Adults, Book 1*
- *Living Values Education Activities for Young Adults, Book 2*
- *Living Values Education Parent Groups: A Facilitator Guide*
- *Living Values Education Training Guide*

Living Values Education Activities for Children Ages 3–7, 8–14, and ***Young Adults*** — LVE utilizes a wide range of modalities and activities, with the hope that each young person will be inspired to love values and experience their strength and beauty. Reflection points teach the importance of valuing all people, discussions help students grow in empathy, role playing builds conflict resolution skills and a myriad of facilitated cognitive, artistic, and experiential activities increase positive intrapersonal and interpersonal social and emotional skills. Reflective, imagining and artistic activities encourage students to explore their own ideas, creativity and inner gifts. Mind mapping values and anti-values builds cognitive understanding of the practical effect of values and encourages a values-based perspective for analyzing events and creating solutions. Other activities stimulate awareness of personal and social responsibility and, for older students, awareness of social justice. The development of self-esteem and respect, acceptance and inclusion of others continues throughout the exercises. Educators are encouraged to utilize their own rich heritage while integrating values into everyday activities and the curriculum.

Sixteen Values Units — and Related Values

The updated Living Values Education Activities books have sixteen values units, eight in Book 1 and eight in Book 2. This allows schools to easily plan to implement one value a month during the school year, rotating through eight values a year. The universal values explored in all three books are peace, respect, love and caring, tolerance, honesty, happiness, responsibility, simplicity and caring for the Earth and Her Oceans, cooperation, humility, compassion, freedom and unity. The value unit exploring freedom for children ages three to seven is titled "Brave and Gentle".

There are two values units on both peace and respect as these values are so important to young people and present the opportunity to help them build important intrapersonal and interpersonal social and emotional skills. It is recommended that educators in schools begin with the Peace I and Respect I values units in Book 1 during the first year of implementation and Peace II and Respect II values units in Book 2 during the second year, rotating through eight values each year.

The sixteenth values unit is titled "Another Value We Love". This offers activities on a few values and an invitation to educators to explore a value they feel is needed locally or nationally.

The sixteen values units in the updated Living Values Education Activities books also include many related values such as kindness, fairness, determination, integrity, appreciation, diversity, human rights, valuing education, trust, gratitude, inclusion, equality and social justice.

Living Values Education Parent Groups: A Facilitator Guide — This book offers both process and content for facilitators interested in conducting LVE Parent Groups with parents and caregivers to further understanding and skills important in encouraging and positively developing values in children. The first section describes content for an introductory session, and a six-step process for the exploration of each value. The second section offers suggestions regarding values activities the parents can do in the group, and ideas for parents to explore at home. In the third section, common parenting concerns are addressed, and parenting skills to deal with those concerns. Parent group facilitators are encouraged to use *Nurturing with Love and Wisdom, Disciplining with Peace and Respect: A mindful guide to parenting* in conjunction with the parent group facilitator guide.

Living Values Education Training Guide — This updated guide contains the content of sessions within regular LVE educator workshops as well as staff building activities. It contains the content of sessions within regular LVE educator workshops. This includes introductory activities, an LVE overview, values awareness reflections, the LVE Approach and skills for creating a values-based atmosphere. LVE's Theoretical Model, Developing Values Schematic, and sample training agendas are included.

Materials for Young People At Risk

There are special LVE programs for young people at risk. These materials are restricted, made available only to educators who undergo LVE training for these particular modules. The ability to create a values-based atmosphere, and use active listening and validation skills, are an important part of the process. These educational

resources are:
- *Living Values Activities for At-Risk Youth*
- *Living Values Activities for Children Affected by Earthquakes Ages 3–7*
- *Living Values Activities for Children Affected by Earthquakes Ages 8–14*
- *Living Values Activities for Drug Rehabilitation*
- *Living Values Activities for Refugees and Children Affected by War Ages 3–7*
- *Living Values Activities for Refugees and Children Affected by War Ages 8–14*
- *Living Values Activities for Street Children Ages 3–6*
- *Living Values Activities for Street Children Ages 7–10*
- *Living Values Activities for Street Children Ages 11–14*
- *Living Values Activities for Young Offenders*
- *Living Values Education Supplement, Helping Young People Process Difficult Events*

Living Values Activities for At-Risk Youth (LVAARY)* and *Living Values Activities for Young Offenders (LYAYO) — These resources for youth 14-years and older weave in values activities on peace, respect, love, cooperation, honesty, humility and happiness, with lessons related to crime, violence, drug use, gang involvement, negative influences and concomitant emotional issues, along with the building of social and relapse-prevention skills. Based on LVE methodology, educators are asked to create a values-based atmosphere. Participants are encouraged to explore and develop values in a group-facilitated process by first exploring their own dreams for a better world. Lessons on peace and respect build self-confidence and a supportive values-based atmosphere in the group, prior to beginning choice-related lessons in which participants are asked to explore and share their journey and the consequences in their lives. The 90 lessons in LVAARY and the 103 lessons in LVAYO include experiences to help young adults deal with their pain and anger, learn to self-regulate more effectively, and learn life-lessons. Positive intrapersonal and interpersonal social skills are taught, encouraged and practiced in the facilitated activities. In LVEAARY, a series of stories is related to engage the young adults in a process of healing and to learn about a culture of peace and respect. Through discussion, art, role-playing and dramas, participants explore many aspects of their experiences and build relapse-prevention skills.

Living Values Activities for Children Affected by Earthquakes — These resources were developed at the request of educators in El Salvador after the earthquake. This was developed specifically for that situation and culture; hence, the materials would need to be adapted for use by other cultures and for other sets of circumstances.

Living Values Activities for Drug Rehabilitation — The 102 lessons in this curriculum weave in values activities on peace, respect, love, cooperation, honesty, humility and happiness from *Living Values Activities for Young Adults*, with lessons related to drug use, emotional issues that arise with addiction and concomitant behaviors, and the building of social and relapse-prevention skills. It is designed for use with young people 14- through 26-years old but has been used in rehabilitation clinics with adults in their 40s.

Living Values Activities for Refugees and Children Affected by War — These supplements contain activities that give children an opportunity to begin the healing process while learning about peace, respect and love. Designed to be implemented by refugee teachers of the same culture as the children, there are 49 lessons for children three to seven years old and 60 lessons for students eight to fourteen years old. The lessons provide tools to begin to deal with grief while developing positive adaptive social and emotional skills. A section on camp-wide strategies offers suggestions for creating a culture of peace, conducting values-education groups for parents/caregivers, cooperative games, and supporting conflict resolution monitors. Teachers are to continue with the regular Living Values activities after these lessons are completed.

Living Values Activities for Street Children (LVASC) Ages 3–6, 7–10 and 11–14 — These three resources contain adapted Living Values Activities on peace, respect, love and cooperation and a series of stories about a street-children family. The stories serve as a medium to educate about and discuss issues related to domestic violence, death, AIDS, drug sellers, drugs, sexual abuse and physical abuse. The issues of begging, being scared when adults argue, safety, being safe from unsafe adults, sex, being scared at night and wanting to learn are also addressed. The 70 lessons in the LVASC 3–6 book include discussions, activities, and the development of positive adaptive social and emotional skills and protective social skills. In addition to the issues just mentioned, the 77 activities in the LVASC 7–10 book also address caring for younger siblings, eating in a healthy way, cleanliness, lack of food, stealing, the effects of drugs and the right to education. The 80 LVASC 11–14 activities, in addition to the above, addresses female and male maturation, prostitution, sex trafficking, labor trafficking, corruption, eating in a healthy way and hygiene. The issues of the risk of dying quickly from diarrhea, cycles of violence versus non-violence, child rights and making a difference are also addressed. The materials also include suggestions for greater community involvement in the area of vocational training as well as educating the community about AIDS and other relevant issues through dramas/skits.

LVE Supplement, Helping Young People Process Difficult Events — Originally developed in response to a request from educators in Afghanistan, this special supplement contains 12 lessons to help young people express and process their reactions to violence and death. Designed to be used with *Living Values Education Activities for Children Ages 8–14*, it also contains guidelines to help children begin to process their reactions to other circumstances which may be emotionally traumatic. The lessons can be done in a classroom setting by educators that have undergone an LVE Workshop and learned the skills of active listening and validating and how to create a values-based atmosphere.

Living Green Values

Living Green Values Activities for Children and Young Adults — A special Rio+20 edition, this supplement is dedicated to the Earth in honor of the United Nations Conference on Sustainable Development convened in Rio de Janeiro, Brazil, in June 2012. Living Green Values activities help build awareness of the importance of taking care of the Earth and her resources. Stories and lessons for children 3 to 7, 8 to 14 and young adults infuse love for nature and her creatures along with learning specific ways to be a friend to the Earth. This is downloadable free of charge from the LVE international website.

LVE Distance for Adults, Families and Study Groups

LVE Distance for Adults, Families and Study Groups — Several activities have been selected from each of the 12 value units featured in *Living Values Activities for Young Adults*, along with additional material from *LVEP Educator Training Guide*, to provide a *Living Values Education Home Study Course for Adults* who wish to explore their values in a personal, family or community environment. Using both enjoyable practical values

Living Values Education Activities for Children Ages 8–14, Book 1

activities and awareness building techniques for which LVE is known, these attractive downloadable booklets make LVE accessible to adults, families and groups. The LVE Distance webpage also includes supporting audio files, a guide to *Running an Effective Group*, together with the *LVE 12-Week Self Reflection for Adults*. All are available free of charge on the LVE international website.

Extent and Variety of Use
. . . and some of LVE's partners in different countries

The Living Values Education approach and materials are producing positive results in more than 40 countries at thousands of sites. While most implementation settings are schools, others are day-care centers, boarding schools, community centers, centers and informal settings for children in difficult circumstances, drug rehab facilities, centers, camps, homes, and prisons. The number of people doing LVE at each site varies considerably; some involve a few people with one teacher or facilitator while other sites have involved 3,000 students.

In some countries LVE is implemented by a small number of dedicated educators who feel values education is important for the wellbeing of students, the community and the world. In other countries, ALIVE Associates have expanded into several areas while other ALIVE Associates have found partners to implement LVE widely, serving local and country-wide needs. There are many examples of collaborative partnerships. A few examples are below:

Vietnam — LVE has been disseminated widely, to more than 18,000 educators, through partnerships with the Hanoi Psychological Association, PLAN International, World Vision International, the Ministry of Labor, Invalids and Social Affairs, Drug Rehabilitation Department and VTV2 Education Channel, a television station in Vietnam.

Israel — The ALIVE Associate works with the Informal Education Department within the Ministry of Education, AMEN — Youth Volunteering City, and JOINT Israel. They have jointly developed a project to implement values in schools and in the communities and reinforce the values base of volunteering as a way of life.

Brazil — The Brazilian ALIVE Associate has provided training to thousands of teachers, including street educators and youth detention authorities. Many large

Living Values Education Activities for Children Ages 8–14, Book 1

networks of regular schools or NGOs that work with children in difficult circumstances have received LVE training through these collective programs: São Sebastião, São José dos Campos, Itápolis, São Bernardo do Campo, Campinas, Valinhos, Guarujá, Araraquara, Limeira in the state of São Paulo, Três Corações, in the state of Minas Gerais, Recife, in the state of Pernambuco, and the social networks: Nossas Crianças, Rede Fiandeiras, Rede Oeste, Bompar — Centro Social Nossa Senhora do Bom Parto in the city of São Paulo. Also, trainings have been held in São Paulo for the Young Offenders agency and the CASA Foundation. These educators from numerous outside agencies and private and public schools have facilitated the exploration and development of values with more than 500,000 young people in normal schools and 75,000 street children. The Itau Foundation, Santos Martires Society and the public regular schools Boa Esperança, Peccioli and Josefina have given tremendous assistance to children, young adults and the community through an LVE project in an especially vulnerable neighborhood in Sao Paulo.

Indonesia — The ALIVE Associate, Karuna Bali Foundation, works with a number of organizations in line with the LVE vision, one of which is The Asia Foundation with its implementing partners in Jakarta, Paramadina Foundation, Paramadina University, PPIM UIN Jakarta and LSAF, in Yogyakarta, LKiS, Mata Pena and Puskadiabuma UIN Yogyakarta, and in Ambon, ARMC IAIN Ambon and the Parakletos Foundation. Another cooperating organization is Jesuit Refugee Service which works with internally displaced people, refugees and asylum seekers in several nodes of Indonesia.

From 2009, The Asia Foundation and its partners have actively supported LVE development through its Pendidikan Menghidupkan Nilai program, with LVE workshops for teachers and lecturers of madrasah, Islamic boarding schools, schools, and universities. Now in 50 Islamic boarding schools, one of the program's goals is mainstreaming high quality values-based education where values can be implemented directly in daily life. Great attention is given to character-based education by integrating the approach in all subjects.

During the program, at least 10,119 teachers and 1,423 lecturers from schools and universities all over Indonesia were involved. The evaluation of this program was published in a book format titled *Success Stories* by TAF in the Indonesian language. Parallel to TAF programs, JRS since 2009 also intensively used LVE methods in its work with post disaster and post conflict communities in Aceh province. From 2012, the Peace Education program in Ambon, a collaboration of The Asia Foundation, State's Islamic

Institute of Ambon, and Parakletos Foundation, has been working hard to sow the seeds of peace in the land broken up with strife. More than 300 facilitators of LVE and Peace Education have been trained, and more than 10,000 students, teachers, and members of communities have been involved in peace education activities.

Karuna Bali Foundation also implements LVE in its program, especially with Campuhan College, a one-year program for high school graduates who wish higher education, and EduCare, doing workshops for schools in rural areas. A lot of lessons have been learned, especially the need for educators to live their values before facilitating values awareness in students. There are many requests for training from schools and institutions from all over Indonesia. In 2015, there were 48 LVE workshops, from the eastern most point of Palembang to the western most point of Ambon. In 2016, there were 41 workshops involving 1055 people. This only counts three-day LVE Educator Workshop. There are many more one-day seminars and professional development courses. Since the 20th Anniversary of LVE Conference hosted by ALIVE Indonesia in November of 2016, the requests for workshops have grown even more.

History of Living Values Education

LVE was initially developed by educators for educators in consultation with the Education Cluster of UNICEF, New York, and the Brahma Kumaris. This came to pass as Cyril Dalais, a Senior Advisor with the Early Childhood Development Program Division at UNICEF, read the "Sharing Values for a Better World: Classroom Curriculum" chapter written by Diane Tillman in *Living Values: A Guidebook*, a Brahma Kumaris publication. In June of 1996, he called the Brahma Kumaris to say, "The world needs more of this." Feeling that children would benefit by values education and safe, nurturing quality learning environments, UNICEF and the Brahma Kumaris invited 20 educators from five continents to meet at UNICEF Headquarters in New York in August of 1996.

The group discussed the needs of children around the world, their experiences of working with values, and how educators can integrate values to better prepare students for lifelong learning. Using the values concepts and reflective processes within *Living Values: A Guidebook* as a source of inspiration, and the *Convention on the Rights of the Child* as a framework, the global educators identified and agreed upon the purpose and aims of values-based education worldwide — in both developed and developing countries.

Diane Tillman, a Licensed Educational Psychologist who became the primary author of the LVE Resource Materials, had worked for 23 years as a School Psychologist in public schools in a multi-cultural area of southern California. Having traveled widely internationally, she appreciated many cultures and religious traditions. She was well versed in keeping the educational process separate from religion as that is required by the public education system in the U.S.A. The team of 20 professional educators from around the world agreed that they wanted the approach to be global, infused with respect for each person and culture. They worked cooperatively together to make sure the books had a variety of values activities from diverse cultures, religions and traditions. Several educators contributed substantially, including Marcia Maria Lins de Medeiros from Brazil, Diana Hsu from Germany and Pilar Quera Colomina from Spain. As LVE spread to different countries and the books were translated into different languages, LVE educators in different countries added in their own cultural stories and activities.

Twenty-two years later, the directors and advisors of the Association for Living Values Education International (ALIVE) wish to offer their deep appreciation to the numerous organizations and individuals who have contributed to the development of LVE, and who have implemented LVE in countries around the world. Many dedicated LVE coordinators, trainers, artists and even film makers around the world have served as volunteers. The approach, materials, training programs and projects continue to be developed as new requests for special needs populations are received, and as different countries well versed in the LVE methodology create new materials for their context.

In the early stages of development of LVE, the Brahma Kumaris contributed extensively. They helped edit the initial pilot materials and disseminated LVE through their global network of centers and their relationships with educators. A peace organization deeply interested in values, the Brahma Kumaris continue to provide support or partnership when such is desired by a national LVE group.

Other organizations which also supported LVE in its beginning stages were the Educational Cluster of UNICEF (New York), UNESCO, the Planet Society, the Spanish Committee of UNICEF, the Mauritius Institute of Education and the regional UNESCO Office in Lebanon.

An Independent Organization

In 2004, LVE created its own independent non-profit organization, the Association of Living Values Education International (ALIVE). ALIVE was formed with the aim to benefit more educators, children, young adults and communities through the involvement of a host of other organizations, agencies, governmental bodies, foundations, community groups and individuals. LVE educators in some countries formed their own non-profit LVE associations in order to become an ALIVE Associate while other NGOs became ALIVE Associates. ALIVE Associates and Focal Points for LVE act as the lead for LVE in their country and train educators in schools and agencies to implement LVE. Examples of NGOs who became ALIVE Associates are: Club Avenir des Enfants de Guinée in Guinea Conakry, Yayasan Karuna Bali in Indonesia, Hand in Hand in the Maldives, and the National Children's Council in the Seychelles.

None of the above cooperation would have been possible without the dedication, work and love of the educators who believe in Values Education, the LVE national teams around the world, the ALIVE Associates and Focal Points for LVE, the LVE trainers and volunteers, and those who serve on the ALIVE board and International Advisory Committee. We would like to thank each one of you for your work towards safe, healthy, caring, quality learning environments for children and a better world for all.

Results — Reports, Evaluations and Research

Educator evaluations collected from teachers implementing LVE in countries around the world frequently note positive changes in teacher-student relationships and in student-student relationships both inside and outside the classroom. Educators note an increase in respect, caring, cooperation, motivation, concentration, and the ability to solve peer conflicts on the part of the students. Within a matter of months, educators note that students spontaneously begin to discuss challenges in the language of values, become aware of the effects of values on the self, others and the community, and strive to live their values by making positive socially-conscious choices. Bullying and violence decline as positive social and emotional skills increase. Research also notes academic gains. LVE helps educators co-create with students safe, caring, values-based atmospheres for quality learning.

A Few Observations and Stories

From Kenya: Catherine Kanyi noted, "With LVE the children changed so quickly you could notice which value worked well. Parents also notice the difference in schools implementing LVE. There is no fighting at school. The teacher-pupil relationship is good; there is polite language at school. The parent-teacher relationship is good. Children miss being at school all the time for there is love, peace, freedom and unity."

From Malaysia: Shahida Abdul-Samad, the Focal Point for LVE in Malaysia, wrote about an educator's reaction to an LVE workshop she and Diane Tillman facilitated in 2002. Shahida wrote: "I remember vividly Rahimah's comments after the LVE training ended. She said, 'Shahida, I promise you I will try and implement what I have learnt from you and Diane and see if it works. I will do that. If I see results, I will let you know. That's my commitment to you.'

Every school Rahimah Sura headed she implemented LVE school wide. From inner city schools with major disciplinary problems, to rural schools with drug addiction problems, to the best boarding schools with teachers challenging her positive teaching strategies, she was able in every instance to turnaround each and every school to become the best schools in Malaysia attaining national awards. Children who were drug abusers became actively involved in drama and dance and won competitions locally and nationwide. Teenagers who used to destroy toilets and common facilities changed over a new leaf and took responsibility for the cleanliness of their toilets. They took pride in what they did. Destruction and vandalism dwindled down to zero.

Today these schools are the Exemplary schools. They are rated highest amongst school rankings. From being in the worst band, they moved to the highest band, i.e., from D to A. Not only did this positive environment impact the school and its inhabitants, the positive energy overflowed to their homes and communities, bringing parents, community leaders together — all lending their support to further Rahimah's effort in the 'magic' she created. It wasn't easy for her in the beginning. As usual there was resistance to change. She persisted in the belief that this was the way forward — to bring about change using LVE's Theoretical Model as her compass.

The use of canes was thrown out; students were given the freedom to move from classroom to classroom without being monitored; teachers who refused to follow the LVE approach were counseled and encouraged to use the techniques and activities from the LVE activity books.

With Rahimah's skill set and experience in implementing LVE through PBB, values activities and setting clear guidelines that everyone adhered to, the teachers' hearts and minds began to change. Rahimah once again proved that LVE wasn't just magic or something that happened by chance, it was actually a systematic and well-designed program that brings out the best that is in all of us — our innate values. Rahimah went on to be honored and recognized by the Ministry of Education and was awarded the highest award a civil servant can achieve due to her untiring efforts to bring about positive change through LVE."

From Egypt: A teacher in El-Menia explained that one day she had to leave her class of primary level children unattended for some time. As she was walking back to the class she expected to hear a lot of noise, but to her surprise there was no sound coming from the class. When she reached the class, she found that one of the students was standing and conducting an LVE guided relaxation/focusing exercise for the rest of the class while all the other students were quiet and calm and enjoying the experience!

Another teacher reported that a girl in her class who used to have the highest record of absences in previous years, recorded the highest rate of attendance after using LVE activities with the children. Another student who was on the verge of leaving the school due to his poor educational performance, became attentive in class and scored better academic results after implementing the LVE program.

From Indonesia: An observation team wanted to know why corporal punishment was not used in an Islamic boarding school at which LVE was being used. The reply: "If you want change for two days, use physical punishment; if you want long-term transformation, use LVE.

From China: Peter Williams worked with students for several months in a middle school in Beijing. When he asked his Chinese colleague, Ms. Ao Wen Ya, why she thought a peace visualization was successful, she said: "It helped the children to find peace by themselves. It helped the children to feel happy and relaxed. It made them really want to be happy and motivated to build a better world and be kind to each other." She additionally noted, "Sometimes the children can be naughty in class; they don't concentrate. Now they are more engaged in their subjects because they are interested. They are motivated to learn because they are valued as people ... they are now calmer and not as naughty. The quality and standards of work are higher. They are willing to take risks to express themselves well with more confidence." Mr. Williams added, "The lessons REALLY DID something. Their attitude is more positive, and they are better organized both individually and as a group." An observer from the Chinese Academy of Sciences commented that the motivation of the children had been greatly enhanced, and it transferred to other lessons.

From Canada: Lisa Jenkins, a grade 6 teacher from Canada wrote. "I went to my first LVE workshop a few days before the most challenging school year I have ever faced, began. I knew the history of the class I was to have. There were eight students who were very challenging. The behavior of this group had been a concern since grade one. They were routinely in the hall, or office, and many of the class members had been suspended on a regular basis. The many and varied discipline initiatives were done to them and had become a meaningless joke to the students. The other children in the school were unsafe and staff, parents and the members of the community were frustrated.

Every day, I see evidence all around our school and community that the anti-bullying programs are not effective. The kids realize it is the next bandwagon and go through the motions but don't put it into practice. After the workshop I felt hope. I began the year with the unit on respect and it took us almost five months to explore it fully. The changes were dramatic but came slowly. The language the children used to speak to each other was the biggest change I witnessed. Instead of 'put downs,' foul language and words of hate, they progressed to passionate debate. 'I'm not attacking you, but I don't agree with you…' became regular conversation. The discussions we had were awe-inspiring. By naming violence, exclusion, etc. and talking about these kinds of behaviors in reference to respecting self and others, I think we are having more success with students.

Walking the Talk: They see us living what we speak and seeing that peace can be attained, and that there are alternatives to aggressive behavior. When we treat children with respect, listen to them and ensure they have a loving and safe environment and actively name these things they may not be familiar with, we have more chance of reaching them and seeing them explore their own values and asking the difficult questions of themselves and others.

A lot of time was spent on discussing how our playground/school/community was unsafe. Eventually the realization hit that many of them were the cause of this. They began to explore their behavior choices in a whole new light and they initiated a peer helper program that spring. Our administration team noticed a significant drop in the number of visits these children were making to the office. There was only one suspension all year. Other staff members commented that 'something big' had changed the atmosphere of the school. The hallways, bathrooms, playground, bus stops and community hangouts were not seeing the violence and aggression they once had. These were the gauges I used to measure success.

The journey was a long one but well worth the effort. Every child had increased self-worth and self-respect when the year ended. They were not perfect. They were more aware of how they affected the world around them and wanted that to be more positive than it had been. I wish that we could have stayed together another year. The LVE workshop I attended changed my attitude toward how the year was going to go. The LVE activities we did together changed all of us for the better.

The personal changes are major for me. They are a huge part of why I continue using the program. I know the difference it has made in my own life and the lives of my family. I am much more peaceful, and calm. I use the language of values and talk about them in daily life with my children and students. Through working with the LVE program I am more in tune with my own weaknesses and am practicing simplicity to balance things."

Evaluations and Research Results

From Paraguay: Educators rated 3243 students from 4- to 22-years of age who were engaged in LVE. Despite being from many different schools with a variance in adherence to the LVE Model, the educators found that 86% of the students improved in the conflict resolution skills and the ability to concentrate, 87% improved in responsibility, 89% improved in respect shown to peers and honesty, 92% improved in their ability to relate socially in a positive way, 94% showed an improvement in motivation and more interest in school, 95% showed more respect for adults, and 100% had more self-confidence and cooperated more with others.

From Vietnam: Axis Research Company conducted an evaluation on the effects of implementing LVE on teachers and students three months and one year after an LVE training. The summary showed:
- 100% students have more self-confidence, respect toward teachers/adults, honesty, interest in school, and a safe feeling physically/emotionally.
- Considerable improvement in respect toward peers, ability to resolve conflict, ability to cooperate, responsibility, ability to concentrate in class, and ability to share/give opinion. Students are more united and care for each other.
- 90% of teachers see positive improvement in themselves, from better to much better. They can control emotions, feel more peaceful, lighter, and happier.

From Kuwait — A school which implemented LVE for 18 years: Peter Williams, the Head Teacher of Kuwait American School (KAS) and a former President of the Association of Living Values Education International submitted the following report.

"The K-12 Kuwait American School was founded on the Living Values Education Program in 1999 with the fundamental aim of helping to heal the trauma in the hearts and minds of children after the Gulf War. After 18 continuous years of implementing Living Values Education, the school's vision and mission to 'Build Minds, Characters and Futures' within an international context of 'Learning without Borders' has gone from strength to strength.

In addition to delivering a fully accredited and rigorous academic curriculum, the Living Values Education Program with its vision, creativity, clarity, guidance and practicalities has enabled the school to identify and nurture three key principles.

1. The Loving Presence of the Educator in a Values-Based Atmosphere who models and lives their values with Kindness.
2. The Importance of Enabling a Community of Trust and a Family of Learners especially with parents in the promotion of wellbeing, care and high-quality education for their children.
3. The confidence and trust that there is a healing strength in nurturing and educating the heart with Living Values Education.

As the years progressed and as the school went deeper into the benefits of Living Values Education, we all began to wonder if Living Values Education could truly deliver what it set out to achieve. According to our Family of Learners, the answer was 'Yes'.

Some of the evidence indicating the benefits of Living Values Education include:

- ❖ The school has grown to be a family — a community of learners.
- ❖ There is a strong feeling of welcome, joy and acceptance.
- ❖ There is a powerful and peaceful values-based learning atmosphere.
- ❖ The students express their values using their own moral compass
- ❖ The students became ambassadors of how to live their values.
- ❖ There are virtually no referrals for any form of physical violence.
- ❖ Peace Time and Mindfulness are widely practiced.
- ❖ The level of achievement and the academic standards are higher.
- ❖ Living Values Education lessons are supported by unique Etiquette, Public Speaking and Life Skills programs that are "taught" each week.
- ❖ The school's student and teacher assemblies provide an essential focus for the Living Value of the Month.
- ❖ Values-based learning is incorporated into the Middle and High School years.
- ❖ For everyone, the school is a happy and hard-working place to be.

Living Values Education has helped the school to grow to a population of 600+ representing 33 nationalities who speak with one language — the language of values.

A recent visitor from the Ministry of Youth commented: 'Why are these students so happy and learning so well? We responded: "It's a Living Values School."

The school is very grateful to the Living Values Education program for its vision, clarity, guidance and practicalities. It's a great invitational model to explore, experience and express. Living Values Education invites in learning without borders and learning from the heart."

From Brazil: Hundreds of organizations in Brazil have implemented LVE over a 14-year period. Paulo Sérgio Barros, one of the leaders of the ALIVE Associate in Brazil, shares some of the results in the article *Atmosfera de Valores: O Princípio do Programa Vivendo Valores na Educação* (Values Atmosphere: The Principle of Living Values Education). A few excerpts from his article follow; further excerpts are on the Research page of the LVE international website. The full article in Portuguese is available on the Brazil Country Report page, as are other research articles.

"The educational institutions that have effectively inserted LVE methodology into their classes have been surprised at the positive effect on the personal and academic life of students. There are many successful experiences in schools developed from the partnership with LVE recorded in surveys and reports, in reports submitted to the coordinators of the program, or in educator reports during our LVE events in various parts of the country.

After activities with values at the Center for International Education (CEICOC) in Sao Luis, students/boosted their solidarity, cooperation, respect and love and started volunteer activities in the school's project of Action and Social Responsibility. They organized exhibitions on values, produced peace manifestos, etc., and became involved with other activities such as values classes, round-tables on ethics, collective meditation and art events. Motivated by these activities and by the much more humane awareness of their children, many parents were attracted to the school and stressed the importance of an education based on values for the formation of children and youth.

The PH3 Educational Parnamirim Center in RN inserted into its pedagogical program for employees, teachers, students and the community in general the implementation of LVE activities, training courses and seminars. The constant and effective practice of values in the school environment, the subject of academic research (ALVES, 2005; HENRY & ALVES, 2008), has provided clear changes in the ethos of PH3. Deeper experiences and higher-level sharing of values has enabled a dynamic school atmosphere that is more positive and involves everyone who participates in the school. In addition, there has been an increase in concentration, interest, and consequently the students' academic performance and more involvement of parents, etc.

Also noteworthy are the examples of Maria José Medeiros and John Germano schools, both in Fortaleza. The latter is a good example of holistic education that met in LVE a partner to strengthen current projects, inspire others, and systematize the school's educational policy on values that relied on: teacher training, the implementation of LVE activities in the classroom, daily collective moments to strengthen the atmosphere, mediation of everyday conflicts between children, ethos meetings to keep the link alive between the teachers, and the school and community, and various projects within the school and community. Among these projects are: A Values Fair, a human values bank, a loving school honesty bar and a child disarmament campaign. This group of experiments and the support of LVE have proven effective in the development of values for students, and vital for maintaining the direction of the educational policy of the Institution, established in a region with high social exclusion and marked by great violence.

At the School Maria José Medeiros, a group of educators has been devoted to the implementation of LVE activities with some classes. Pereira (2006) and Barros (2008) reported the positive effect of activities on behavioral change for many students. They noted progress in students' cognitive skills. They developed a better aesthetic sense in their assignments when they were able to express their ideas and feelings, their creativity in individual and collective activities their skills in intrapersonal and interpersonal relationships, and interest in issues like human rights and sustainability associated with collective projects at school. The authors concluded that students care about their values and develop them when they have opportunities. Their way of living, their experiences, their individual transformation, their work/products and the student evaluations at the end of academic year, led us to infer that students have developed many skills such as: deeper concentration, greater self-esteem, more harmonious living, an understanding and practice of greater peace, tolerance and respect, and knowing how to contribute to a better world.

A researcher from the Department of Foundations of Education, Federal University of Ceará, Dr. Kelma Matos, in a recent publication (MATOS, BIRTH, JR NONATO, 2008) recorded some experiments and inferences about the LVE proposal in some schools in Fortaleza, citing it as: "a new way to tune the school into a more welcoming and humanizing environment, where the aspect of emotion is the mediator in knowledge construction and the building of human relationships (BIRTH & Matos, 2008, p. 75), and as a way to recover the meaning of life," which is "the challenge for any education in values, and the act of driving students to regain their confidence and hope and sense of sacredness of life" (Mendoca, 2008, p.199). Scholars of educational practices weave the web of "peace culture" in schools, and a significant number of the articles that make up the book, point out that LVE is an effective program for the process of both individual and social transformation."

"The experiments reported here illustrate a little of what has happened in hundreds of institutions where LVE is, or has been implemented in its 14 years in Brazil. … The program is a live and effective magic for those who have worked with it.

LVE weaves a network of a 'culture of peace' for those who believe that sowing these seeds in education is essential if we are to harvest the changes that will create a better world. LVE has inspired schools and educators to continue to open doors and hearts of students with a humanizing education which focuses on an atmosphere of peace, cooperation, understanding, dialogue and sharing. It is an invitation to the macro-structure of the education system to continue revising the curricula for the training of our children and youth; it is not focused exclusively on the rational, the "analytical thinking", but is in balance with emotion, intuition, spirituality — with all dimensions of our limitless human capacity."

Results in a Refugee Camp and with Street Children

There are also wonderful stories from educators in special circumstances. In Thailand, one year after implementing LVE in a Karen Tribe refugee camp, nine out of 24 refugee-camp teachers working with children and youth, reported 100-percent improvement in violent behavior; the others cited an 80-percent reduction in aggressiveness. Within two years of initiating the program, the high frequency fights between young people from different sections of the camp had completely ceased. In its place was spontaneous play, creative play, caring, happiness and cooperation.

The LVE program for street children is bringing in very positive reports. In Brazil, incarcerated youth that had been so violent that they were housed separately were able to return to the regular setting after three months of the *Living Values Activities for Street Children* materials. They were much more peaceful and compliant with authority. Other street children who were attending a government educational facility were able to obtain a regular job; others were able to learn to care for their children in a nurturing way.

In Vietnam, educators reported considerable decreases in aggression and at-risk behaviors. They noted about the young people: "Now they are confident and friendly with adults and their peers. There is almost no conflict in the classes and they now do not get into trouble after school either. The students have also developed many skits on how to keep safe from dangerous adults and really enjoy performing them. Now when they are on the streets and see children that are new to the streets they give support and advice to the new children and invite them to meet their teacher and join their classes."

Results with LVE's Drug Rehabilitation Program

Living Values Activities for Drug Rehabilitation are used in many government drug rehab centers in Vietnam. The Ministry of Labor reported in March of 2008 that LVE's program for drug rehabilitation was the most successful program in government drug rehabilitation clinics. They had been using it for three years.

A story from Vietnam: "Visitors to Binh Minh Village Drug Rehab Center in HCMC are amazed to see patients reading in a relaxed manner and walking around with smiles on their faces. They feel the secret lies in the Living Values Education program which has been applied at PLV since 2006. Binh Minh Village's English name is Peace and Light Village, or as they also call it, People and Living Values (PLV).

PLV is a private rehab center established in May 15, 2002. Using education as the key approach, the management here considers 80% of the success of the treatment process to be due to 'mental therapy'. Based on the results achieved since its inception, PLV now applies two education programs simultaneously to change the behavior of drug addicts: a 12-step program and the Living Values Education's program for drug rehabilitation. They have observed that these two programs together produce the best rehabilitation effect for even long-time drug users, especially during the two final stages of the rehab process: building a new life style, new behaviors, and helping peers. The LVE program has very practical skills which can be applied in reality.

The founders of PLV had attended LVE workshops conducted by Trish Summerfield since 2000. At that time, they found LVE a simple but scientific, highly educative method, which could fit quite well with Vietnamese culture, especially for drug addicts. *Living Values Activities for Drug Rehabilitation* was created in 2005. They began implementing it in 2006. By the end of 2008, the positive results had won their hearts and infused them with inspiration. They then assigned a board member to focus on LVE to become PLV's trainer of LVE."

For More Research Results and Success Stories

For research studies on LVE, and more success stories, kindly refer to those pages on the LVE international website: www.livingvalues.net.

EXPLORING AND DEVELOPING VALUES

Teaching Values

The choices of young people are critically important, not only for their own happiness and wellbeing at this vulnerable time in their lives, but also for their future. If they are to resist the powerful messages of negativity ubiquitous in our society and on social media, and move toward a love for values and positive socially-conscious choices, they need positive role models and the opportunity to cognitively discern the difference between the impact of values and anti-values on their lives, the community and the world.

LVE values activities are designed to motivate students, and to involve them in thinking about themselves, others, the world in relevant ways. The activities are designed to evoke the experience of values within, and build inner resources. They are designed to empower, and to elicit their potential, creativity and inner gifts. Students are asked to reflect, imagine, dialogue, communicate, create, write about, artistically express and play with values. In the process, personal social and emotional skills develop as well as positive, constructive social skills. This is done most effectively when there is a values-based atmosphere and when teachers are passionate about values.

The Living Values Education Activities resource books are arranged to present a series of skills that build sequentially. However, it is important for educators to integrate values throughout the curriculum; each subject opens a window to view the self and values in relation to the world.

Three Core Assumptions

LVE resource materials are built on three assumptions. The first assumption is drawn from a tenet in the Preamble of the United Nations' Charter, "To reaffirm faith in fundamental human rights, in the dignity and worth of the human person . . ."

Living Values Education Activities for Children Ages 8–14, Book 1

- Universal values teach respect and dignity for each and every person. Learning to enjoy those values promotes wellbeing for individuals and the larger society.
- Each student does care about values and has the capacity to positively create and learn when provided with opportunities.
- Students thrive in a values-based atmosphere in a positive, safe environment of mutual respect and care — where students are regarded as capable of learning to make socially conscious choices.

Developing Values Schematic — the LVE Method

How are values "taught?" How do we encourage young people to explore and develop values and the complementary social skills and attitudes that empower them to reach their potential? We would all like our own children as well as our students to be peaceful, respectful and honest. How can we let them know they can make a difference in this world and feel empowered to create and contribute?

Students need many different skills if they are to be able to love values, commit to them, and have the social skills, cognitive discernment and understanding to carry those values with them into their life. It is with this intention that the LVE Theoretical Model and the Living Values Education Activities were constructed. LVE provides methods and activities for educators to actively engage and allow students the opportunity to explore, experience and express 12 universal values.

After a few months of implementing LVE, dedicated educators find school cultures are infused with more communication, respect and caring. Often even students with very negative behaviors change dramatically. In an effort to understand why this approach works, some educators have asked to know more about LVE's theoretical basis. What methods are used within LVE? The schematic below describes the values exploration and development process. There are two complementary processes. The first is the creation of a values-based atmosphere; the second is the process within the facilitation of the activities.

Developing Values Schematic — the LVE Method

Explore ... Experience ... Express

```
Values-based Atmosphere
          ↓
   Values Stimulus
```

- **Reflecting Internally** ~imagining and reflective activities
- **Exploring Values in the Real World** ~through news, games and various content subjects
- **Receiving Information** ~through stories, reflection points and literature

↓

Discussion
~ sharing, cognitive exploration and affective understanding

↓

Exploration of Ideas
~ *further discussion, self-reflection, small group study, and mind mapping*

↓

- **Creative Expression**
- **Skill Development**
  - Personal social and emotional skills
  - Interpersonal communication skills
- **Society, Environment and the World**

↓

Transfer of Learning
~ integrating values in life

Values-based Atmosphere
Feeling Loved, Valued, Respected, Understood and Safe

As values must be "caught" as well as "taught," the adults involved are integral to the success of the program, for young people learn best by example and are most receptive when what is shared is experienced. The establishment of a values-based atmosphere is essential for optimal exploration and development. Such a student-centered environment naturally enhances learning, as relationships based on trust, caring, and respect have a positive effect on motivation, creativity, and affective and cognitive development.

Creating a "values-based atmosphere" is the first step in LVE's Developing Values Schematic. During LVE Educator Workshops, educators are asked to discuss quality teaching methods that allow students to feel loved, respected, valued, understood and safe.

LVE Theoretical Model

The LVE Theoretical Model postulates that students move toward their potential in nurturing, caring, creative learning environments. When motivation and control are attempted through fear, shame and punishment, youth feel more inadequate, fearful, hurt, shamed and unsafe. In addition, evidence suggests that repeated interactions loaded with these emotions marginalize students, decreasing real interest in attending school and/or learning. Students with a series of negative school relationships are likely to "turn off"; some become depressed while others enter a cycle of blame, anger, revenge — and possible violence.

Why were these five feelings — loved, valued, respected, understood and safe — chosen for the LVE Theoretical Model? Love is rarely spoken about in educational seminars. Yet, isn't it love and respect that we all want as human beings? Who doesn't want to be valued, understood and safe? Many studies on resiliency have reinforced the importance of the quality of relationships between young people and significant adults in their lives, often teachers.

What happens to the learning process when we feel loved, valued and respected? What happens in our relationships with educators who create a supportive, safe environment in the classroom? Many people have had the experience as a child of an educator who they found positive, encouraging and motivating. In contrast, how do we feel when an educator, at school or home, is critical, punitive and stressed or when the peers are derogatory or bully? While an interesting stimulus can heighten the creative process, high anxiety, criticism, pressure and punitive methods slow down the learning process. Simply the thought that others may be critical or have dislike can distract one from a task. Neurophysiologists have found positive effects on brain development when a child is nurtured, and deleterious effects when there are traumatic experiences. Lumsden notes that a caring, nurturing school environment boosts students' motivation, that is, students' interest in participating in the learning process; their academic self-efficacy increases as well (Lumsden, 1994). A caring, nurturing school environment has also been found to reduce violent behavior and create positive attitudes toward learning (Riley, quoted in Cooper, 2000).

Currently in education, in many countries there is considerable pressure on teachers to raise student achievement levels. Constant pressure and an emphasis on memorization and test scores often reduce "real" teaching as well as distract teachers from focusing on nurturing relationships with students. Much of the pleasure inherent in teaching well is lost. It is also harmful to levels of motivation and the classroom atmosphere. Alfie Kohn writes of "… fatal flaws of the steamroller movement toward tougher standards that overemphasize achievement at the cost of learning. Kohn argues that most of what the pundits are arguing for just gets the whole idea of learning and motivation wrong, and that the harder people push to force others to learn, the more they limit that possibility" (Janis, quoted in Senge, 2000).

Real Learning Comes Alive in a Values-Based Atmosphere

Achievement automatically increases as real learning increases. Real learning and motivation come alive in values-based atmospheres where educators are free to be in tune with their own values, model their love of learning and nurture students and the development of cognitive skills along with values. This is not to say that excellent teaching will always occur when there is a values-based atmosphere; a values educator must also be a good teacher.

As Terry Lovat and Ron Toomey concluded from their research: "Values Education is being seen increasingly as having a power quite beyond a narrowly defined moral or citizenship agenda. It is being seen to be at the centre of all that a committed teacher and school could hope to achieve through teaching. It is in this respect that it can fairly be described as the 'missing link' in the quality teacher … and quality teaching (2006)."

Modeling the Values from the Inside

In LVE Workshops, educators are asked to reflect on the values in their own lives and identify which are most important to them. In another session, they are asked to share quality teaching methods they can use to create their desired class climate.

Modeling of values by adults is an essential element in values education. Students are interested in educators who have a passion to do something positive in the world and who embody the values they espouse, and are likely to reject values education if they feel teachers are not walking their talk. LVE educators have shared amazing stories of change with angry and cynical pre-teens and teens, when they were able to stick to their values in challenging circumstances.

Teaching values requires from educators a willingness to be a role model, and a belief in dignity and respect for all. This does not mean we need to be perfect to teach LVE; however, it does require a personal commitment to "living" the values we would like to see in others, and a willingness to be caring, respectful and non-violent.

Skills for Creating a Values-based Atmosphere

The Theoretical Model and LVE's workshop session on "Acknowledgement, Encouragement and Building Positive Behaviors" combine the teachings of contingency management with a humanizing approach, that is, understanding that it is love and respect that we want as human beings. Showing interest in and giving respect to students while pointing out well-done relevant characteristics over time can be used to build the ability of students to analyze their own behavior and academic skills, and develop positive self-assessment and intrinsic motivation. In this approach, there is a focus on human relationships as well as sensitivity to the level of receptivity and needs of the students.

Skills for creating a values-based atmosphere also include: active listening; collaborative rule making; quiet signals that create silence, focus, feelings of peace or respect; conflict resolution; and values-based discipline. Active listening is useful as a method of acknowledgement with resistant, cynical and/or "negative" students. A key tool of counselors and therapists, active listening is an invaluable tool for teachers. Thomas Gordon's understanding of anger as a secondary emotion is a concept that is useful to educators in dealing with resistant students.

Collaborative rule making is a method to increase student participation and ownership in the rule-making process. Many educators have found that when students are involved in the process of creating, they are more observant, involved and willing to be more responsible in monitoring their own behavior and encouraging positive behaviors in their peers.

LVE training in values-based discipline also combines the theories of contingency management with a humanistic understanding of students and the belief in the importance of healthy relationships and wellbeing. Some people use the methods of contingency management as though the young person is a machine; the need for feeling accepted and valued as a person — by teachers and/or peers — is not factored into the behavioral plan. When social and relationship needs are considered as part of the intervention plan, outcomes are far more successful.

Educators can use the LVE Theoretical Model to assess the positive and negative factors affecting one student, a classroom, a school or an organization, and adjust the factors to optimize young people experiencing being loved, valued, respected, understood and safe rather than shamed, inadequate, hurt, afraid and unsafe. In conflict resolution or disciplinary settings, the emphasis is on creating a plan which supports building positive student behavior. Educators focus on treating the student in such a way that she or he feels motivated to be responsible in regulating their own behavior. There are occasions when students hold onto a negative attitude and logical consequences are needed; during the time period in which that consequence is paid it is recommended that the student not be treated as a "bad person." While at times an educator may find it best to be firm, serious or even stern, opportunities are looked for to build the young adult's ability to self-monitor and build relationship while the consequences are being carried out. This reflects back to Virginia Satir's work; people feeling full of love and wellbeing are more positive in their interactions and behaviors.

LVE Workshops

The creation of a values-based atmosphere facilitates success with young people, making the process of education more enjoyable, beneficial, and effective for both students and teachers. LVE Educator/Facilitator Training for all members of the school or an organization's staff is highly recommended whenever possible, however workshops are often given to educators from many different schools and educational organizations. Depending on the student population, consideration of additional training for the use of the LVE at-risk materials may be appropriate.

Components of Living Values Education Activities Units

The sixteen values units in *Living Values Education Activities for Children Ages 8–14*, Book 1 and Book 2, allow regular schools to easily plan to implement one value a month, that is, eight values a year. Peace and respect are important to young people and provide a wonderful opportunity to build intrapersonal and interpersonal emotional and social skills as well as a solid basis for understanding and loving values. As the values of peace and respect provide such a rich perspective from which to view the self, others and the world, and develop the social and emotional skills to live those values, there are Peace I and Respect I units for the first year of implementation and Peace II and Respect II units for the second year. If you are in an organization that invites people to explore and develop values for twelve months a year, simply facilitate a value a month.

Each values unit is designed for all students with the wellbeing of marginalized and resistant students in mind. The sequence of activities is aimed to maximize the fullest engagement/path of least resistance — by making the value relevant and beneficial to the student and his or her life. For example, lecturing to students about not fighting in school is an ineffective method to create peace and respect and can serve to further the apathy or resentment of already disenfranchised students. In contrast, beginning a lesson on peace with an imagination exercise elicits the natural creativity of all students. Once students develop a voice for peace they are more empowered to discuss the effects of peace — and violence. Each value unit is designed to begin with a values stimulus to create relevance/meaning.

Far too often, values are only taught at the awareness level, without building the cognitive understanding and social and emotional skills important in being able to "live" those values. For this reason, it is recommended that educators use all or almost all the lessons found in each value unit that they wish the students to explore. They are more likely to develop a love for values and be committed to implementing them if they explore values at many levels and develop the personal and social skills that allow them to experience the benefits of living those values. As students' backgrounds and needs vary, please feel free to adapt the activities to their needs and your style.

A lesson on values can be launched in many learning settings. Educators are encouraged to relate values to the subject matter they are teaching or relevant events. For example, a lesson on values can be launched in relation to literature, history, etc., or in response to current local or world news about which students are concerned.

Living Values Education Activities for Children Ages 8–14, Book 1

Values Stimulus

Each LVE Activity begins with a values stimulus. The three types of values stimuli noted in the schematic are receiving information, reflecting internally, and exploring values in the real world.

Receiving Information — This is the most traditional way of teaching values. Literature, stories and cultural information provide rich sources for exploration about values. Care is taken in the LVE Activities to provide stories about the use of holding or developing a positive value. Stories about failures because of holding an anti-value can be instructive at this age level, if they are perceived as socially relevant by the students. However, it is important to also create motivation through positive examples of people succeeding with values. Educators are asked to find relevant literature or media that they feel the students will relate to, and will help them see the effect and importance of values and their own actions.

Within each value unit there are reflection points which provide information about the meaning of the value being explored. The reflection points are at the beginning of every unit, and are incorporated in the lessons. "Understanding core values is essential to teaching values if students are to develop lifelong adherence to high principles" (Thomas Lickona, 1993). The reflection points are intended to be universal in nature, while holding an interdependent perspective of the importance of dignity and respect for each and every one. For example, a point in the unit on Respect is: *Everyone in the world has the right to live with respect and dignity, including myself.* A Tolerance Reflection Point is: *Tolerance is being open and receptive to the beauty of differences.* This universal perspective is important if we wish to create a better world for all.

The teacher may wish to add a few of his or her own reflection points, or use favorite sayings from the culture of the community and historical figures. Students can make up reflection points or research favorite sayings of their own.

Reflecting Internally — Imagining and reflective activities ask students to create their own ideas. For example, students are asked to imagine a peaceful world. Visualizing values in action makes them more relevant to students, as they find a place within where they can create that experience and think of ideas they know are their own. The process of creation, ownership, and a sense of hope are essential if students are to be motivated about living their values.

Reflective exercises ask students to think about their experiences in relation to the value. Students are also asked to reflect about different aspects at a later step within the lessons. It is important for students to be able to work as reflective learners if they are going to be able to discern and apply values most appropriately to a particular situation.

Exploring Values in the Real World — Some LVE Activities use games, real situations, news or subject matter content to launch the lesson. Too often in today's world, local and national events can be of concern to students. Please look for areas in which they have concern or interest, be it bullying, poverty, violence, drugs or the illness or death of a classmate or neighbor. Providing a space to air their concerns is helpful and allows meaningful discussion about the effect of values and anti-values and how our actions do make a difference.

Discussion — Meaningful and validating sharing

Creating an open, respectful space for discussion is an important part of this process. Sharing can then be more meaningful and validating. Talking about feelings in relation to values questions can clarify viewpoints and develop empathy. Discussions in a supportive environment can be healing; students who are often quiet can experience that others hold the same viewpoint. Shame can be released and/or diminished when students discover that others feel the same way. Children who think that everyone holds the same viewpoint can learn otherwise; those who bully can find out what others think about their behavior. The discussion process is also a space within which negativity can be accepted and queried. When this is done with genuine respect, students can begin to drop the defenses that necessitate their negativity. When the positive values under the negativity are understood and validated, a student can feel valued; gradually he or she can then experience the freedom to act differently.

In many of the LVE Activities, questions to discuss are provided. Some of these are to query about feelings; others are to open the cognitive exploration process and the generation of alternatives. Educators can use questions to delve into important emotional issues or alternative understandings. Feel free to adapt the questions to your personal style and the local usage of language.

One reason why LVE can be used in many different cultures is that the questions are open-ended. For example, "How do you give respect to your parents?" would be answered a little differently in different cultures, yet the desired outcome is the same.

Within the activities there are only one or two questions to which an absolute or "right" answer is given. The most important one is: "Is it okay to hurt others?" LVE's answer is "no". If a "yes" answer is given, the educator is to explain why it is not okay to hurt others. The other questions are truly open, allowing the students to discuss the values and their application in ways that are appropriate to their culture and way of life. The reflection points, however, create a standard of dignity and respect around which the activities are built.

Exploration of Ideas

Some discussions are followed by self-reflection or small group planning in preparation for art projects, journaling, or dramas. Other discussions lead into mind-mapping values and anti-values. These methods are useful to view the effects of values and anti-values on the self, relationships and different segments of society. Contrasting the effects of values is an important step in seeing long-term consequences. Mind-mapping is also an introduction to systems thinking.

Discussions are often a lead-in to activities regarding the effects of values in different subjects. Values activities can often awaken real interests in students. To acknowledge their passion and to facilitate the exploration of the subject is the type of teaching that allows real learning and furthers intrinsic motivation. This is where a few questions from an educator can create enthusiasm: "Why do you think that happens?" "What is the relationship between . . .?" "What value do you feel would help resolve this situation?" "What do you think should be done?" "How could you show this by Walking your Talk?"

Creative Expression

The arts are a wonderful medium for students to express their ideas and feelings creatively — and make a value their own. Drawing, painting, making mobiles, games and murals combine with performance arts. Dance, movement and music allow expression and build a feeling of community. For example, students are asked to make slogans about peace and put them up on walls, sculpt freedom, draw simplicity, and dance cooperation. As they engage in the medium they often must refer back to the value and discern what they really want to say. The creative process can also bring new understandings and insights; the value becomes more meaningful as it becomes their own. A similar process occurs as students are asked to write creative stories or poetry. The completion and beauty of the finished products can be a source of pride and act to enhance the self-esteem of students. A variety of creative arts can serve to let different students shine at different times. A school climate that can allow each person to shine at different times and through different modalities is a place where all can move toward their potential.

Music is also an important medium. Not only can it act to build a sense of community, but it can be healing. Provide the opportunity for students to create songs about values. Educators may wish to bring in traditional songs of their culture, or the cultures present in the area, and sing those with the students. Students could bring in popular songs which contain values themes or ideas.

Skill Development

It is not enough to think about and discuss values, create artistically or even to understand the effects of values. Emotional and social skills are needed to be able to apply values throughout the day. The youth of today increasingly need to be able to experience the positive feelings of values, understand the effects of their behaviors and choices in relation to their own wellbeing, and be able to develop socially conscious decision-making skills.

> **Personal Social and Emotional Skills** — There are a variety of intrapersonal skills taught within the LVE Activities. The Peace, Respect and Love units introduce Relaxation/Focusing exercises. These Relaxation/Focusing exercises help students "feel" the value. Educators have found that doing these exercises helps students quiet down, be less stressed, and concentrate more successfully on their studies. While there is initial resistance sometimes, usually that resistance disappears after several trials, and our experience has been that students begin to request quiet time. Once they are familiar with this strategy they can make up their own Relaxation/Focusing Exercises. The ability to self-regulate one's emotion and "de-stress" is an important skill in adapting and communicating successfully. Self-regulation or self-modulation helps a person regain calmness more quickly when a threat is perceived and be able to stay more peaceful in daily life.
>
> Other LVE Activities build an understanding of the individual's positive qualities, develop the belief that "I make a difference", enable exploring their own feelings and learning about the feelings of others and increase positive self-talk, and responsibility. Students are asked to apply those skills in a variety of ways.

Interpersonal Communication Skills — Skills for building emotional intelligence are included in the above set of activities and furthered in activities that build understanding of the roles of hurt, fear and anger and their consequences in our relationships with others. Conflict resolution skills, positive communication, cooperation games and doing projects together are other activities that build interpersonal communication skills. Conflict resolution skills are introduced during the Peace Unit, and reinforced during the Respect and Love Units. During the Love Unit, students are asked to think back to when the problem began and imagine what would have happened if they had used the value of love. The development of cognitive skills paired with probably consequences is aimed to help students "think on their feet" in difficult circumstances. Educators are encouraged to create the opportunity for students to be conflict resolution managers.

Students are provided the opportunity to role play different situations about which they are concerned. They may also make up their own situation cards. In the cooperation unit, students are asked to adapt their suggestions for good communication skills after games. One skill in the tolerance unit is to create assertively benevolent responses when others are making discriminatory remarks. Combining creativity with discussion and practice helps students feel comfortable in using the new skills, increasing the likelihood that they will use them.

Society, Environment and the World

To help youth desire and be able to contribute to the larger society with respect, confidence and purpose, it is important for them to understand the practical implications of values in relationship to the community and the world. One value can have a tremendous effect on the wellbeing of a community and social justice. A few activities are designed to build emotional awareness and cognitive understanding of this relationship. For example, students mind map the effects of a loving world and a non-loving world, mind map the effects of honesty versus corruption, explore the effects of corruption on the wellbeing of different countries and collect examples and stories of tolerance and intolerance.

The aim of developing social cohesion is constant throughout the material. However, the units on tolerance, simplicity and unity bring elements of social responsibility that are interesting and fun. Students explore the variety of cultures using the colors of a rainbow as an analogy. The unit on simplicity includes suggestions for conservation and respect for the earth. Further activities are in Living Green Values.

Transfer of Learning — Integrating Values in Life

"Integrating values in life" refers to students applying values-based behaviors in their life — with their family, society and the environment. For example, LVE homework activities increase the likelihood of students carrying new positive behaviors into their homes. Students are asked to create special projects that exemplify different values in their class, school and/or community. Parents and businesses can be involved as resources, for example, helping students learn organic gardening, how to clean up a stream and assist in the promotion of entrepreneurship and ethical leadership skills. Students are encouraged to share their creative dramas and music with their peers and younger students. Please do involve your students in service-learning projects. The ability to make a difference builds confidence and commitment to values.

Bringing in the Values of Your Culture

As you take LVE Training and facilitate LVE activities, you will understand the LVE methodology more deeply. At that point, you may wish to add ideas generated from your own experience, creativity, and cultural and educational resources, to help students explore, experience and express values meaningfully.

A group of teachers may want to get together before the introduction of each values unit to share their own material and ideas for students about that value — traditional stories, fiction or non-fiction articles, salient history units, web research projects, news stories, or relevant movies. Insert cultural stories at any time within the units. The students may enjoy acting out the stories. Ask the students to create their own plays and songs. They might even want to do an informal skit where the lines are improvised and are used to dramatize the situation being discussed. Perhaps older adults can tell traditional tales and teach traditional forms of music. Community based service-learning projects help strengthen students' commitment to values, and the understanding that they can make a positive difference. Educators are welcome to contribute the activities they create on the international web site. Kindly send them to content@livingvalues.net.

Making Values Education a Practical Reality

Step 1

A first step you may wish to do while considering the implementation of Living Values Education is inviting interested teachers and principals, or the leadership team of the organization, to reflect on and discuss the purpose of education. What values do you feel would benefit the students or group of people with whom you work? What values do you feel are needed in society and the world? What values would you like to be part of the culture of your school or organization?

Perhaps discuss the vision statement of the LVE Approach. Or, share that education has always been the primary method of change for society. What change would you like to see in your community and the world? Do you agree that the way to peace is peace? What would a culture of peace, respect, love, tolerance/acceptance of all, and honesty create in your community? Perhaps define together the culture or ethos you would like to create.

"At the core of values education lies the establishment of an agreed set of principles, deeply held convictions, that underpin all aspects of a school's life and work" (Hawkes).

Step 2

Engage yourself and your entire faculty/all the adults in your community in an LVE Educator/Facilitator Workshop, to explore the kind of values-based atmosphere you would like to create, learn about skills to do such, and think about how you can make values an important, integral part of your school culture and curriculum. Plan to engage in an ongoing dialogue about values, as you make your organization one which thinks about values when making decisions about, for and with, students and teachers.

Step 3

Find time slots to integrate LVE Activities. It is hoped that the activities in this resource generate further ideas from teachers in all subject areas, for all educators within the school can contribute to the exploration of values. Values education is most effective when the entire school community is engaged and values are integrated throughout the curriculum.

The staff of each educational community implementing LVE will need to decide how, when and by whom the LVE lessons will be taught. This is more easily done in primary schools, and with middle schools that have ample homeroom periods or dedicated periods for social skills development, citizenship, civil leadership, moral education, social responsibility or ethics. Schools without such time slots, are advised to creatively find a place to integrate two core lessons a week, at least for the first several months. For example, as many of the activities for peace and respect contain discussion and writing activities, they could be integrated and/or done during literature or language classes.

The lessons in the honesty unit could be done in history classes. The cooperation lessons could be done by physical education teachers.

Two or three lessons a week, suitably adapted to the age and background of students, are highly recommended during the first four months of LVE to obtain student "buy-in." This may not be possible for all educators to do, especially when only one teacher or a few teachers are implementing LVE within a school. Do not be concerned if you are the only educator doing values education. Many educators implementing LVE are in a similar situation. They have found that their way of being, and their passion for values, creates the needed "buy-in."

Implementation Details

LVE's sixteen values units are designed to allow you to easily plan values education at your site by focusing on one value a month during the school year. Book 1 includes eight values units for the first year of implementation and Book 2 includes another eight values units for implementation during the second year. A "value of focus" each month for the entire school facilitates planning for special subject areas, assemblies and special projects.

The universal values explored in all three books are peace, respect, love and caring, tolerance, honesty, happiness, responsibility, simplicity and caring for the Earth and Her Oceans, cooperation, humility, compassion, freedom and unity. The value unit exploring freedom for children ages three to seven is titled "Brave and Gentle". Another unit is titled "Another Value We Love". This offers activities on a few values and an invitation to educators to explore a value they feel is needed locally or nationally.

There are two values units on both peace and respect as these values are so important to young people and present the opportunity to help them build important intrapersonal and interpersonal social and emotional skills. It is recommended that educators begin with the Peace I and Respect I values units in Book 1 during the first year of implementation, and alternate years, and the Peace II and Respect II values units in Book 2 during the second year, rotating through eight values each year.

This book contains at least three values activities for each week. Facilitating at least two values activities a week is highly recommended to create student "buy in". Young people also benefit by relaxation/focusing times several times a week, or daily.

If a school is planning to begin values education with *only* two grades in a school, it is recommended that you start with the older students/higher grade levels. It is much healthier for younger students to "catch" values from older students who are benefiting from values education, than to have younger students who are into values education being bullied by older students who are not in the program. However, school-wide implementation is more effective and beneficial for all.

Assemblies and Songs

When the entire educational community is exploring the same value at the same time, assemblies are an excellent way to sustain the enthusiasm. Different classes or various clubs can take turns presenting values creatively at assemblies through drama, music, art, poetry, etc. Allow them to share their concerns about values and anti-values, and the service-learning projects with which they become involved.

Please begin with the Peace Unit!

Beginning each school year with a Peace Unit is always recommended. Young people are deeply concerned about peace — even those who may be externally aggressive. At the beginning of the unit, facilitators ask them to imagine a peaceful world. This allows them to look inside themselves and explore what they would like their world to be like. After a visualization, they are asked to express their ideas in words and artistically. What they create is always beautiful. The opportunity to explore what they would like in the world creates interest ... and a bit of needed hope for the cynical or marginalized youth.

While young children are then engaged in activities with stories and the making and playing with peace puppets, older students are led in mind mapping peace and violence. Lessons with relaxation/focusing exercises and art allow students a chance to explore peace at a personal level before a series of conflict resolution activities are begun. Discussions in those lessons help build understanding of others and allow them to further their communication skills.

Throughout each values unit, reflection points educate in a universal manner, that is, in a manner which models respect for all. Usually within six weeks, with just two or three lessons a week, students are doing conflict resolution successfully. Teachers report that students find the peace unit relevant; they note reduced resistance in students often considered unmotivated.

Is there a recommended order of values units?

We suggest beginning with the Peace I and Respect I Units as they build intrapersonal and interpersonal social and emotional skills in a sequential manner.

Living Values Education Activities for Children Ages 8–14, Book 1

Conflict resolution and Bullying No More lessons begin in the Peace I unit and are revisited in the Respect I Unit. Mind mapping peace and conflict, relaxation/focusing exercises and conflict resolution skills developed during the Peace I and Respect I lessons are important building blocks in creating a values-based atmosphere. If students are able to solve their own conflicts, peacefully and respectfully, there is much more time for teaching.

You may wish to do further values units in the order presented in the book, or you may wish to decide a different sequence depending on perceived needs. The Love Unit continues to reinforce communication and conflict resolution skills. For example, in the Love Unit, students are asked, "What was the starting point of the conflict? How will a loving attitude change the situation?" The Tolerance Unit invites appreciating each other and other cultures.

The Honesty Unit is also important, especially as it is helpful for older students to begin to comprehend the why's and how's of corruption. Young adults are asked to engage in activities about social justice in several of the values. Each one of the values units are designed to build personal skills as well as understanding of the value and the effects of the anti-value on the self, others and the community.

If you are implementing LVE independently, it may be easier to focus on the values that fit best into your curriculum. A bit of reflection about values or an interesting discussion here and there, can help students become more engaged — and see the difference values make.

Do I need to do every activity?

No. While it is good to include a variety of values activities, educators may choose not to do some lessons or may wish to substitute material. In many of the lessons you will find scripted questions and content. This has been provided as many educators have requested such specificity. Please feel free to adapt the questions to your own personal style, the needs of the students, the culture, and your particular setting.

Incorporating Values into the Existing Curriculum

All educators are encouraged to incorporate some values exploration into the regular curriculum. As the content expert, you know which materials on hand best portray the values or their contrast. History and social studies easily lend themselves to values discussions. You may wish to stop at critical points during lessons when one individual or a group of people exercise choice. Ask students, "What is this person or group valuing so much that this choice is being made? What are the values of the other group? What are the consequences of having this value and the challenges in achieving it? How do you see a particular value or its lack being portrayed?" For example, a historical unit about independence is an ideal time to look at what kinds of freedom people want. Ask, "Did they hold that same value in their treatment of other groups?" Ask students to recognize and discuss the application of a particular value or the consequences due to lack of that value.

In literature and language classes, the teacher can select reading materials that relate to the value being explored. Ask students to react to the material they just read, write about the value, or create poems. You may wish to use journal writing to bridge students' personal experience and the experiences of characters or themes in the text or ask them to write in the role of one of the characters to see what values motivate them.

The arts are a wonderful medium in which to incorporate values while teaching skills the students need to learn. You may wish to select plays that have to do with the value of focus. In music, while teaching students how to play and harmonize their instruments, discuss, for instance, the dynamics of unity. In art class, ask students to express the values while learning how to paint, draw, and sculpt.

Values webs are useful. Ask the team of teachers planning the values program to discuss the value in the context of their culture and the subjects in which they are planning to teach values. An example of a value web on Freedom follows.

Values Web

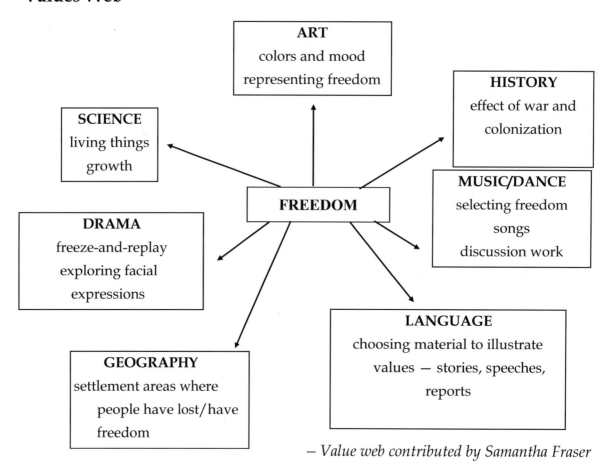

— Value web contributed by Samantha Fraser

Share Your Values Creations with the World!

Students

Students around the world are invited to share their murals, videos, poems, essays, songs, drawings, activities and experiences with students of similar age. Ask your teacher if there is an LVE social media site in your country through which young adults can share. Or send in the digital files of your artistic creation for posting on an LVE website to website@livingvalues.net.

Educators Share

Educators are invited to share their experiences or the artistic creations of their students with other educators around the world through LVE web sites. Please send in your contribution to the national ALIVE Associate, Focal Point for LVE or lve@livingvalues.net. Country Report pages, a Success Stories page and a Research page are on the livingvalues.net site.

Annual Evaluation

An important part of any program is evaluation. Your evaluation of the program and observations about changes with students are very important. Please do request an evaluation form at lve@livingvalues.net or send us your comments.

We hope you and the young people with whom you work
enjoy Living Values Education.

Thank you for your dedication to nurture young people
and educate hearts as well as minds.

UNIT ONE: PEACE I

Peace I Lessons

We recommend beginning with the Peace I Unit. This is suggested as the activities in this unit create the opportunity for students to reflect on what a peaceful world would be like, contrast peace and violence, learn to relax and fill the self with peace, and learn conflict resolution skills as well as other social emotional skills. Our experience is that young people care deeply about peace. Beginning with this values unit creates student buy-in and builds intrapersonal and interpersonal skills which help them contribute to a values-based atmosphere. And, their conflict resolutions skills will soon make the life of the educator easier!

Consider playing a song about peace every day at the beginning or end of "Living Values Education time". Playing and singing songs builds the feeling of community and is a great time to relax, to build the feeling of the values being explored, or to provide time for the students to contemplate the Refection Points on the board. Choose a song you feel the students will relate to; one that is appropriate for their age or one from their culture. "Teaching Peace" by Red and Kathy Grammer is a great song. Favorites with older students are "Imagine" by John Lennon and "We Are the World" by USA for Africa. A YouTube video of "A Song of Peace" by Pebblespash694 has lyrics and would be great for small or large groups: www.youtube.com/watch?v=mxidrVmwznU

This is also an opportunity to learn traditional songs and music from your culture or the culture of others. If the entire school is involved with the values program, your school may wish to do assemblies on peace to build enthusiasm and a feeling of belonging.

Peace Reflection Points

- Peace is more than the absence of war.
- Peace is living in harmony and not fighting with others.
- If everyone in the world were peaceful, this would be a peaceful world.

- Peace is being quiet inside.
- Peace is a calm and relaxed state of mind.
- Peace consists of positive thoughts, pure feelings, and good wishes.
- Peace begins within each one of us.
- To stay peaceful requires strength and compassion.
- Peace is a qualitative energy that brings balance.
- World Peace grows through nonviolence, acceptance, fairness and communication.
- Peace is the main characteristic of a civilized society.
- Peace must begin with each one of us. Through quiet and serious reflection on its meaning, new and creative ways can be found to foster understanding, friendships and cooperation among all peoples.
  – *Mr. Javier Perez de Cuellar, Secretary-General of the United Nations*

Peace I Unit Goals and Objectives

Goal: To think about peace and experience peace for the self.

Objectives:
- To think about and appreciate peace.
- To experience what peace feels like and to draw, paint or write about it.
- To identify thoughts and actions that allow them to feel peaceful.
- To write a poem or short story about their most peaceful moments.
- To relax, let go of tension, and enjoy being quiet and peaceful during Relaxation/Focusing exercises in the classroom.
- To experiment with experiencing the qualities and values that they have identified as a group as most important.
- To help students increase their ability to concentrate.
- To express peace artistically.
- To participate in singing songs about peace.
- To participate in a small group to create songs or poems about peace or peace versus violence.

Goal: To increase knowledge about the feelings and consequences of peace and peacelessness and a peaceful school and a school of conflict.

Objectives:

- ❏ To imagine a peaceful world and communicate their ideas through words and a drawing or a short essay.
- ❏ To think about small actions people can do to contribute to a peaceful world.
- ❏ To participate in making a drawing of a Peace Cake of human qualities, choosing the qualities that they think are most important for a peace and sharing the results with family and/or friends.
- ❏ To participate in a discussion about words and actions that would exist in a peaceful school versus a school culture of conflict.
- ❏ To select the qualities and values in small groups that they would like to have in their own Peaceful Classroom.

Goal: To express their feelings and build positive, peaceful methods of creating peace and dealing with conflict, including conflict resolution skills.

Objectives:
- ❏ To identify thoughts that create peacelessness and thoughts that create peace.
- ❏ To participate in a group process to choose three practical ways to make their classroom more peaceful.
- ❏ To participate in a discussion about how they feel when people are mean or hurtful.
- ❏ To be able to listen to others during a conflict resolution exercise and repeat key phrases of what they say.
- ❏ To participate in a conflict resolution exercise, stating how they feel and identifying what they would like others to do and not do. They may participate by playing a role in the exercise, or as a participant in a real conflict, or as a peer mediator.
- ❏ To demonstrate understanding of how hurt or fear moves into anger by being able to state two examples.
- ❏ To identify two thoughts or actions that allow negativity to grow.
- ❏ To identify two thoughts or actions that allow peace to grow.
- ❏ To participate in creating a negative story and a positive story to understand more clearly the effect of thoughts.

Goal: To express their feelings about bullying, think of what qualities and understandings are important to not be a bully, and learn methods to avoid being bullied and help their peers if they are bullied.

Objectives:
- ❑ To learn the definition of bullying.
- ❑ To identify feelings of the person being bullied and participate in a discussion about how they have seen people bullied.
- ❑ To identify values, qualities and beliefs that help us not be a bully.
- ❑ To learn two assertive responses if they encounter someone bullying, create their own responses, and role play giving those responses with self-respect and confidence.
- ❑ To learn about benevolent-assertive responses as a method of disarming someone bullying in a non-offensive and non-defensive manner.
- ❑ For 11-year old students and older to learn about the increasing suicide rate of children their age in response to meanness on social media and discuss values and guidelines for kindness on social media.
- ❑ To learn about and role play safe strategies for peer intervention when a peer is being bullied.

PEACE I LESSON 1
Imagining a Peaceful World

Play a song on peace. You may want to teach a song to the younger students. Play a song for the older students to which they will relate. Invite them to bring in a couple of their favorite songs. Tell them that in the next few weeks the school/class will be exploring something very important, peace.

Discuss/Share
- Who can tell me about peace?
- What is peace?
- What does it mean to have a peaceful world?

Acknowledge all responses and thank them for sharing. Continue with Imagining a Peaceful World exercise.

Imagining a Peaceful World

Lead the students in this imagining exercise. Say the following, pausing at the dots:

"A wonderful thing about people your age is that each one knows about peace. I'd like to start our unit by asking you to use your mind to imagine a peaceful world. Let yourself be very still. I want you to picture in your mind a beautiful, big bubble — this bubble is so big that you can step inside — it's like a small, silent plane that you can travel in to imagine going into the future, to a better world. . . . You step inside the bubble and float to that world that is completely peaceful. . . . The bubble rests on the ground of this world, and you step out . . . . What does it look like there?. . . . Imagine how you would feel. . . . How does nature look? . . . What is the air like? . . . How do the houses look? . . . As you take a walk around a lake, let yourself feel how peaceful that place is and how you feel. . . . Look in the lake and see your reflection . . . You can feel your body relaxing in this peaceful place. . . . How do you feel? . . . As you pass by a group of people, notice the expressions on their faces and how they relate to one another. . . . You see a group of young people your age playing. . . . What are they doing? . . . How are they treating each other? . . . Soon a couple of them see you. . . . They smile and call to you to come over and join them. . . . You spend some time with them. . . . Soon it is time to go, and you say goodbye . . . and they wave as you step back into your bubble plane to return here. . . . The bubble floats back to this time and this class. . . . As you experience yourself seated here, the bubble disappears, leaving you with a feeling of stillness within."

Share

Give the students time to share their visualization. Some may wish to share their experience. Or, the teacher may wish to ask them to share first about nature, then the self, and then about what they imagined about relationships with others. Acknowledge and actively listen to their responses.

Activity

Eight to Eleven Activity: Divide the class into small groups three or four students, so each group can draw a large picture of a peaceful world. Allow each group of students to bring their large picture up to the front and share it with the rest of the class.

Twelve to Fourteen Activity: They may enjoy drawing a peaceful world in small groups as in the above activity. Or, ask them to share their thoughts about a peaceful world in writing. Or, they may write a few lines and illustrate it.

Homework: Ask them to think about one small thing people could do to contribute to a peaceful world.

PEACE I LESSON 2
Mind Mapping Peace and Peacelessness

Begin with a peace song. If you are up to a bit of fun and you think your students would enjoy some movement, invite them to move slowly around the room with the music, making peaceful movements. Or lead them around the room or open space, making peaceful movements. Perhaps during the next LVE activity, one of them could lead.

Homework follow-up: Ask the students if they thought of small things anyone could do to contribute to a more peaceful world. Acknowledge all responses and thank them for sharing.

Mind Mapping Activity

Say, "Today, let's explore the differences between a peaceful world and a world of conflict through mind mapping."

Mind Map: Begin by drawing a large circle on a white board, putting Peace on the right side and Peacelessness/Conflict/Violence on the left side. If you are not familiar with Mind Mapping, you will find information in the Appendix (Item 1). Start with a branch for Self on the Peace side of the circle, asking them what happens when there is Peace in the Self and writing in brief their responses. Then ask them what happens when there is a lack of peace, conflict or violence in the Self. The students are to supply all the answers. Also do branches for Families, Friends and the Neighborhood.

Discuss the Reflection Points:
- Peace is more than the absence of war.
- Peace is living in harmony and not fighting with others.
- If everyone in the world were peaceful, this would be a peaceful world.

Creative Activity

Divide the students into groups of four to six. Ask each group to create a song or poem about peace or peace versus peacelessness, conflict or violence. It could be a rap song. Allow them to perform their creation for the group.

PEACE I LESSON 3
If We Were All Peaceful

Play, teach, or sing with the students a peace song that they created, one from your culture, or share your favorite peace song.

Write the Reflection Points on the board:

- ♦ Peace is being quiet inside.
- ♦ Peace is a calm and relaxed state of mind.
- ♦ Peace consists of positive thoughts, pure feelings, and good wishes.

Discuss/Share

- If every single person in this world were peaceful inside, would this world be more peaceful? How?
- What does peace feel like?
- What types of thoughts do you think people have when they feel peaceless?
- What types of thoughts or activities do you think help people feel peaceful?

Introduce the Physical Relaxation Exercise: Say, "Many people in the world today feel stressed. Do you experience being stressed sometimes? . . . One way to help get rid of stress and feel more peaceful is doing a physical relaxation exercise. When we get rid of some of the tension, we can relax and be at our best. Let's try it." Play some relaxing music, if possible. Read the following slowly.

Physical Relaxation Exercise

"Sit comfortably . . . and relax. . . . As you relax, let your body feel heavy and focus your attention on your feet. . . . Tighten all your muscles for a moment . . . and then relax them . . . let them stay relaxed. . . . Now become aware of your legs, letting them be heavy . . . tightening the muscles . . . and then relaxing them. . . . Now the stomach . . . tighten the muscles for a moment . . . and then relax. . . . Be aware of your breathing, and take in a deep breath. . . . As you breathe out, let go of any tension. . . . Be in the present moment. . . . Breathe in deeply again . . . let the air out slowly . . . and let go of any tension. . . . Now tighten the muscles in the back and the shoulders . . . and then relax them. . . . Tighten the muscles in your hands and arms . . . and then relax them. . . . Gently move your neck . . . first to one side, then to other . . . relax the muscles . . . now tighten the muscles of the face . . . the jaw . . . and then relax the face and the jaw. . . . Let the feeling of wellbeing flow through the body. . . . Focus again on your breathing, breathing in deeply . . . and then letting go of any tension. . . . I am relaxed . . . I am peace . . . I am ready to be at my best."

— *Contributed by Guillermo Simó Kadletz*

Eight to Ten Activity: Choose one or more colors and draw or paint peace.

Eleven to Fourteen Activity: Write about a time you felt really peaceful — or paint or draw peace.

NOTE TO EDUCATOR

An LVE supplement, *Helping Young People Process Difficult Events* is available. Originally developed in response to a request from educators in Afghanistan, this special supplement contains 12 lessons to help young people express and process their reactions to violence and death. Designed to be used with *Living Values Education Activities for Children Ages 8–14*, it also contains guidelines to help children begin to process their reactions to other circumstances which may be emotionally traumatic. The lessons can be done in a classroom setting by educators that have undergone an LVE Workshop and learned the skills of active listening and validating and how to create a values-based atmosphere. You may write your LVE Trainer or content@livingvalues.net to access this free resource.

PEACE I LESSON 4

Baking a Peace Cake

Make a Peace Cake of human qualities and characteristics. This activity provides an opportunity for students to think about a peaceful environment, create, and discuss what they think is important with their peers, parents, and teachers. Allow students to work in small groups of four or five.

Begin with a song.

Discuss/Share

- What are the finest human qualities you think should be in the Peace Cake?

Activity

Step 1. Each small group is to choose the ingredients. Ask them to make a list of the finest human qualities you would like to put into your Peace Cake.

Step 2. Choose the amount of each ingredient: The amount of each ingredient can be measured in grams, kilograms, percentages, or any other suitable way.

Step 3. Mixing and baking the cake: Describe the order in which you would put the ingredients into the cake mix and explain how you would mix and bake the cake. (The evening before Lesson 5, younger students may wish to look at a recipe book with their father or mother.)

Step 4. Presenting your work: You can record your work in any way you wish. Your presentation can be as simple, imaginative, creative, and illustrated as you wish. Allow each group a large piece of paper on which to draw their cake.

Step 5. Sharing your work: Allow each group to share their recipe and picture with the class. Talk about your Peace Cake with family and friends. Explain that the ingredients and the way it is baked make it taste the way it does. Invite them to share their feelings about your cake.

– Contributed by Peter Williams

Display: Allow each group to put their work on the wall. Perhaps in another couple of weeks they can put them in shop windows in the community.

Another possibility: Send copies of your recipes and jpg files of your Peace Cake pictures to website@livingvalues.net for posting on the LVE international website.

PEACE I LESSON 5
A Special Place

Begin with a song.

Discuss/Share

- Do you have a special place where you can sit quietly and think?
- Why do you like to be quiet and peaceful?
- How do you feel inside when you are quiet and peaceful?
- What sorts of things prevent us from feeling peaceful?

– Contributed by West Kidlington School

Discuss the Reflection Points:

♦ Peace consists of positive thoughts, pure feelings, and good wishes.

♦ Peace is a qualitative energy that brings balance.

Living Values Education Activities for Children Ages 8–14, Book 1

Peace Relaxation Exercise

Read the following slowly, pausing at the ellipses. You may wish to play some music softly. Allow the students at least eight minutes to relax and be.

"Let the body be relaxed and still. Let go of thoughts about the day, and slow down within. . . . Be in the present, focusing on this moment in time. . . . Breathe in deeply . . . and let go of any tension through the bottoms of your feet. . . . Breathe in deeply . . . and let go of any tension through the bottoms of your feet. . . . Breathe in deeply . . . and let the mind be still. Slowly absorb waves of peace. . . . Imagine being outdoors. . . . You might imagine sitting under a tree, looking at the sky . . . or being by the ocean . . . or in a meadow. . . . (Pause for a full minute.) As you picture the beauty of nature in front of you, absorb waves of peace. . . . Let the self feel totally safe and relaxed. . . . Enjoy being still inside and absorbing peace. . . . You are naturally peaceful . . . still. . . . Now surround the self with love . . . surround the self with peace. . . . You are important . . . you are part of creating a peaceful world. . . . Now bring your attention back to the room. . . . You are peaceful . . focused . . . alert."

Activity

Ask students to write a short story or a poem about their most peaceful moments. "I feel most peaceful when _____." Perhaps a few of them would like to share what they created.

PEACE I LESSON 6
Increasing Peace at School

Begin with a peace song.

Discuss/Share

Introduction: "The other day we mind mapped the differences between peace and peacelessness. Today, I'd like you to think about the differences between a Peaceful School and a School with Conflict."

Step 1. Put the words Peaceful School and School of Conflict at the top center of the white board or on flip chart paper and prepare to write their answers to the following two questions in the appropriate column.

Ask:

- What kinds of things happen in a Peaceful School?
- What kinds of things happen in a School of Conflict?

Step 2. Add another column on each side of the two center columns. Title them *Feelings*

Ask:
- How do you think the people feel who are arguing, bullying and fighting in the School of Conflict? (Record their answers in the appropriate column.)
- How do you think the people feel in the peaceful school? (Record their answers in the appropriate column.)

Step 3. Add another column on each side of the four center columns. Title them *Words and Actions*. As before, record their answers in the appropriate column.

Ask:
- What kind of words would you hear from people who are arguing and bullying in the School of Conflict?
- What kinds of actions would you see from people who are arguing, bullying and fighting in the School of Conflict?
- What kind of words would you hear from people in the Peaceful School?
- What kinds of actions would you hear from people in the Peaceful School?
- Which of the words and actions that we have here on the board would you like to try in our classroom? (Circle the words and actions that they voice wanting.)

Say, "Just as people create their world and students create what happens on the playground, so we are creating what happens here in this class."

Small Group Action

Step 1. Say, "Now I would like you to look at the Peace Cake recipes and pictures that you made. Everyone, please form the same small groups of people you were with when you made the pictures. I would like each group to gather around your picture and decide which values or qualities you would like to have in our own Peaceful Classroom. I will give each group ten minutes to write down the eight values or qualities you think are most important for a Peaceful Classroom."

Step 2. As they gather, please make a header for another column titled Our Peaceful Classroom. Perhaps put it on a large piece of paper so it can be kept on a wall.

Step 3. Invite each group to call out their eight values or qualities. Underline the values or qualities when they are repeated by another group. In this way you can find out which qualities or values are most important for the entire group.

Step 4. When all the groups are finished, circle the six values or qualities that have the most "underlining". Double circle the top three values or qualities. (Please keep this list and make it visible to the students.)

Step 5. Putting their thoughts into action: Ask the class to think of three practical things they would like to try based on the most frequently mentioned values or qualities. For younger students, help them make the suggestions practical, e.g., after lunch, we could play a peace song, or we could really listen when other people are sharing.

Step 6. Try the ideas the rest of the day and the next day and then ask the students to evaluate the process. Allow them to decide if they want to try it for another week. Ask them if they would like to create other ideas from the Our Peaceful Classroom list.

Close with the Peace Relaxation Exercise. At the end of the exercise, add another two minutes while you name three or four values or qualities they identified as the most important. For each one say, "I value _____. I am _____. I let the light of _____ enter my mind." Then pause before doing the same with the next two values or qualities.

PEACE I LESSON 7
Bullying No More — Creating Assertive and Benevolently Assertive Responses

Begin with a song.

Discuss/Share

Say, "In the last couple of Living Values Education lessons we talked a little bit about bullying. Let's explore bullying a little more." Please share a definition of bullying. You may wish to adapt the below definition, as appropriate for the age of the young people with whom you are working.

> "unwanted, aggressive behavior among school aged children that involves a real or perceived power imbalance. The behavior is repeated, or has the potential to be repeated, over time. . . . Kids who bully use their power — such as physical strength, access to embarrassing information, or popularity — to control or harm

Living Values Education Activities for Children Ages 8–14, Book 1

others. … Bullying includes actions such as making threats, spreading rumors, attacking someone physically or verbally, and excluding someone from a group on purpose." (U.S. Department of Health and Human Services)

Ask:
- What are different ways you've seen people bullied?
- Have you seen people bullied in different ways in other places? How?
- Have any of you ever been bullied?
- How do you feel when you are bullied?
- Have any of you seen someone else bullied?
- How do you feel when that happens?
- Have any of you acted like a bully? How did that feel?
- Would anyone like to share anything else about bullying?

Accept and acknowledge all responses of the students. Comment: "Yes, being bullied destroys our feelings of peace, safety and happiness."

Ask:
- Do you want our class/school/club to be a bully-free zone? (Great!)
- Who is the one person you can always affect? (Yourself.)
- The first step in creating a bully-free zone is to not be a bully! What values and qualities help you to not act like a bully?
- What beliefs help you to treat all others kindly?
- Why do you think people sometimes act like bullies?

Say, "Thank you for sharing. Yes. And, often when people don't feel good about themselves, they are mean to others."

Ask:
- What can we do to feel better about ourselves when we're not feeling so good?

"Great ideas." Say, "Now let's look at bullying, and what to do and not do. Generally, when someone is mean, people react passively or aggressively. There is a third option which is called assertive."

Ask:
- When someone calls you a name, what is an aggressive response? (Yes, to call him a name back or hit him.)

63

- And what does it lead to? (Yes, more name calling or a fight.)
- When someone calls you a name, what is a passive response? Looking sad or looking frightened.)
- How would that feel?

Say, "People who act as bullies will usually continue to be mean to someone who acts passively, that is, who looks sad or frightened. People who act as bullies want to feel they are powerful, so when the target they are bulling looks upset they feel more powerful. Other people who act like bullies are simply so miserable inside that they want others to be miserable too."

Say, "So if you respond passively to a bully, he or she may bully you again. If you respond aggressively to a bully, the name calling or fighting is likely to get worse. The third type of response is an **assertive response. It begins with staying in your own power of peace and self-respect.** It might look like:

- ★ Looking confident, shrug your shoulders like it doesn't matter because you know who you are, and walk away. (Please act it out for the students.)
- ★ An assertive verbal response: "I don't like it when you do that, I want you to stop." (Please act it out for the students, stating the sentence clearly and with self-respect and confidence.)

Activity

- ➢ Say, "Everyone, please stand up and let me see the first 'It doesn't matter because I know who I am' response." . . . . . "Again! Great!"
- ➢ "Now I'm going to call all of you a name. When I do, I want you to give me your first assertive 'I know who I am' confident response. Are you ready? (Call them a not-so-bad name and positively reinforce them for their 'I know who I am' confident response.
- ➢ "Great. Now everyone together, the assertive verbal response: I don't like it when you do that, I want you to stop."
- ➢ "Great. Say it one more time, a little louder and with self-respect."
- ➢ "Okay, I'm going to call you a name. Ready?" Call them a no-so-bad name, softly, prompting them to give their assertive response.
- ➢ Do this again a couple more times, calling them a name a little more loudly each time.

> When finished, smile at them, tell them "Well done!" And then tell them that's the last time you want to hear any name calling in your class!"

Introduce benevolent-assertive responses: With a benevolent-assertive response, the student is deliberately not agreeing with the offending person by letting the person know in a non-offensive and non-defensive manner of a different view. The comment may include an acknowledgement of the goodness of the offending person or change the direction of the interaction to values, qualities or relationship. This can be quite effective for it communicates a lack of fear and changes the dynamic. It is also a more peaceful and respectful response.

Share examples of benevolent-assertive responses . . .
When someone attempts to start a fight:
  ★ Fighting stinks. Can't we think of anything better to do?
  ★ I think there's enough fighting in the world. Fighting or friends … what a choice!
  ★ Peace is a better choice than fighting.

When someone makes a discriminatory remark:
  ★ Life wouldn't be so interesting if we were all clones.
  ★ God is a great artist. I think both of our colors are beautiful.
  ★ I was hoping to be purple this birth, but it didn't work out!
  ★ I think all the religions of the world are cool.

Share examples that could be used by the "target", or by another student who wants to stop the bullying of someone else and feels it is safe to do so.
  ★ Kindness is cool. Peace is cool. Come on, I know you have at least one of those inside.
  ★ <u>All</u> people deserve respect — that includes everyone.
  ★ The world has enough wars. Do we really need another one here?

> Tell the students you will say the examples again. This time you would like them to give you a thumbs-up if they think it might work for their situation.
> Then ask them to generate a few more benevolent-assertive responses.
> Then invite them to share examples of different situations that happen at your school or in the neighborhood. Ask everyone to generate responses to those

situations as a group.

Role Play: Divide the students into small groups of three or four and ask them to role play, acting out the two assertive responses and trying out one or two of the benevolent-assertive responses to the situations of their choice. Each student is to get a turn.

For older students who are using social media:
If there is time, please continue with the following. If there is not enough time, please continue at the beginning of the next lesson.
Ask:
- Have any of you seen someone bullied or treated badly on social media?
- How do people bully on social media? (Some of the students are likely to want to share some stories. If so, ask them not to use anyone's name.)
- Are you sometimes frightened that might happen to you?
- Would anyone like to share anything else about bullying?

For students eleven and older: "There have been a few very, very sad cases where children as young as 11 killed themselves because of what was written about them on social media."
Ask:
- What values or qualities would have prevented these tragedies from taking place? (Actively listen, as always, to their responses and reactions.)
- What guidelines can you think of that would help someone decide whether to text or post something?

Ask one of the students to write on the board the examples the students generate. Examples are:
- ★ Is this kind or helpful?
- ★ Would I like to get this?
- ★ Never hit send when I'm angry!

Before closing: Remind the students that if they are being bullied, it is important to go to a responsible adult for help. Discuss who they would go to in your particular setting.

Close with an uplifting song, and perhaps ask them to get up and move to the music, shaking out any tension. End with a peace relaxation exercise.

NOTE TO EDUCATOR
Please read prior to lesson 8

Lessons in conflict resolution are simple, develop good communication skills which are useful in life, and have proved to be successful. There are many excellent resources, each one varying to some degree. In some schools, students serve as peer conflict resolution managers during break and playtime. The students often wear a special sash, cap, or armband to identify their role.

Conflict Resolution Process

First, the students in conflict are asked if they want help in resolving the problem. If they do, one or two conflict managers sit with them. One can sit by one upset student, the other by the other upset student. It is more comfortable for two conflict managers to be together so they can give each other moral support.

If one or both students say they do not want help, they are not willing to listen and talk, ask them if they would like a few minutes to quiet down by listening to a relaxation/focusing exercise, meditating, or doing some art work to express their feelings. If they say no, then they are choosing the standard disciplinary procedure of the school.

The "conflict resolution managers" or "peer mediators" are there to help the students solve the conflict. They are to listen to their replies and direct them to listen to each other rather than interrupting. The peer mediators are to encourage the students to listen carefully without interruption, and then repeat to each other what they heard the other say. Their job is to appreciate the disputants' listening and problem-solving skills, and to avoid taking sides. They are not to blame, accuse, moralize, or judge. They are there to help the students resolve the conflict. It is easy to slip into old verbal patterns, so be careful!

> ➤ A conflict resolution manager starts with the more visibly upset student, asking him or her to state <u>what happened.</u>
> ➤ Ask the second student to listen and repeat back what he or she heard. (He or she is not to contradict, argue, or blame, but simply repeat.)

- The same question — What happened? — is then posed to the second student, and the first student is to listen carefully and repeat.
- The next question asked each student is, "How were you feeling?"
- Again, each listens and repeats what the other said.
- Next, they are asked: "What would you like to stop?"
- After they each answer and have repeated back what the other said, then they are asked: "What would you like to happen instead?"
- The students are then asked if they can agree to do what the other suggested.
- If they are not happy with that suggestion, they are asked to generate other solutions.
- They are then asked if they can make a firm commitment to try to behave in the way they both agreed.
- When both have agreed to another behavior, the conflict resolution managers compliment them and tell them to return to the regular school activity.

Starting Conflict Resolution in Schools: All students are taught the same communication process. Tell the students about the process, demonstrate it for them, and lead them in practice. One person may want to visit the different classes and do all the training, or teachers can be taught how to do this at a teacher training session. **Post the conflict resolution questions/process in each classroom.**

Conflict resolution managers might want to take the questions with them to the playground and even take notes during the process. If so, the questions can also be found in Item 2 of the Appendix. Let all students know that if they have a conflict on the playground, they may go to the student conflict resolution managers, or other students can call the managers to come over. As part of giving the students more ownership in this process, you may wish to have a contest for re-naming the conflict resolution managers. Perhaps you would get suggestions to call them peacemakers, stars, or _____? The students could submit possible names, and there could be a school-wide selection of the name.

Conflict resolution has had dramatic effects in teaching students how to mediate disagreements and fights. Several teams of students can rotate as conflict resolution managers. Adults should positively comment on the courage and qualities of the students — both of the conflict resolution managers and of the students who are willing to communicate and listen to help resolve a problem.

Conflict Resolution Process: Summary of Steps

The mediator asks each student the question:

"Are you willing to work on a solution?" If the answer is "yes," continue. Ask each student one question at a time, and wait for their response. The other student listens and repeats what was said.

Then ask:

- Please tell us what happened.
- How did you feel when that happened?
- What would you like to stop?
- What would you like her/him to do instead?
- Can you do that?
- Can you make a firm commitment to try to act the way you both have agreed?

Compliment them for the qualities they demonstrated during this peace process.

PEACE I LESSON 8
Introducing Conflict Resolution

Educator Preparation: Be familiar with the above information, and list the six questions used during conflict resolution on a poster or board.

Are you willing to work on a solution?
Each person has to be willing to
LISTEN to Each Other
and repeat what the other says.

1. Please tell us what happened.
2. How did you feel when that happened?
3. What would you like to stop?
4. What would you like him/her to do instead?
5. Can you do that?
6. Can you commit to trying to behave in the way you two have agreed?

Begin the session with a peace song.

Ask:
- What would happen in the world if everyone learned to communicate and solve problems instead of fighting? (Acknowledge their responses.)

Say, "People all over the world are learning about conflict resolution. The more people learn it, the more there is hope for peace. I really believe that people can solve their problems."

Say, "Today, we're going to learn one method of conflict resolution. These are the steps." Review the 6 steps you have written on a poster or board.

Go back to the first question and the sentence under it.
Ask:
- Willingness to work on a problem really helps, doesn't it? Why?
- What does it mean about you as a person if you are willing to work on a problem? (If they have not included the following answers, please do include them: "It takes courage to work on a problem. It means that you believe you are capable of finding a solution, and it means you believe other people are capable, too."

Say, "It's good to start with the problems we know about. Let's list them.
Ask:
- What kinds of things do people your age fight over? Listen and list their responses. (In classes with older students, ask them to write the responses on the board.) *Note to Educator:* Keep the list for future lessons.
- How do you feel when _____ (one event mentioned) happens?
- If the feeling is anger, ask: What feeling is underneath that feeling?
- How do you feel when _____ (another event mentioned) happens?
- If the feeling is anger, ask: What feeling is underneath that feeling?
- How do you want to feel? Accept all responses. Ask them if they want to feel valued, respected, and loved (if they have not given those responses).

Demonstration: Ask for two volunteers to try the conflict resolution exercise. Let them pretend to have a common conflict or else enact a recent conflict. The teacher models asking each student the six questions and asks them to listen to each other.

Thank the volunteers. Ask for questions or reactions.

Living Values Education Activities for Children Ages 8–14, Book 1

> **NOTE TO EDUCATOR**
>
> Actively listen to their replies, direct them to listen to each other and repeat what the other says. Appreciate their listening and coming up with solutions. If a student blames, interrupts or accuses the other during the dialogue, say "Please listen," or "Please answer the question." Restate the question again, such as, "How did you feel when that happened?"

The students may want to learn the peace rap song "Cool Off", or make up their own song.

Ask for two more volunteers and demonstrate the conflict resolution process again.

Song: Cool Off

This peace rap song was created by Max and Marcia Nass.

Cool off, cool off, cool off, cool off!
Solving problems is hard when you're mad,
Walk away, cool off, you'll be glad.
(Repeat)

When you're angry at someone, it's not easy to have fun,
You'll get madder if you stay. Get smart and just walk away.

You don't need to start a fight to prove who's wrong and who is right.
Remember the good times you had, and then you won't feel so bad.

Take deep breaths and cool off. Find a friend to listen to you talk.
You just want peace, my friend, to make your anger end.

Cool off, cool off, cool off, cool off!
Solving problems is hard when you're mad,
Walk away, cool off, you'll be glad.

Mind your own business. Don't make threats.
Play with people who don't fight.
Don't call names, just be kind. Everything will be alright.

When you're angry at someone, it's not easy to have fun.

Living Values Education Activities for Children Ages 8–14, Book 1

You'll get madder if you stay. Get smart and just walk away.

You don't need to start a fight to prove who's wrong and who is right
Remember the good times you had, and then you won't feel so bad.

Take deep breaths and cool off. Find a friend to listen to you talk.
You just want peace, my friend, to make your anger end.

Cool off, cool off, cool off, cool off!
Solving problems is hard when you're mad,
Walk away, cool off, you'll be glad.

Close with a relaxation exercise.

PEACE I LESSON 9

Conflict Resolution Continues: What We Like and Don't Like — Under the Anger

Begin with a song.

Discuss/Share

Say, "Yesterday, we were discussing some of the things people have conflicts over and we made a list of those. Let's look at them in relation to the questions asked during the conflict resolution process."

Take one item from the list, for example, name-calling, and ask the following questions:

- How do you feel when that happens? (If the response is anger, ask: What feeling is underneath that?)
- What would you like the other person(s) to stop doing?
- What would you like the other person(s) to do/say instead?

Repeat the above process with another couple of items from the list.

Say, "In some ways, people are simple. When we get angry, there is hurt or fear or embarrassment underneath. The hurt and fear come first when people do not feel valued, respected, or loved. Some people stay feeling hurt and others handle it by getting angry." Repeat what you just said and illustrate it on the board:

Living Values Education Activities for Children Ages 8–14, Book 1

Anger
Hurt, Fear, Shame or feeling Unsafe
Everyone wants to be valued, respected or loved.

Apply concept: Ask the students to think of examples of things that happen or a time they felt this way when something happened to them. If they are unable to think of an example, use examples from the list of conflicts made previously.

Activity

Instruct the students to form pairs or small groups and ask them to create a poster on what others should not do, or what behaviors they would like from others. The students may need another day to finish their posters and have those who wish to share do so.

End with the Peaceful Star relaxation/focusing exercise below, adding in the additional class-identified values or qualities.

Peaceful Star Relaxation Exercise

Read the following slowly, pausing at the ellipses. You may wish to play some music softly. Allow the students at least eight minutes to relax and be.

"One way to be peaceful is to be silent inside. For a few moments, think of the stars and imagine yourselves to be just like them. They are so beautiful in the sky, and they sparkle and shine. They are so quiet and peaceful. Let the body be still. . . . Relax your toes and legs. . . . Relax your stomach . . . and your shoulders. . . . Relax your arms . . . and your face. . . . Be still . . . be in the present. . . . Let the feeling of being safe emerge . . . and a soft light of peace surround you. . . . You, the tiny star, are full of peaceful light. . . . Relax into the light of peace. . . . Let the self be still and peaceful inside . . . You are focused . . . still . . . concentrated. . . . You are peace . . . a star of peace."

PEACE I LESSON 10
Listening as Part of Conflict Resolution

Begin with a peace song.

Demonstrate: Ask a couple of volunteers to role play the conflict resolution process.

Discuss/Share

Say, "One of the most important things in solving problems is to listen to others and really hear what they have to say."

Ask:

- How do you feel when you try to talk to someone and he or she turns away?

Acknowledge: "Yes, when people don't listen and are rude, problems usually get worse."

"Sometimes people do other things that interfere with solving a problem." Ask:

- "Would anybody like to guess what some of those things could be?"

Acknowledge their responses and add any of the following not mentioned.

- ❖ Blaming
- ❖ Telling the person he or she is silly or stupid
- ❖ Interrupting
- ❖ Accusing
- ❖ Contradicting
- ❖ Trying to make him or her feel guilty
- ❖ Getting angry because the other person is angry

Explain: "For effective listening, it is important to do two things:"
1. To really (genuinely) pay attention to what the person is saying, and
2. To let the other person know that you understand what he or she is saying.

Listening Activity

Form groups of three students. Ask them to count off one, two and three. For Round One: Person One will be the Talker, Person Two the Listener, and Person Three the Observer. See the chart below.

	Person One	Person Two	Person Three
Round One	Talker	Listener	Observer
Round Two	Observer	Talker	Listener
Round Three	Listener	Observer	Talker

- For Rounds One, Two and Three, each Talker shares something positive that happened to him/her.
- Do the rounds again, this time asking each Talker to share something that is important to him/her or something that makes him/her feel peaceful.
- Do the rounds again, this time asking each Talker to share something that he or she felt a little angry or sad about a long time ago. (If there is not sufficient time, continue this activity during the next lesson.)

During each round, the Listener should be encouraged to listen, occasionally reflecting the feelings or emotions of the Talker, or restating or paraphrasing the content of the message. The Observer in each round can provide feedback.

Discuss/Share

- How did you feel when someone really listened to you?
- Did anyone notice that anger automatically started to decrease when the person was genuinely listened to?

Say, "Real listening is giving respect. People who listen well have self-respect."

Close with a relaxation exercise, adding in the additional class-identified values or qualities.

Options: A Peace Circle and/or a Peace Club

A Peace Circle can be a regular time once a day or once a week when students and the teacher name actions they saw during the day/week that contributed to peace. It is also a wonderful idea when there is a conflict in the classroom, or when students come into the classroom with an unresolved conflict. A Peace Circle can be called into session as needed. It is wise for the teacher to be the mediator of a real conflict in the classroom. While it may seem to some teachers that this would take time away from teaching, most teachers who try it report that dealing with the conflict ends up saving time. Students learn that real conflicts are very solvable. Additionally, the teacher is demonstrating that peace is important to him or her — and the feelings of the students. When there is harmony it is much easier to feel and do our best.

Students and a teacher who is willing to be an advisor can set up a Peace Club. Students can create their own activities. Peer mediators could continue to refine and practice their methods with the help of the advisor as well as share with other mediators.

Living Values Education Activities for Children Ages 8–14, Book 1

Members of the Peace Club could create assemblies and dramas, create messages of peace, give Peace Awards, and acknowledge others.

PEACE I LESSON 11
Conflict Resolution — Peers as Mediators

Begin with a peace song.

Discuss the Reflection Points:
- Peace begins with each one of us.
- To stay peaceful requires strength and compassion.

Activities

Demonstrate: Ask four students to volunteer for a conflict resolution demonstration. Two are to act as mediators and two to pretend to have a conflict. The peer mediators will take over the role the teacher had been playing in asking the six questions and helping the students in conflict resolve the problem. Instruct each peer mediator to sit by the students who have the conflict. When one demonstration is finished, ask the four students to reverse roles.

Note to Educator: There is a conflict resolution sheet for the mediators to use in the Appendix.

Contrast Poetry Activity: If time remains, ask students to brainstorm vocabulary associated with the above activities. They can use a dictionary and thesaurus to find synonyms and antonyms. As a group, or as individuals, students can write poetry to take the reader from one feeling or idea to its opposite. The point is to use words to show a change in feelings as a conflict is resolved. For example:

Anger

Hot resistance

Eyes bright, throat too tight

Nails digging deep into fists

Itching to fight

Eyes meet

A tear trickles down an inflamed check

"I'm sorry"

"Me too"

Acceptance

– Contributed by Ruth Liddle

Allow those who wish to do so to share their poetry.

Close with a relaxation exercise, adding in the class-identified important qualities and values.

PEACE I LESSON 12
Bullying No More — Peer Intervention

Begin with a song.

Say, "We've been talking about peace in different ways. We've been exploring personal peace through thinking about when we feel most peaceful and doing the peace relaxation exercises. We've been exploring how to create peace when there's been a conflict with someone else by learning conflict resolution. You've also learned about assertive responses as that helps stop bullying."

Ask:

- Who remembers the assertive responses we did several lessons ago? (Lesson 9: "I know who I am", "I don't like it when you do that, I want you to stop," and a benevolent- assertive response.)
- May I have a couple of volunteers to role play them?

Note to Educator: Please give each of the volunteers a turn as the target and the person bullying.

Practice previously learned assertive skills: Ask everyone to stand up and form groups of two, each pair acting out all three responses.

Humor as a Strategy to Counter Bullying: Say, "Sometimes humor works in a bullying situation when you can be humorous with confidence. For example, a humorous response which usually disarms when delivered confidently with a smile is: 'If I had feelings, they'd be hurt!'

Ask if they have any humorous responses that have worked for them and invite them to share.

Note to Educator: Do comment if their humorous responses are mean, as the intent is not to be aggressive but to be assertive. The rule: When people don't get defensive and stay in self-respect, the bullying usually stops as there is no pay-off for the person bullying. A non-aggressive response can open the door of change for the person who is bullying."

Activity

Peer intervention — Working together to deter bullying

Educator information: Canadian research indicates that bullying stops 57 percent of the time within ten seconds if a peer intervenes. Bystanders passively watching bullying take place can add to the feeling of power the person who is bullying wants, so standing and watching can unwittingly reinforce bullying. Peer intervention is important as adults are rarely around when bullying occurs. Other children are frequently around when bullying occurs: 85 percent of the time.

Introduce the topic:

- I was thinking that as you are all working together so well with peace, you might be interested in learning simple ways to protect your friends and have them protect you if there's bullying. Would you like to hear about it?

Say, "When someone is bullying another person, if someone speaks up for the target, the bullying stops more than half of the time. If people just stand there and do nothing, the person bullying feels more powerful. In this lesson, we are going to look at safe things you can do that will help the person being bullied.

Say, "I am going to tell you about three different situations. I want you to think about which one you would prefer if you were the target of the person who is acting like a bully.

"**Response One:** You are being bullied and your classmates walk away from the bullying scene."

Ask:

- How do you feel? (Actively listen to their responses.)

"The good thing is that the person bullying is deprived of an audience, but the target feels unsupported and may fear the bystanders think less of him or her. It is important for the target to walk away, but to walk away alone might be difficult."

"**Response Two:** It's the same situation. You are being bullied but one of your classmates calls out to you, 'Come on, Sema. Don't listen to her.' Or, 'Come on, Tom, it's no fun listening to this.' 'Hey, Mira, let's go. This is totally uncool.' Your classmates walk away from the bullying scene *with* you."

Ask:
- How do you feel? (Actively listen to their responses.)

"The good thing is that the target feels supported by his or her classmates so does not feel as bad, and it is successful in stopping the bullying."

"In the situation, I just read there was:"
- ✯ Come on. Don't listen to her.
- ✯ Come on, it's no fun listening to this.
- ✯ Hey, let's go. This is totally uncool.

Ask:
- What kinds of things could you call out to the target to let him or her know you are helping them be safe?
  ➢ Make a list of their statements. As the children call out a statement, ask everyone in the group to echo them. Ask them to read aloud all the statements with self-respect when they have finished generating ideas.

Role Play: Tell them you would like them to role play this.
Ask:
- Who wants to be the person bullying?
- Who wants to be the target?
- Who wants to be the helpful bystander? What shall we call the helpful bystander?

Say, "The rest of you will play the bystanders watching the bully and the target."
Ask:
- Person bullying, what are you going to say? …… Got it? Allow the students to generate a bullying statement and/or action they have witnessed before.

Say, "Okay, person bullying, stand here. Target, please stand a few feet away and look surprised when he says something that is bullying. Helpful bystander (or whatever name they have decided upon), stand with the group. You can pick your lines from the list we made."

Living Values Education Activities for Children Ages 8–14, Book 1

Divide the students into groups of four or five so they all get to practice the helpful-bystander role. Positively reinforce efforts and encourage them to say their statements with self-respect and confidence.

"Response Three: It's the same situation. You are being bullied but one of your classmates calls out to you, 'Come on, Sema, it looks like Pam is grumpy today. Maybe she'll be nicer tomorrow!' 'Come on, Tom, it's no fun listening to this. It looks like Mack isn't his usual self today.' Then your classmates walk away from the bullying scene *with* you."

Ask:

- How do you feel? (Actively listen to their responses.)

"The target feels supported by the bystanders and you have been successful in stopping the bullying. But also, the person bullying has not been completely alienated. He or she has been offered a reason for their behavior. This opens a door for possible change."

A caution: Say, "*Sometimes* if we are a little kind a few times, the person bullying will stop bullying. *Not all the time, but sometimes*! Some people get stuck in being mean for a few years. But some people who bully can feel stuck in needing to be mean. So, when someone is a little kind, it can open a door for the person bullying to change. So be kind, and then step away. Don't be too kind — just a little! The most important thing is always to stop the bullying and help the target get away feeling supported."

Ask:

- Can you think of other things you could say to a person bullying?

Write down the benevolent-assertive responses the students come up with for the situations they are encountering and have them echo each statement. Perhaps decide together which responses might work for one person who is bullying and which might work better with another person bullying. Have a good time role playing Response 3 and the benevolent-assertive response scene until they can deliver the helpful-bystander statements with self-respect and confidence.

Close with a peace relaxation exercise of their choice.

PEACE I LESSON 13
Creating Verbal Stories — Growing Peace or Conflict

Begin with a relaxation exercise.

Discuss/Share

Discuss the Reflection Points:

- ◆ Peace begins within each one of us.
- ◆ Peace is a qualitative energy that brings balance.
- ◆ If everyone in the world were peaceful, this would be a peaceful world.

Ask:

- What allows the negative to continue to grow?
- How can feelings escalate so that small upsets become big and out of control?
- What type of thoughts keep conflict alive?
- How can we try and control these angry feelings and replace them by calmer, peaceful ones? (the help of friends, etc.)
- What allows peace to grow?
- What types of thoughts help peace grow?
- How does being at peace with oneself and one's friends make for a happier life?

Activity

Invite the group to create a story. Instruct the students to start with a peaceful situation that changes to a negative situation. Then start with a negative situation that changes to a positive one. Have fun! Find original ways to transform/solve the negative situations. The students may wish to create a reference book on solutions the students have found.

Eight to Ten Variation: This could be done as a continuous verbal story. The students create the story themselves, with one person starting, the next continuing, etc.

Eleven to Fourteen Activity: Depending on time, you may want students to create a verbal story as above, or small groups could create and enact a play. After each play, ask the students to comment on what gestures convey negativity or aggressiveness and what gestures convey peace.

– *Contributed by Sabine Levy and Pilar Quera Colomina*

Close with a peace relaxation exercises of their choice.

PEACE I LESSON 14
Collaborative Painting

Living Values Education Activities for Children Ages 8-14, Book 1

Note to Educator: This last Peace Lesson of the Peace I Unit could be the last lesson you are doing on Peace for the year. If so, you may wish to do the below activity, or create skits. Perhaps ask the students what they would like to do. There may also be a peace service learning activity they would like to carry out at school or in the community.

Begin with a song.

Discuss/Share

Ask the students what they enjoyed about the unit on peace and what they learned. Admire the work around the room and their accomplishments.

Eight to Ten Activity: Discuss what the students would like to put on a collaborative painting — symbols of peace, peace star, a picture of a peaceful world? Provide students with a long piece of colorful paper and individual small pots of paint and a brush. Play peaceful music. As they stand close to each other, they can paint their own small planned pattern. When the music stops, each student moves one step to the left or right.

— *Contributed by Linda Heppenstall*

Eleven to Fourteen Activity: Divide the class into five groups of students. Each group is responsible for painting the sky, earth, buildings, people, and animals. Provide students with a long piece of paper and enough individual small pots of paint and brushes for two groups. Play peaceful music and begin the Imagining a Peaceful World exercise from Lesson 1. Start to read the visualization very slowly. Each group can get up in turn to draw and paint its part of the picture. One person from each group can add to the visualization — adding verbal commentaries that include descriptions of what the group is painting. Everyone should have a good time while enjoying the music and staying in a state of peace. (This is intended as an experience — not a polished piece of art!)

Close with a relaxation/focusing exercise.

Additional Peace Lessons and Activities

PEACE I LESSON 15 for Ages 8 and 9
Dove Game

Discuss the following Peace Point: Peace begins within each one of us.

Activity

Make squares for the Dove Game or for an adaptation of a children's board game in your country. The Dove Game is an adaptation of a game from Spain, called the Goose Game. The Spanish board game has squares that form a spiral. Small groups of students can make the board game, drawing objects on small pieces of paper that can be later pasted onto a larger piece of paper in the form of a spiral. Or each member of the entire class can make one square, and then the squares can be laid on the floor of the classroom or outside in a large spiral. In the former, students would use dice and markers when they play. In the latter, they would use dice, but then stand by the square on the ground as they advance toward the finish.

Discuss

Ask the students to think about what pictures they would like to make for their game. One out of every five pictures should be a dove. Two out of every five pictures can be something that disrupts peace. For these, ask the students to draw pictures about what things they do not like other people to do. Arrange the pictures so that the fifth square is a dove, and then the tenth, fifteenth, and twentieth, etc. The last picture should be a picture of a completely peaceful world.

Game Rules: To play, the student rolls the dice. When a student lands on a picture of a dove, he or she says "Dove to dove, I fly above," and then moves to the next dove (five spaces up). If a student lands on a disrupting-peace square, he or she gives a solution. For example, if it is a picture of someone calling a name, the student can say, "I don't like it when you do that; I want you to stop." Or, if it is a picture of someone gossiping, he or she can say, "I feel ____ when you talk about me because ____." When a student thinks of a solution, he or she advances to the next peace square. The game is over when everyone reaches the last square of a peaceful world. Allow the students to encourage and help each other. The teacher can lead the applause when everyone reaches the last square.   *– Adapted from an activity contributed by Encarnación Royo Costa*

Activity

Play the Dove Game made in the previous lesson. First explain the rules, then ask the students to practice verbal responses in preparation for landing on the dove and conflict squares. Then ask them to play the game. Enjoy!

Celebrate with a happy song when everyone has reached the last square.

Activities

Dance peace to music as part of a picnic or open space time.

Dance free style or experiment with your culture or other cultures' traditional peace dances. Perhaps do an interpretive dance for an assembly, starting with a group of dancers who begin with peace, a few dancers who try to persuade them to escalate into violence, and the triumph of the peace dancers getting those who are violent into valuing peace.

Do an assembly on peace. Share your favorite peace songs and poems. Create a play of a peaceful school versus a school of conflict.

Create a peace sculpture. Provide the students with silly putty or clay. Ask the students to form groups of three and give each group some clay. Invite them to decide on the ultimate symbol of peace and create a small sculpture. Encourage them to be creative and let them know to be sure each person has a chance to work with the clay so it's a shared experience. — *Contributed by Janardhan Chodagam*

Paint a peace mural. Consider surrounding it with peace slogans or your Classroom Qualities and Values List.

UNIT TWO: RESPECT I

Respect I Lessons

The Respect Unit continues to help educators and students co-create a culture of peace and respect. This unit builds on the social and emotional skills begun in the Peace Unit. Please always begin with the Peace Unit.

As in the Peace Unit, please play or sing a song at the beginning of "values time" and end with a relaxation/focusing exercise. You may want to teach traditional songs or ask students to bring songs that relate to the theme. A list of Reflection Points is provided. Students may want to make up their own respect points or slogans. Also use favorite sayings from your culture, from legends, or quotes from respected individuals.

Respect Reflection Points

- The first respect is to respect myself — to know I am naturally valuable.
- Part of self-respect is knowing my own qualities.
- Respect is knowing I am unique and valuable.
- Respect is knowing I am lovable and capable.
- Respect is listening to others.
- Respect is knowing others are valuable, too.
- Part of respect for the self is taking care of the body.
- Respect for the self is the seed that gives growth to confidence.
- When we have respect for the self, it is easy to have respect for others.
- Those who give respect will receive respect.
- To know one's worth and to honor the worth of others is how one earns respect.
- Everyone in the world has the right to live with respect and dignity, including myself.
- Part of respect is knowing I make a difference.

Respect I Unit Goals and Objectives

Goal: To think about and experience self-respect.

Objectives:
- To state and be able to discuss two Respect Reflection Points about respect for the self.
- To identify times when they have a feeling of respect for the self.
- To identify six qualities of the self.
- To enjoy the Respect Relaxation/Focusing Exercises by the end of the unit, as demonstrated by sitting quietly during it and appearing content to do so.
- To identify positive and negative examples of self-talk and how it feels.
- To learn that it is okay to make a mistake; it is an opportunity to try and learn something new.
- To participate in a group story game and gain more awareness about the impact of respectful versus disrespectful self-talk.
- To paint respect or be part of a dance portraying respect.

Goal: To increase knowledge about respect.

Objectives:
- To state and talk about two Respect Reflection Points on respect for others.
- To participate in a discussion about feelings when people give respect and disrespect.
- To identify how people give respect and disrespect.
- To write a few lines of advice on how people should treat each other.
- To learn several greetings or polite phrases in other languages.
- To explore learning how to take good care of their body as part of self-respect.

Goal: To build respectful relationship skills.

Objectives:
- To identify five or more qualities that they like in others.
- To write down one positive quality for each student participating in the "Our Qualities" activity.
- During a conflict resolution discussion, to be able to generate an alternative respectful behavior that would help solve the problem.

- To learn the response, "I don't like it when you call me names. I want you to stop" and to be able to apply that response or another appropriate response if the situation arises.
- For students 10 and older, to be able to fill in the blanks to the problem-solving communication skill: "I feel _____ when you _____ because _____."
- To give respect to others by listening when they are speaking, as demonstrated by being able to listen to others during the values discussion time.

Goal for students 11 to 14: To learn about the art of distraction as a nonviolent method of stopping bullying and explore what to do in threatening situations.
Objectives:
- To hear that joining a fight is dangerous and never recommended.
- To learn about the art of distraction as a nonviolent method to stop bullying or to break up a fight.
- To practice different verbal "art of distraction" responses and apply that knowledge to any local situations about which they are concerned.
- To think about threatening situations they may encounter, learn about staying calm in the face of danger, possible non-defensive and defusing responses, and when to flee or protect the self in other ways.
- To role play local situations they may encounter with a variety of responses.

RESPECT I LESSON 1
Respect, Disrespect and Qualities

Begin with a song about respect or knowing yourself that the students like.

Discuss/Share

Explain that in the next few weeks the school/class will be exploring respect.
Ask:
- Who can tell me about respect?
- Why is respect important?

Activity

Step 1. Ask six students to volunteer to come to the front of the class and stand in a

Living Values Education Activities for Children Ages 8–14, Book 1

row. Give a pencil to the first student and ask her or him to hand it to the next student and so on down the row.

Step 2. Then, give the pencil to the first student again, and ask all the students in the line to hand the pencil to each other with disrespect.

Step 3. Then ask the six volunteers to hand the pencil to each other with respect.

Step 4. Ask:
- Was there a difference in the way the pencil was being given?
- What was different?
- How did you feel when the pencil was given with respect?
- How did you feel when the pencil was given with disrespect?
- What do you all prefer?
- Do you think everyone in the world would prefer respect?

Discuss the following two Reflection Points:
- The first respect is to respect myself — to know that I am naturally valuable.
- Respect is knowing others are valuable, too.

Ask:
- When do you feel good about yourself?
- When do you have a feeling of respect for yourself?

Students will sometimes mention specific things they do that are helpful to others as a time when they feel good about themselves. Confirm that when we do good things we feel good about ourselves. They will often mention a time when they look pretty/handsome or have something new. If they are mostly focusing on times when they feel good when they look good or have something new, prompt for responses about how they feel when they are helpful, friendly, kind, giving, etc. Accept and acknowledge all responses.

Step 5. Say, "Today, we are going to think about personal qualities, the things that are good about us. We all have many things that are the same, but one of the wonderful things about humans is that each has a personality of his or her own. Each person comes with a unique combination of qualities. Let's start by listing good qualities that people can have."

Living Values Education Activities for Children Ages 8-14, Book 1

The teacher can lead the students in brainstorming personal qualities, such as friendly, loyal, nice, kind, caring and compassionate. Depending on the vocabulary of the students, you may want to include creative, gentle, witty, cooperative, confident, humble, trustworthy, fun, hardworking, honest, benevolent, artistic, generous, economical, sensible, sweet, loving, patient, and tolerant. Keep the list of qualities you create together on the board.

Step 6. Ask the entire class the following questions, writing down the qualities they mention on the board.
- What qualities do you like in your friends?
- What qualities do you like adults to act with?
- Think about someone you admire. What qualities do you admire in that person?
- Who are your heroes? You may think of real people or characters in cartoons or movies. What positive qualities do they have that you like?

NOTE TO EDUCATOR

If some of the students mention negative qualities or actions as something they admire in people or their heroes, acknowledge their responses respectfully with actively listening. For example, "So you admire _____ when he _____." Then ask: "What value or quality do you see in him/her that allows him/her to do that? (For example, "He is not afraid of what people think," or "She has courage to fight for what is right.")

Reflection

Say, "Now, I would like you to think about three times when you felt really good about yourself. What quality or value were you showing at that time? Just write one line to remind yourself of that time. (Give them several minutes to do this.)

Now, I want you to think of the quality that you showed you had on each one of those times. (Give them several more minutes.) Give a few examples if they need it, such as: "If you remember a time when you helped someone, you might put down loving, caring, or compassionate. If you remember a time you returned something to someone who lost it, you might put honest."

I want you to add to the list of qualities that you are writing down by adding the qualities that you like in your friends, in adults, and in your heroes. (Give them three to four minutes to do this.)

- Think about someone who made a positive difference in your life. (Pause) What quality did he or she have that made a positive difference for you? Please write down that quality.

Say, "It is said that any quality you admire is really yours. So, you have just written down a list of your qualities. Now I want you to write down six qualities that are most important to you." Please give them a couple of minutes to do this.

Discuss the Reflection Points:

- Part of self-respect is knowing my own qualities.
- Respect is knowing I am unique and valuable.

Eight to Nine Activity: Instruct the students to draw a picture of a time they felt full of respect. Ask them to add their six qualities to the picture, writing, "I am _____ _____.

Ten to Fourteen Activity: Invite the students to draw symbols that represent some of the qualities and/or values that are important to them. Ask them to write their six qualities on their drawing, perhaps around the symbols or make them part of the picture.

Homework: I would like you to quietly read your six qualities to yourself every day. Each person has wonderful qualities deep inside, and we can silently make them more present in our lives when we remember them.

Close with a peace relaxation exercise.

RESPECT I LESSON 2
Feeling Disrespected — and My Advice about How People Should Treat Others

Begin with a song about respect or knowing yourself that the students like.

Share a Story

Read "Lily the Leopard" by John McConnel to students ages 8 and 9 (Appendix, Item 3) or another story that you like on respect. For older students, you may wish to read "Pillars of the Earth" by Pedro Pablo Sacristan (Appendix, Item 4) or select a story from your culture or curriculum. Another option is to see a video about respect and disrespect.

Discuss/Share

Mention the following Reflection Point in relation to the story:

♦ Respect is knowing I am unique and valuable.

Discuss the story read. The first two of the following questions are for the story, "Lily the Leopard." You may wish to begin with: "Lily knew she was unique, but at first she did not realize she was valuable." The other questions can be used with many stories. Ask:

- Why did they treat Lily without respect? (Lily was different.)
- How did Lily feel when the others were mean?
- How did the characters in the story give disrespect?
- How did the characters in the story give respect?
- How do kids your age sometimes give disrespect? What types of things do they do?
- How do you feel when people give you disrespect?
- How do you feel when that happens to other people?
- What are different ways people give respect?
- Why do people sometimes not give respect?
- Do you think everyone has times when they feel full of respect and other times when they feel down on themselves? (You might say something personal, such as, "Everyone I know feels down on themselves sometimes.)
- What's the moral/significance of the story?

Mention if they have not: "Sometimes kids who give disrespect don't know better. Maybe someone older treated them with disrespect. It's important to know that people who give disrespect don't have real respect inside."

Share the Reflection Points: Those who give respect will receive respect."
Ask:

- Can you think of examples of that?
- What would be your advice to people who give disrespect? How would you like people to treat each other?

Eight to Eleven Activity: Divide the students into groups of three to five. Instruct the students to write a few lines of advice about how people should treat each other. Allow each group to share their sentences with the class. Younger students may enjoy illustrating their advice with a picture.

Twelve to Fourteen Activity: Discuss in small groups of four or five how you would like people to treat each other. Write up your advice on a poster and present it to the class.

Introduce another Relaxation/Focusing exercise: "Relaxation/Focusing exercises are one way to enjoy and strengthen the feeling of respect inside. The one we are going to do today uses the image of a garden. Perhaps later one of you would like to make up one using the image of an ocean or another image."

Flowers of Respect Relaxation/Focusing Exercise

"Sit comfortably and let your body relax. . . . As you breathe slowly, let your mind be still and calm. . . . Starting at your feet, let yourself relax. . . . Relax the legs . . . the stomach . . . the shoulders . . . the neck . . . the face . . . . Let your mind become still . . . calm. . . . Breathe deeply. . . . Concentrate on stillness. . . In your mind, picture a flower. . . . Imagine the smell. . . . Enjoy its fragrance . . . . Observe its shape and color. . . . Enjoy its beauty. . . . Each person is like a flower. . . . Each one of us is unique . . . yet we have many things in common. . . . We are all naturally good inside. . . . Picture a garden around you with many varieties of flowers . . . all of them beautiful. . . . Each flower with its color . . . each flower with its fragrance . . . giving the best of itself. . . . Some are tall with pointed petals, some with rounded petals, some are big and others little. . . . Some have light colors and others have bright colors. . . . Some attract the eye because of their simplicity. . . . Each one of us is like a beautiful flower. . . . Enjoy the beauty of each one. . . . Each adds beauty to the garden. . . . All are important. . . . Together they form the garden. . . . Each flower has respect for itself. . . . When one respects the self, it is then easy to respect others. . . . Each one is valuable and unique. . . . With respect, the qualities of others are seen. . . . Perceive what is good in each one. . . . Each has a unique role. . . . Each is important. . . . Let this image fade in your mind, and turn your attention to this room again."

— Reflection contributed by Amadeo Dieste Castejon

Living Values Education Activities for Children Ages 8-14, Book 1

RESPECT I LESSON 3

Talking to Myself and the "It's okay to make a mistake" Rule

Begin with a song. Perhaps the students would like to perform one they created during the last lesson.

Discuss/Share

Say, "Everyone talks to themselves inside. Our talk to ourselves can be positive and respectful or negative and disrespectful."

Ask:

- What positive or respectful things do people say to each other?
- What positive or respectful things can you say to yourself?
- Would it be respectful to tell yourself you did a good job or tried your best, if you did do a good job or tried your best? (Yes.)
- What disrespectful things do people say to each other?
- Name calling is disrespectful. What names do you not want to be called?
- Is it disrespectful to call yourself a name? (Yes.)
- If you didn't do a good job, what would be a disrespectful way to talk to yourself about it?
- If you didn't do a good job, what would be a respectful way to talk to yourself about it?
- What do you say to yourself when you're afraid that you'll miss the ball during a ball game or fail a test?
- If you make a mistake, do you feel better if you call yourself "Stupid," or if you say, "It's okay to make a mistake, all I have to do is correct it"?[1]

Say, "There's no need to feel angry or sad or feel like a bad person when you make a mistake — mistakes are simply things through which we learn.

- Does it help if you get angry at yourself?
- What happens to your feelings when you say, "I'll never be able to do it" or "I'll never make it"?
- Are the feelings different when you say, "This is a bit scary, but I'll do my best"?

---

[1] This useful rule is from Thomas R. Bingham's <u>Program for Affective Learning</u>.

Living Values Education Activities for Children Ages 8–14, Book 1

Say, "Repeat the mistake rule with me, please: It's okay to make a mistake, all I have to do is correct it."

Say, "You're all being asked to read or remember your positive qualities every day. We know we all have positive qualities, but sometimes when we get hurt, scared or angry, we don't use them. That doesn't mean we don't have those positive qualities, it just means that we weren't full of the strength of self-respect."

Discuss the Reflection Point:
- ♦ Respect is knowing I am lovable and capable.

Activity

Group Story Game: Each person is invited to contribute one, two or three sentences to the story — no more — and then the next person continues the story. In the first group story game ask the students to make up something about someone who uses negative or disrespectful self-talk. As the facilitator, you can start: "One day there was a little _____." Allow them to continue to go around until everyone who wishes to do so has contributed to the story. (Have a good time! The story can be ridiculous and create a lot of laughter.)

Now do a group story game asking the young people to use only positive or respectful self-talk.

Expressive Activity

Eight to Nine Activity: Paint/color respect, or paint/color the value of respect on one-half of a piece of paper and its anti-value, disrespect, on the other half. Or draw a picture about one of the stories you created.

Ten to Fourteen Activity: Write a thought and feeling chain of positive self-talk versus negative self-talk. Starting from a mid-point on the paper, the positive chain can create an upward spiral and the negative chain a downward spiral. If you wish, ask them to keep this and continue to add to it during the time you are working on respect.

Close with the Flowers of Respect Relaxation Exercise.

RESPECT I LESSON 4
Colors of Respect and Disrespect — and Mobiles

Educator Preparation: Colored strips of paper for armbands and supplies to create mobiles will be needed.

Living Values Education Activities for Children Ages 8–14, Book 1

Begin with a song.

Say, "Today we're going to experiment with respect and disrespect. I'm going to give half of you these strips of green paper to wear around your upper arms, and half of you purple strips to wear around your upper arms." Tell them in this experiment a "pretend" government has declared the green group to be the elite group. Elite means the best. The government notices that the greens have a disrespectful attitude toward the purples.

Note to Educator: Please assess what remaining time you now have in the period. At the mid-point ask the purples be the "elites".

Activity

Instruct the green group to only give respect to other greens, while being disrespectful (in attitude, not words) to the purples.

At the mid-point inform the students that the government has changed and now the purples will be the elite!

Create the opportunity for students to make Me Mobiles for two sessions of Living Values Education time as they do the "Colors of Respect and Disrespect" experiment.

Me Mobiles

Say, "Part of learning to have respect for yourself is knowing your qualities and knowing yourself. During this session and the next session of Living Values Education Time you are invited to make a mobile about yourself. Over here there is string, paper, colored pens, colored paper, and little sticks. You can bring in tin cans or cartons to hang and decorate them with colored paper. Each object on the mobile is to represent an aspect of you."

- ❖ Favorite pastimes.
- ❖ Your qualities.
- ❖ Your family.
- ❖ What you like about nature.
- ❖ Your favorite animals.
- ❖ How you give to others.
- ❖ What you believe in.
- ❖ Your favorite food.

➢ List the above categories on the board.

Ask:
- Does anyone have another area to add?

Review the list: Do this slowly for younger students so they have time to think about their answers in each area. Circulate among the student as they work on the mobile, listen, and positively affirm their output.

Construct the mobile: An easy way to construct the mobile is to tie two sticks together in an "x" and then hang objects from the ends of the sticks at different lengths. Students can use three sticks if they wish. A string from the middle — where the two or three sticks are tied — then goes to the ceiling. A coat hanger may be used instead of the sticks.

Discuss/Share

At the end of the period of time in which all of the students have had a turn being the elite and non-elite, have a brief discussion.

Ask:
- How did you feel when you were the elite?
- How did it feel to be the "non-elite"?
- What didn't you like?
- Would you like a world in which everyone has respect for all?
- How would the world be different?

Close with the Flowers of Respect Relaxation/Focusing Exercise.

RESPECT I LESSON 5

The Colors of Respect — Princes and Princesses

Begin with a song.

In this session, randomly distribute a whole rainbow of colored armbands. Tell them that now they are all princes and princesses from different kingdoms. Or, they could be different superheroes or another set of characters that they admire. Ask the students to give respect to everyone through their looks, attitudes, and behavior. Perhaps they could each make something for another person's mobile if they are done with their mobile.

Share

Invite the students to share their mobile in a small group of five or six, each one staying in the self-respect of a prince or princess and giving each other that same respect.

Ask the students of the entire class what happened to the respect level in the room when they were all asked to consider themselves and everyone else a prince or princess.

At the end of the session, do the Star of Respect Relaxation/Focusing Exercise.

Star of Respect Relaxation Exercise

"Let's think of the stars and imagine ourselves to be just like them. . . . They are so beautiful in the sky, they sparkle and shine. . . . They are so quiet and peaceful. . . . Be very still. . . . Breathe in peace. . . . Breathe out any tension. . . . Relax your toes and legs. . . . Relax your stomach . . . and your shoulders. . . . Relax your arms . . . and your face. . . . Feel safe . . . and allow a soft light of peace to surround you. . . . Inside you are like a beautiful little star. . . . You are a star of respect. . . . You are lovable and capable. . . . You are who you are. . . . Each person brings special qualities to the world. . . . You are valuable. . . . Enjoy the feeling of respect inside. . . . You are a star of respect. . . . Be still . . . peaceful. . . . Focus . . . . You are concentrated . . . full of respect . . . content. . . . Now, slowly bring your attention back to the room."

RESPECT I LESSON 6

The Colors of Respect — and Discrimination

Begin with a song.

Activity

The students are to continue to wear the variety of armbands. However, tell them that blue means they are people working for healthy rivers and oceans, green means they are medical people working to prevent disease, orange means they are peace makers working to create a peaceful world, and purple means they are musicians creating songs about respect and dignity for all, etc.

Small Group Presentations: Ask the students to divide into groups based on the color of their armbands. Give them ten minutes to prepare a short one to three-minute presentation to the entire class about how their group contributes peace and respect to their community based on the profession indicated by their armband. The rest of the class may ask them questions after their presentation. Remind them to stay in their self-respect and have respect for all others.

Discuss/Share

- How did you all give respect? (Listening carefully to what others said, etc.)
- Were you all able to give everyone respect?

Say, "In classrooms, schools, neighborhoods and communities around the world, often some people are given respect and others are not. This is called discrimination. Sometimes people judge other people as better than them, or less than them, based on skin color, if they wear nice or not-so-nice clothes, or if they're shinny or fat."
Ask:

- What else do people discriminate about?

Acknowledge their answers and write a list on the board. Then ask:
- What are we learning in class? What did you learn in the last few lessons?
- What does it feel like when you get disrespect?
- What does it feel like when you get respect?
- What does it feel like when everyone respects everyone else?
- What does this group, and all of humanity, have in common? (All are human beings, each one has something to offer, etc.)

Say, "Sometimes people don't give respect to themselves. Do you sometimes discriminate against yourself by judging yourself and talking mean to yourself rather than talking respectfully to yourself?" Ask:
- Would calling yourself a name be respectful to yourself or disrespectful?
- Has anybody ever called yourself stupid?

Say, "I want you to continue with your homework of reading your eight qualities every day. But, I also want you to notice your tone of voice as you talk to yourself inside during the day. Check and see if your tone of voice is kind and respectful. It's important to encourage ourselves and be kind to ourselves."

Written Expression

Ask the students to write a short personal essay on their experience. How did they feel when receiving disrespect, how did they feel when receiving respect, how did they feel when everyone was a prince or princess? Or, what would they like to tell the world about respect?

Close with a respect relaxation exercise.

RESPECT I LESSON 7
The Colors of Respect and Disrespect — Creative Expression

Begin with a song.

Creative Expression Activity

Divide the students into groups of five to eight. Invite them to write a poem, a song or create a small play/drama to express their feelings about and reactions to any part of the Colors of Respect experiment. Give them the opportunity to share their artistic creations in class.

End with the Star of Respect Relaxation Exercise.

RESPECT I LESSON 8
What stories about respect would you like to share?

Begin with a song.

Share a Story

Read stories about people who learn to have self-respect or who maintain their self-respect. For students eight to ten, you may wish to read "A Christmas I'll Never Forget" by Linda DeMers Hummel. The Joy of Reading Project kindly gave their permission to post this story on the international LVE site, www.livingvalues.net. You will find it under For Schools /Children Ages 8–14 / Download Free Stories / Respect 8–10. In this story a migrant boy whose family picks fruit stays in his self-respect and teaches his classmates and teacher about respect and kindness.

Ask older students to bring in their favorite books or stories, including real stories from the newspaper, web or social media. Or, share or investigate real stories of your culture's heroes.

Living Values Education Activities for Children Ages 8–14, Book 1

Discuss/Share

- What qualities or values did the hero in the story have that allowed him or her to act with self-respect?
- What lessons did he or she teach others around him or her?

Close with the Physical Relaxation Exercise.

RESPECT I LESSON 9
Greetings of the World

Begin with the Peaceful Star Relaxation Exercise.

Introduction: One way of showing respect to others is learning about their culture and learning to say things in their language. Learn about different ways around the world of greeting others with respect.

Activity

Depending on the age group and language skills of the class, learn several greetings and polite phrases in two to four languages. Perhaps students in the class have a variety of languages to share and can share gestures or a dance. Enjoy practicing.

— *Contributed by Dominique Ache*

Continue to share stories about respect from your culture or the world.
Close with a relaxation/focusing exercise of your choice.

RESPECT I LESSON 10
Conflict Resolution and Listening with Respect

Begin with a song.
- ➤ Practice the greetings and phrases in the different languages from Lesson 9.
- ➤ Ask the students how it is going with peace and respect and discuss with them their current situation in terms of bullying or any need for conflict resolution.

Activity

Review the conflict resolution steps, found in Lesson 8 of the Peace I Unit.
Demonstrate: Ask for volunteers to practice the conflict resolution process, with

Living Values Education Activities for Children Ages 8-14, Book 1

peers as their mediators. Ask the mediators to use the value of respect.

In the second demonstration ask the mediators and those with the conflict to all listen and actively listen with respect.

Ask:

- What is the difference when the other person listens to you with respect?
- How does it feel different?

Small Group Practice: Divide the students into groups of three or four and ask them to practice giving respect as they communicate about a conflict — pretend or real.

Debrief with the entire group, asking them to share what is easy and difficult and dialoguing about the process.

Close with the Flowers of Respect relaxation/focusing exercise.

RESPECT I LESSON 11
Strategies to Stop Conflict

Educator Preparation: Bring out the list of things students fight about that the teacher and class made during Peace I Lesson 8.

Begin with a song.

Practice the greetings and phrases in the different languages from Lesson 9.

Introduction: Say, "Very often conflict occurs when someone shows disrespect to someone else. Today we're going to take a look at the list we made of the things people do that cause conflicts/fights when we were exploring Peace. Sometimes when people do the things that are on this list, we get hurt or angry. We feel bad when people treat us without respect. But, always remember that you define who you are. You are the one that knows your qualities. If someone calls you "stupid," does that mean you are stupid? "No." Every single one of you is a valuable and worthwhile human being. Okay, let's look at this list in the light of respect."

Discuss/Share

Take one item on the list, and ask:

- Would this have occurred if the person were showing respect?
- What would you like/advise this person to do instead? What would have been a respectful way to handle it?

- Would the problem have occurred then?
- If the person this was done to stayed in his or her self-respect, how could he or she handle it differently so the problem does not build?

Help students problem-solve: See what alternatives they generate. Let them know when they come up with a good idea. Ask them to come up with several ways to handle the situation. Help them create sensible strategies.

If someone offers an idea that is hurtful to someone, ask what the consequences might be of that action. Allow the students to supply the answers. If some feel that it is okay to hurt others, ask how they would feel if that were done to them.

Reinforce the social skills introduced during the Bullying No More lessons in the Peace Unit as follows.

- ➢ *Ages eight to nine:* When someone does something you don't like (such as calling you a name), one thing you can do is tell him/her, "I don't like it when you to call me names. I'd like you to stop." Ask the class to repeat that several times with you, and then ask them to pair up and practice saying that in self-respect (firmly, clearly, but not aggressively).
- ➢ *Ages nine through fourteen:* Ask the students to generate clear and assertive things they can say in addition to "I don't like it when you call me names. I'd like you to stop." Perhaps, "Hey, it's not cool to do that," "I'm not into fighting," or (to a friend), "Are you angry today? What's the matter?" Let them pair up and practice saying that in self-respect.

Introduce a new social emotional skill:
- ➢ *Teach the following formula:* This is a good idea to use when somebody you know does something you do not like, such as gossiping, name calling, etc. "I feel _____ when you do _____ because _____."

Give a couple of examples, such as:
- ☆ "I feel bad when you talk to me about Marsha that way because she is my friend. I like you and I like Marsha, too. I think it's okay to like both of you."
- ☆ "I feel pressured when you keep asking me to smoke because I already told you I don't want to do that. I know what I want to do, and I want you to respect that."

- ➢ Ask the students to create "I feel" strategies for each situation they bring up.

Note to Educator: The "I feel" communication skill may be a little difficult for eight- and nine-year-olds. If necessary, begin by helping them identify their feelings, such as happy, angry, sad, or hurt.

Take several more items from the list made during Peace I Lesson 8 and ask the same four questions above, helping the students develop strategies.

Discuss the following Reflection Point:
♦ When we have respect for the self, it is easy to have respect for others.

Practice: Ask the students to use the "I feel _____ when you do _____ because_____" formula and fill in the blanks for two situations.

Close with movement/dance around your space/room to a song or two — and then do the Flowers of Respect Relaxation/Focusing Exercise.

RESPECT I LESSON 11B for Ages 11 to 14
Bullying No More — The Art of Distraction

Note to Educator from the author: A few years ago, I read in the *Los Angeles Times* an article about a police department that used distraction as a method to help them deal with domestic-violence disputes. Tragically, sometimes policemen and policewomen are killed when they are called to a home to intervene. Using planned distraction, this police department was able to reduce mortality. The example given was a policeman arriving as a couple were screaming and yelling. If the couple continued the argument after the police officer arrived, he would start talking about how tired he was, go into their kitchen and start rummaging through the cupboards to find a cup and some coffee. The couple would often stop their argument to follow him and ask what he was doing. One of them would usually help the officer make a cup of coffee. It changed the dynamics and decreased the level of violence. Sometimes we come upon a situation where we don't know the person bullying or the target. Distraction can be quite useful in such a situation.

LVE has educational resource books for children in difficult circumstances. Distraction as an art of nonviolence is introduced to 11- to 14-year-olds as a method to stop violence. **If you think your students might benefit from distraction as a method to** reduce bullying, you might wish to read the story "Crazy Like a Fox" which can be found in the Appendix (Item 5). This story is taken from *Living Values Activities for Street Children Ages 7–10*.

Begin with a song.

Introduce concept to students: "We had a couple of lessons on Bullying in the Peace Unit. In this lesson on Bullying No More, we are going to talk about the art of distraction as a method of nonviolence.

When people are fighting, fists are flying, hormones are pumping and peace and respect aren't anywhere in the picture. Trying to restrain someone can result in the helper being hurt, sometimes quite seriously. Joining a fight to stop it is dangerous and *never* recommended. For serious violence, the first action should be to withdraw to safety and call the emergency number for police intervention.

I'm going to read you a story from Living Values Education's activities for children in difficult circumstances. The story is part of a series of stories about a street-children family who love and care for each other."

Share a Story

Read "Crazy Like a Fox". It can be found in the Appendix, Item 5.

Discuss

- What did Fred, Marion and Mohammed do instead of joining the fight?
- What method did they use? (Distraction. Staying peaceful. Giving respect to all. Not taking the side of one over the side of another.)
- What did Keemen want Fred and Mohammed to do?
- What did Fred say to explain why they did not join the fight? (They beat you up, you beat them up. They knife you, you knife them. They shoot you, you shoot them. It only gets worse.) What do you think about that?
- Can you think of some examples of people that happened to?
- What do you think Mohammed meant when he said, "What comes around goes around?"
- What values did Fred, Marion and Mohammed use?

Say, "Distraction can be used as to tool to stop low-level fighting and bullying, if you are comfortable doing so — and it is safe. Your protection is acting in a clearly nonthreatening manner. You are de-escalating tension, not increasing it. "

Ask a student to read out the following examples.

When someone at a distance is bullying a person you know — Call out to the target in a loud voice:
- Dana, could you come over here? I need your help right away!
- Hey, Dana! Mr. Murphy (name of a teacher) wants to see you right now!
- Dana, have you seen Mrs. Tey? I can't find her anywhere!
- Hey, did you see the really cool _____ Sam has?
- Hey, guys, is that a snake over there?

When someone close by is bullying someone you know — Call to the target:
- I can't find my phone! Have either of you seen it? If I lose it my father's going to be soooooo upset. I'll probably be working for a year to get another one. Have either of you lost your phone? Have you seen mine? Harry, would you help me look for it?
- Hey, have you guys seen that really cool new movie, _____? The part I like best was _____.
- Did you see the raccoon over by room 3? Awesome! Today it was just one, but the other day I saw one with two cubs….
- Do either of you remember what Mrs. Rami said about the _____?

To strangers:
- Do you know where _____ is?
- Excuse me. I'm trying to find _____.

Activity

Divide the students into small groups and ask each one to select a situation that they would like to portray, and generate statements, questions or dialogues which could work as a distraction and allow them to be safe. Facilitate a learning process, helping them learn how to be safer in their local setting. Discuss their concerns and help them generate some practical, non-violent solutions.

Close with a respect relaxation/focusing exercise.

Living Values Education Activities for Children Ages 8–14, Book 1

RESPECT I LESSON 11C for Ages 11 to 14

Keeping Your Head in the Face of Danger

Begin the session with a song.

Share a Story

Read "Samosas and Peace in the Face of Danger". This is Item 6 in the Appendix.

Discuss

Read them the story again if they wish.
Ask:
- What happened in the story?
- What did Marion think to herself to stay calm when the two boys with the knives appeared? (Just stay peaceful she told herself. Be still. Be peace. Give peace.)
- What did Mohammed say happens with him when he stays calm and gives respect when someone threatens him? (The threatening one calms down.)
- What did Mohammed say happens when you get nervous, scared or angry at the threatening one? (It makes them feel more nervous. That's when they can get violent. If you don't get all scared — but stay peaceful and steady . . . and they don't feel threatened . . . then they usually calm down.)
- What did Mohammed suggest doing if they get "crazed" or are mean through and through? (Run.)
- When did Mohammed say your head works better? (When you can stay peaceful.)
- Have you ever had anyone threaten you before? How did you feel?
- What happens when you get scared or angry? Would anyone like to tell a story about that?
- What can happen when the threatening person gets angrier or more scared? (They get more dangerous and likely do something that is more violent.)
- Have you ever seen anyone stay calm in a dangerous situation and have it get better?
- What can you do better when you stay calm? (You can think better.)

Explain: "Your brain has a thinking part and an emotional part. The cortex, the thinking part, stops working when your emotions get all excited. If you stay calm and full of respect for yourself and the other person — your mind will be able to think clearly. When you can think clearly, you are more likely to be able to get out of a dangerous situation."

Ask:
- What are the threatening or dangerous situations that you have encountered or are likely to encounter on the streets around here?

Activity

> Divide the students into small groups and ask each one to select a situation that they would like to portray. Take the same beginning scene and then have the actors play out three different ways to respond to the situation:
> > 1) with anger
> > 2) with fear
> > 3) staying calm and using their head.
> > > Part of staying calm and using their head may be knowing when it is time to flee or protect themselves in another way.
> Ask them to apply a value.
> Facilitate a learning process, helping them learn how to be safer in their local setting. Discuss their concerns and help them generate some practical, non-violent and safe solutions.

Close with a relaxation/focusing exercise.

RESPECT I LESSON 12
Different Ways of Giving Respect

Begin with a song.

Discuss/Share

Share the Reflection Points.
- Respect is knowing others are valuable, too.
- To know one's worth and to honor the worth of others is how one earns respect.
- Everyone in the world has the right to live with respect and dignity, including myself.

Ask:
- What are the different ways we give respect to adults?

- What are the different ways we give respect to nature?
- What are the different ways we give respect to objects?
- What are the different ways we give respect to common spaces?
- What can we do to make sure respect is given?

Ask the students to divide into groups to analyze one or two of the topics and make suggestions. Invite them to make posters or slogans.

— *Contributed by Sabine Levy and Pilar Quera Colomina*

Allow each group to share their poster or slogan.

End with the Star of Respect Relaxation Exercise.

RESPECT I LESSON 13
Our Qualities

Begin with a song.

Activity

Make sure the list of qualities generated during the first Respect I Lesson is in plain view.

Pass out paper to everyone. Ask each student to write his or her name at the top of the paper. The objective is for students to pass around the paper, each writing the quality he or she sees in the person whose name is at the top. Everyone's paper should be passed to everyone else before being returned to the rightful owner. Allow the students to read their list of qualities for a couple of minutes before continuing.

Discuss with the students what they have enjoyed and learned about respect.

Expressive Activity

Paint respect as a group or put on music and dance respect for a few minutes, then disrespect, then respect, then peace. Or, go to the next lesson and create a skit/drama on respect.

Close with the Flowers of Respect Relaxation/Focusing Exercise.

Additional Respect Lessons

RESPECT I LESSON 14
Paint a Picture with a Friend in Another Country

Begin with a song.

Activity

Step 1. Join up with a school in another country and make friends — perhaps as pen pals.

Step 2. Invite your partner school to take part in a joint Art project.

Step 3. Each child in each country starts to draw/paint a picture but leaves the center box of the picture completely blank.

Step 4. The pictures are sent to the other country.

Step 5. The children complete their pen pal's picture.

Step 6. Share the complete picture with each other.

Step 7. Display the pictures in a local shopping mall.

Reflection: We each see our world differently — or do we?

Post Script: This activity is especially powerful when shared with children who have been affected by the traumas of war or conflict. The concept of the joint pictures from either a peaceful to a war-torn country or war-torn country to war-torn country often carry the same message — "Let us live in Peace".

— *Contributed by Duaa Mansour*

RESPECT I LESSON 15 . . . and more!
Health — Respect is Taking Care of Your Body

Begin with a song.

Share/Discuss

Share the Respect Reflection Point:

♦ Part of respect for the self is taking care of your body.

Ask:

- Why is part of self-respect taking care of your body?
- How do you take care of your body?

- What do you think people your age can do to take care of their body in terms of exercise?
- What about in terms of eating?
- What foods are good for the body?

Note to Educator: The situation will be very different in some countries than in others, and in most countries, the situation will vary in different areas. Please start with which health aspect you think is most important for the students — and doable.

Exercise: For example, perhaps the students in your class may need to exercise more. Let them know that exercise is important for the health of their brain and body, and that people feel better emotionally when they exercise. Have fun trying out some exercises. Brain gym exercises are fun and are helping in synchronizing the left and right hemispheres. Incorporate a few minutes of brain gym as a regular part of the day and encourage them to play a sport or do something that is doable in their circumstance. If possible, go outside.

Healthy Eating: As the educator, you know the situation of your students and what is available. Perhaps set up the lesson to discuss healthy eating choices and perhaps plan to cooperate together in bringing in different things for all to try. Or, you may notice that the young people are eating too much sugar.

With twelve- to fourteen- year-olds, perhaps invite them to investigate foods that fall into the alkaline or acidic categories and look at the health benefits of eating to create an alkaline state in the body. They may discover that coke has a pH factor of 3.5 which is quite acidic.

Note to Educator: The topic of healthy eating could be expanded indefinitely. Student could research the topic, and as a class you could experiment with making or sampling different foods, or adding healthy foods to the diet and eliminating unhealthy goods as a class experiment.

Close with a relaxation/focusing exercise or perhaps spend time doing hatha yoga or Chi Gong exercises.

Living Values Education Activities for Children Ages 8–14, Book 1

Unit Three: Love and Caring

Love and Caring Lessons

Love is at the core of the human being and an essential part of our human experience. Nurturing love in the home helps children thrive. Educators are valued and prized by untold millions around the world as providers of not only knowledge but love, and creators of nurturing, caring and safe places to learn.

In this updated book, we have retitled the Love Values Unit as the Love and Caring Values Unit. While caring and kindness are always part of love, in some cultures it is easier to talk about love by using the word "caring". Please feel free to use the word that you feel is most appropriate for your culture or the culture of the young people with whom you work. You may simply wish to substitute the word "caring" for "love".

Songs: Play a song about love each morning as students are entering class or at the beginning of values time. Pick out some songs about love that students like. This will vary in different countries and with different languages. "Heal the World" by Michael Jackson one choice. The lyrics and cords for "Someday" are below. There are lots of wonderful songs and videos of young people singing on YouTube. The teacher may want to have a Love Reflection Point already on the board so students can enter silently and reflect as they listen to the music.

Please include a relaxation/focusing exercise during "values time". Many students greatly value this time to relax and "be", hence you may wish to do one daily. You may wish to use relaxation/focusing exercises from the Peace and Respect units. All of the exercises can be found in the Appendix.

Love and Caring Reflection Points

- Everyone in this room is lovable and capable.
- When I am full of love, anger runs away.
- Love is the value that makes our relationships better.
- When my words give flowers instead of thorns, I create a better world.

- I can have love for myself, love for my family, love for others, love for my country, love for my goals, and love for the world all at the same time.
- Love for others means I want what is good for them.
- Love means I can be kind, caring, and understanding.
- When we feel strong inside, it's easy to be loving.
- Love is caring, love is sharing.
- Love is being a trustworthy friend.
- "Our task must be to free ourselves . . . by widening our circle of compassion to embrace all living beings and all of nature." — Albert Einstein
- "The real law lives in the kindness of our hearts. If our hearts are empty, no law or political reform can fill them." — Tolstoy

Love and Caring Unit Goals and Objectives

Goal: To increase the experience of love and caring.
Objectives:
- To listen to stories about caring and love, to tune to the value and create an affinity for love and caring.
- To think of kind ways to relate to the self.
- To think about widening their circle of compassion.
- To participate in relaxation/focusing exercises on sending love and on experiencing the self as lovable and capable.
- To participate in creating a mural as a group, staying in the experience of love or caring.
- To create three of the following on the values of love and caring: a story, song, dance, slogan, banner, or poem.

Goal: To increase knowledge about the effects of the values of love and caring.
Objectives:
- To participate in discussions about the Love and Caring Reflection Points and be able to talk about three or more of them.
- To imagine a loving world and discuss the elements of that world.
- To identify what leaders/rulers in a loving world would want for the citizens.
- To think about and express their ideas about the components of a loving world versus the components of a non-loving world by making a Mind Map as a group.

- To think about the different ways the opposite of love can exist: as lack of love, unkindness, meanness, fear or hate.
- To generate combined words to do with the quality of the heart and do a follow-up activity.
- To hear a story about drugs and those who sell drugs, to understand the harmful effects of drugs and learn that those who sell drugs may act friendly but do not care about the people to whom they are selling; they are selfish and care about money.
- To understand the importance of our words, i.e., "When my words give flowers instead of thorns, I create a better world."
- To identify loving and non-loving actions through discussions.
- To participate in a group story,

Goal: To exhibit caring and kind social skills.
Objectives:
- To identify caring and kind things to do and to carry out at least three of their ideas.
- To see part of caring as listening to others and listen to a peer and to listen with appreciation to someone in their family.
- To generate ideas about appropriate or more loving and caring behaviors during a conflict resolution exercise once the starting point of the negativity is identified.
- For students using social media, to generate kindness guidelines for young people their age in relation to the social media used locally.

Song: Someday

Chorus: ^CSomeday on the ^Fplanet,
^{Emin7/C}There will ^{Dmin7/D}be ^{Emin7/C}perfect ^{Dmin7/C}peace and ^{Emin7/C}harmony.
And ^{Eb}all the ^{F/G}people every ^Cwhere
Will ^{Eb}love each ^{F/G}other without ^Cfear.

Verse 1: ^{Bb/F F}I know the ^{Bb/F}day is ^Fcoming soon
^{Ab/Eb}When there ^{Eb}is no more ^Fhate
^{Bb/F}And we ^Fsee ^{Bb/F}every ^Fone with love
^{Ab/Eb}I know ^{Eb} it's not too ^Flate.

Verse 2: ^{Bb/F}There won't ^Fbe a ^{Bb/F}need for ^Fguns
^{Ab/Eb}And we'll ^{Eb} have no more ^Fwar.

Living Values Education Activities for Children Ages 8–14, Book 1

^{Bb/F}And we ^Fcan just ^{Bb/F}play to-^Fgether,
^{Ab/Eb}'Cause that's ^{Eb} what life is ^F for!
(Repeat chorus and verse 1)

Verse 3: ^{Bb/F}So let's ^Ftalk our ^{Bb/F}problems ^Fout,
^{Ab/Eb}Put our ^{Eb} anger a-^Fway.
^{Bb/F}If we ^Fall can ^{Bb/F}join to-^Fgether,
^{Ab/Eb}'We'll get ^{Eb} close to some ^F day.
(Repeat chorus two times)

— *Contributed by Max and Marcia Nass*

LOVE LESSON 1
Imagining a Loving World

Begin with a song.
Introduce the new values unit on Love and Caring.
Ask:
- Who thinks love is important? Why?
- Would it be a different world if everyone were loving towards everyone else?

Imagining a Loving World

Lead the students in this imagining exercise. Say the following, pausing at the dots. "Today, I would like you to think about someone who is loving and kind. It can be a real person in your life now, or a person who helped you before, or it can be a person that you have seen in the movies. Think about that person's attitude. . . . Picture that person helping. . . . Now, I want you to imagine that everyone in the world was that loving and kind. . . . What would the world be like? . . . Now, relax and step into your imaginary bubble — this bubble is so big that you can step inside — it's like a small, silent plane that you can travel in to imagine going into the future, to a world full of caring and kindness. . . . Step inside the bubble and float to that world. . . . The air inside the bubble is clean and fresh as you and your balloon float above different cities . . . and the countryside . . . and now you are floating over different countries. . . . Picture leaders of different nations and how they treat each other. . . . How would they be with the citizens of their countries? . . . Picture friends playing. . . . See students on a playground and in the neighborhood . . . How do they act? How do they feel? . . . Please begin your journey back to our place. . . . Fly the plane over your own neighborhood . . . and now over this school . . . and imagine what would be happening if every person was caring and kind to everyone else. . . . Now the bubble begins to descend . . . it comes into this room . . . and you are relaxed and in your place here again."

Discuss/Share

Give the students time to share what they pictured and experienced. With a class of younger students, the teacher might want to lead this activity. With older students, the teacher may wish to ask them to form small groups to share.

Ask:
- In a loving world, what would everyone want for his or her family?
- In a loving world, how would everyone get along?
- What would be happening in families, schools and neighborhoods?
- In a loving world, what would the rulers/leaders want for the citizens?
- In a loving world, would anybody be interested in war? Why or why not?

Activity

Invite the students to draw a symbol or picture of a loving world or to make up a poem or song about the world they imagined. Allow them to share their songs, poems, symbols or drawings.

Close with a relaxation/focusing exercise.

LOVE LESSON 2
Story — The Four Thrones

Begin with a song.

Read "The Four Thrones" by Wendy Marshall, or another positive story from your culture.

Share a Story: The Four Thrones

Once upon a time there were four benevolent sovereigns who ruled the earth. Each had great respect for the other, and the world was in harmony. At the top of one of the highest mountains, overlooking their kingdoms in all four directions, was their place of four thrones. The four rulers would meet to exchange news of their kingdoms.

But a time came when their people became bored with noble qualities. They wanted the thrill of winners and losers, the contrast of rich and poor. The four sovereigns decided to leave their kingdoms and let their people rule themselves. They all agreed to silently wander the earth and return as sovereigns only when their people wanted to live in peace again.

Many years later, when the earth and its people had become spoiled by greed, ego, and selfishness, a young girl read the story of the four sovereigns. She realized this was not a fairy tale. She vowed that when she grew up, she would search for the four sovereigns and ask them to return to their kingdoms so that harmony could prevail once again.

After many years of searching, she reached the high mountain foretold. There she found the four thrones. She waited there, since in the legend it was said that each year the sovereigns came to the place where the four thrones faced outward over the mountains and valleys to meet and give news of their lands. Months passed.

One day, an old traveler came by and asked the young woman about her quest. The traveler listened intently. He then told her that the sovereigns would only meet her when she had learned to look within and let peace grow in her heart. They would meet her when her eyes radiated love, when her words were guided by wisdom, and when her actions brought only happiness to others.

The traveler agreed to teach the young woman these lost arts, and the young woman studied diligently. On the day she was ready, the old traveler took her leave. At sunrise the next morning, four figures approached. Queen Wisdom took her place on one throne, and then King Love, Queen Peace, and King Happiness assumed their thrones. The young woman entered the circle and told them of her quest.

As Queen Wisdom addressed her, she recognized that this was her teacher, the old traveler. "Go back to your land and teach all who come to you the things you have been taught here. You are the seed that will bear the fruit of harmony throughout the earth once again. Keep courage. There will be many tests. But the seed of hope will soon grow, and when all hearts are ready, we will return."

"Remember, all human hearts contain beautiful qualities. Don't be fooled by bitterness and hatred. These treasures you have found within yourself will touch others deeply. Never stop believing in yourself and the task will be accomplished quickly."

Living Values Education Activities for Children Ages 8–14, Book 1

Perhaps read the story again, asking the students to listen for the lines that are most meaningful to them. Discuss the story with the students, and then share the following Reflection Points to open up any additional discussion.

- "The real law lives in the kindness of our hearts. If our hearts are empty, no law or political reform can fill them." — Tolstoy
- Love is the value that makes our relationships better.

Activity

Ask the students to act out the story, draw it or write a personal journal page in response to the story.

LOVE LESSON 3
Mind Mapping a Loving World and a Non-Loving World

Begin with a song.

Activity

"Today, let's explore the differences between a loving world and a non-loving world."

Mind Map: Begin by drawing a large circle on a white board, putting Love on the right side and Lack of Love, Fear and Hate on the left side. (If you are not familiar with Mind Mapping, you will find information in Item 1 of the Appendix.) Start with a branch for Self on the Love side of the circle, asking them what happens when there is Love in the Self and writing in brief their responses. Then ask them what happens when there is a Lack of Love in the Self. The students are to supply all the answers. Do the same for the branch of Family and Friends.

Say, "For the branch of the Self and Family and Friends, we looked at the difference of what happens when there is love and lack of love. It has been said that the opposite of love is fear. Some people act mean when they have fear inside. Let's look at a school or a neighborhood that is full of love and caring, or full of fear and unkindness or meanness."

Ask: "What branch would you like to do next, a school or a neighborhood?"

Write the name of the branch the students select and continue, asking them several times, "What happens if there is fear in the _____?", drawing out their responses. Then ask, "What happens if there is unkindness or meanness?"

119

Do the same process for the Country or World, but this time contrast love with hate. Say, "Sometimes when people are full of fear, their meanness can grow into hate." If the students are older, you may wish to add other branches.

Discuss the following Reflection Point: "Our task must be to free ourselves . . . by widening our circle of compassion to embrace all living beings and all of nature." — Albert Einstein. Ask:
- What do you think Mr. Einstein meant?
- What happens when the circle of compassion is very small or does not exist?
- What would happen if people all over the world began creating circles of compassion?
- What changes would we see if there were only circle of compassion in our school/community?

Creative Expression

Divide the students into groups of four to six. Ask each group to create a song or poem about love, or love versus lack of love, fear, meanness or hate. It could be a rap song. Allow them to perform their creation for the group.

End the lesson with the following Relaxation/Focusing exercise. You may wish to say, "Many people live in places in the world that are non-loving. Let's experiment with sending love with a relaxation/focusing exercise.

Sending Love Relaxation Exercise

"Let's be peace stars for a few minutes and send love to people all over the world. . . . Think of the stars and imagine yourself to be like them. . . . They are so beautiful in the sky, and they sparkle and shine . . . quietly and peacefully. . . . Relax your toes and legs . . . relax your back . . . and your shoulders. . . . Relax your arms . . . and your face. . . . We are safe . . . a soft light of peace surrounds you. . . . Inside you are like a beautiful star . . . full of peaceful light . . . full of love. . . . We can all send love and peace any time we want. . . . Let the self be still . . . filled with the light of caring and kindness. . . . Allow that love to automatically flow to people all over the world. . . . Let the body relax. . . . Take in more love. . . . You are focused . . . still . . . contributing to a kinder world. . . . Let the mind be still. . . . Begin to bring your attention back to this room. . . . Wiggle your toes, move your legs and let your self be content . . . powerful . . . and alert."

LOVE LESSON 4
Stories about Caring

Begin with a song.

Share a Story

The teacher can select a story or two to read about people's love or caring serving as inspiration to do something special — for another person, for someone who is ill, or for an animal. There are many books. Pick one popular in your culture or one easily accessible. After reading the story, discuss it with the students. Point out how the person's love motivated him or her to act in a courageous or kind way.

A couple of stories about love were selected from The Joy of Reading Project, those creators kindly gave their permission to post them on the international LVE site, www.livingvalues.net. You will find under For Schools /Children Ages 8–14 / Download Free Stories / Love 8-14, "Chicken Sunday" by Patricia Polacco and "The girl with a brave heart: A Tale from Tehran" by Rita Jahanforuz.

In Zimbabwe, LVE educator Natalie Ncube's class of high school boys read Valentin Katayev's short story, "Rainbow Flower." This story is about a girl who became lost and met an old woman. The old woman gave her a magic Rainbow Flower that could make any wish come true. The flower had seven petals, each allowing a wish. The girl wasted six of them and used the seventh, the last one, to cure a crippled boy.

Mrs. Ncube noted: "After the story had been read in class, the development of the girl's character was discussed. The pupils noticed that with the first six petals the girl's character deteriorated because of jealousy, envy, and unnecessary pride. Only when she was left with one petal did she become more thoughtful and try to use the petal 'wisely'. While she was wishing for material things, she felt unhappy, dissatisfied, and unfulfilled. When she saw the lame boy, many values emerged."

Discuss/Share

Discuss the story read. Then ask them to name caring things people can do in daily life.

Activity Options

Draw a table of the negativities and virtues of the central character(s) in a story selected by the teacher. Or, write a story, "What I Would Do if I Had the Rainbow

Flower" or draw the Rainbow Flower and write your words on the petals. Or, write a poem or a story about caring or giving love. Allow those who wish to do so to share.

Close with a relaxation/focusing exercise.

LOVE LESSON 5
Words of the Heart

Begin with a song.

Say, "The value that we will continue to explore today is Love. Let's start by playing with some of the combined words having to do with the heart."

Ask:

- Have you heard of hard-hearted, soft-hearted, big-hearted? What does each mean?
- Can you think of anymore? . . . . . . Great!

(If not mentioned, you may want to add small-hearted, mean-hearted, half-hearted.)

Eight-Year-Old Activity: Instruct students to make a "heart person" from pipe cleaners and to tell their parents what the heart person would say. If there is time, they can draw a couple of heart people and write down what each one would say.

Nine to Eleven Activity: Instruct students to make a small storybook with the characters as hearts of different kinds. They can illustrate the different heart characters on each page and write a statement about what that heart would say. You may want the students to share one page of their completed book in front of the class or group.

Twelve to Fourteen Language Arts Activity: Continue the above discussion by asking students to think of characters in literary works they have been studying recently, movies they have all seen or video games with which they are all familiar.

Ask:

- What actions of the characters reveal they are mean-hearted, big-hearted, etc.?
- Which of those characters would you like to join you in the world now? Why?
- Which characters would be able to introduce more love and caring into the world?
- What are the values or qualities of that character?

If time allows, they could write a short essay on this topic.

Close with a relaxation/focusing exercise, asking those who wish to contribute a sentence one of the characters might say.

Living Values Education Activities for Children Ages 8–14, Book 1

LOVE LESSON 6

Selling Drugs — Caring or Selfishness?

Begin the session with a song about peace or love.

Note to Educator: The following story was adapted from "The Street-Children Family" stories in *Living Values Activities for Street Children Ages 11–14*. It has been adapted in such a way that the characters in the story could be living in homes. In the story, the youngest character is fooled into sniffing glue. You may wish to substitute a drug that is common in your area. While many children eight- and nine-years-old in some areas have the fortune of not being exposed to drugs, it is sensible to do this lesson with young people ages ten and above. If drugs are a pervasive problem in your area, the story has been adapted to be suitable for eight-year-olds as well.

If you would like to continue with drug prevention, please see Love Lesson 18: Drug Sellers Pretend to Be Nice at First.

Share a Story: Joe Got Fooled

Nelson came up to the big tree on the corner just as Joe was racing back with his sister, Marion. "I won, I won!" Joe yelled.

Marion laughed, "Yes, you did!"

"Hey, Marion," said Nelson, "Fred and I get to come to school with you and Joe early this morning."

"Wow. That's great," smiled Marion.

"Joe, run down to the next corner and see if you can find Mohammed. Maybe he can come early too," said Nelson to his little brother. "I'll go look in the other direction."

Soon Nelson was back. "Where is that kid?" asked Nelson. "The one day we get to go early!"

Ten minutes went by and then another ten. What was taking Joe so long? Fred and Nelson and Marion chatted as they waited. Marion caught a glimpse of Joe before Fred and Nelson did. Her face stopped smiling and became pale. She spoke softly but there was an odd serious tone in her voice, "Joe, what is that?"

Joe was walking a little funny and holding a jar in his hand. He lifted it up to his nose and sniffed and gave Marion and Fred a smile.

"My new friend gave me this," he said with a silly look at this face. He stumbled as though he was dizzy and gave them another smile.

Marion's eyes filled with sadness.

Fred jumped up. "What, are you crazy?" he yelled. Fred grabbed the jar from Joe. He threw it on the ground.

Joe looked at him with a shocked look in his eyes and began to cry. "That's mine!" he protested.

For once, Marion did not reach out to comfort Joe. "I do hope this is the first time he's tried that," she muttered to Nelson and Fred.

"I saw some new kids on the street yesterday," said Fred, "but I didn't know they were dealing drugs."

"But, he's so little," said Marion, "only six."

"They don't care how little they are. They only want their money."

"They don't want my money," laughed Joe. "Ha, ha, you're wrong. They gave it to me free. Free!"

"No use talking to him now," said Fred quietly. "He can't think now . . . and won't remember what you say."

Nelson said, "You guys go to school. I'll stay with him." Nelson looked really upset.

"Joe, don't you know any better?" he was saying as Marion and Fred left for school. Joe was giggling and acting goofy.

Joe went to sleep after a couple hours. His legs would sometimes jerk. He didn't feel so good when he woke up a few hours later.

"I have a headache, Nelson," he whined.

"You deserve it, taking drugs," said Nelson.

"Drugs? I didn't take any drugs."

"What do you think sniffing glue is?" asked Nelson.

Later after school, the kids gathered around the tree. They had decided to try to explain to Joe why sniffing glue is such a rotten idea.

"Sniffing glue is a drug, Joe. Drugs are things that people put in their bodies to get high," said Nelson. There are many kinds of drugs. Today a drug seller gave you some glue to sniff. Sometimes they have pills or sell _____." (Note to Educator: Kindly fill in the blank with whatever drug is most common for children in your area.)

"He wasn't a drug seller," pouted Joe. "He's my friend. He gave it free. It was a present."

"Some present," growled Fred. "Makes you dumb for free."

"I'm not dumb. Don't call me dumb," cried Joe.

"Fred's right." said Marion. "You'll be dumb if you take them."

"Why shouldn't I take them, Marion?" asked Joe. "My friend said I would feel happy

Living Values Education Activities for Children Ages 8-14, Book 1

— and I did!"

"Yes," said Marion slowly. "Sometimes a person feels good for a little while. But the drugs make you feel much worse after a while. It ruins your body and your life. Nelson, how did Mama explain it to you?"

"Mama was great at explaining," Nelson said. He sat down next to Joe and said, "Mama explained about drugs to me when I was about your age."

"Those kids that gave you the glue free today aren't really your friends. No kid is your friend that gives you drugs."

"Why are drugs bad?"

"I want you to pretend that you have a glass ball around you," said Nelson.

"A glass ball?" asked Joe.

"Yes," said Nelson, "all around you so even your hands and feet are inside."

"When you take drugs, it's like having a glass ball around you. The person starts looking at the glass ball and watches how the light shines on it. It looks pretty. And because it feels like there is something between that person and the world, sometimes the person feels safer. But, it is much safer not to be in the glass ball. What would happen if you were in the glass ball when a car comes by? You might not notice it's close enough to hit you because you are only looking at the light on the glass ball."

"Oh" said Joe, "so if I'm on drugs I won't see the things I need to see?"

"That's right," said Nelson.

"And if you stay in the glass ball," he continued, "you can't play ball because your arms don't work well. And you can't learn to read because your mind doesn't work well. People get a spacey feeling inside and only focus on little things."

"And after a while, the mind gets really slow and it's hard to learn anything. The person slowly gets dumb and then dumber. And then," continued Nelson, "when you want to get out of the ball you can't, because your body and mind only want the drug. So, you take more drugs and you get trapped in the glass ball."

Joe said, "I don't want to be trapped in a glass ball!"

"Then don't take drugs! It's no fun inside a glass ball after a little while — because you are trapped," said Nelson. "When you are outside the glass ball you are free to grow and are much safer."

Discuss/Share

Questions for ages 8 to 10:

- How did the kids selling drugs get Joe to sniff glue?

- What did Marion say about drugs?
- What did Nelson explain taking drugs was like?
- What can't you do if you are trapped inside a glass ball? (You aren't as safe as you don't notice the things you need to notice.)

Questions for all:

Actively listen to their stories.
- Why do some people take drugs?
- What happens to your mind when you are on drugs?
- Do drug dealers care if you get dumber and dumber when you take drugs?
- What do drug sellers care about?
- Does anyone know someone who took drugs? What happens to them when they take drugs for a long time?
- What drugs are sold in our neighborhood?
- What are the effects of _____ and _____? (The drugs commonly sold in your neighborhood.)
- Would anyone like to tell a story about someone you know that takes drugs?
- Would anyone like to share something else about drugs?

Activity

Invite the students to form small groups to make posters about the harmful effects of one drug and present it to the rest of the class. One group could focus on the effects of sniffing glue, another on speed or _____. Assign them to discuss the drugs sold locally on the streets or that some young people may find at home.

When each group presents, ask them to pretend the drugs can talk. What would the drugs say to you? And, what would you say back?

Close with the Respect Star relaxation/focusing exercise.

LOVE LESSON 7

I Am Lovable and Capable

Begin with a song.

Discuss/Share

Ask the students to think about the Reflection Point:

- ♦ Everyone in this room is lovable and capable.

Ask:

- How do you feel when you feel lovable and capable at the same time?
- How would you feel inside if you felt that this was true for you all the time?
- What would you not worry about?
- Everyone in this room is naturally lovable and capable. What would our behavior be like if we all remembered this all the time?
- What kinds of things would we do?
- What kinds of things would we not do?
- When do you feel lovable?
- When do you feel capable?
- What kinds of things can you do that create those feelings?
- What kinds of things can you say to yourself to help you feel this way?

Activity

Paint an abstract picture of lovable and capable feelings, or write a short essay or poem entitled "I Am Lovable and Capable".

Close with the following relaxation/focusing exercise.

I Am Lovable and Capable Relaxation/Focusing Exercise

"Let the body be relaxed and still. Let go of thoughts about the world outside, and slow down within. . . . Allow yourself to be in the present, focusing on this moment in time. . . . Let the mind be still, and slowly absorb waves of peace. . . . Imagine being outdoors in a world where everyone is kind and caring. . . . Imagine a garden or a meadow . . . or an ocean or river . . . whatever you wish. . . . And in the picture of your mind imagine a world where everyone understands that they are lovable and capable. . . . Breathe in slowly and relax. . . . Know you are lovable and capable. . . . All children are naturally lovable and capable. . . . Sometimes they forget this as sometimes the adults in the world forget that they are lovable and capable . . . . The truth is that you are lovable and capable. . . . Allow yourself to breathe in love. . . . Allow yourself to know that you are capable. . . . Sometimes we don't always act loving to the self or others. . . . Allow yourself to think of a time you were not caring or loving . . . and what you would like to do instead. . . . Think of the quality you would like to have . . . or the value you would like to live. . . . Imagine yourself holding that quality or living your value in a similar situation in the future. . . .

Breathe in that quality or value. . . . Enjoy feeling that quality or value. . . . If you can think of that quality or value it is yours. . . . Each child comes into the world to bring a special gift of his or her qualities . . . and his or her talents. . . . Be still . . . quiet within . . . focused . . . and enjoy feeling full of love and peace. . . . As you begin to bring your attention back to this place . . . know that you are capable and allow yourself to be alert and focused, concentrated . . . ready to do well. . . . Please wiggle your toes and move your legs . . . and bring your attention fully back to this place."

LOVE LESSON 8
Kindness to the Self

Begin with a song.

Discuss/Share

Ask:

- What do you love in yourself?
- How can people be loving or kind to the self?
- How is your self-talk going? Are you remembering to talk to yourself in a kind way?
- What can you say to yourself when you are discouraged to encourage yourself?

Activity

Option One: Write a short letter to yourself, saying what you appreciate about yourself and giving yourself your best advice!

— *Based on a contribution by Marcia Maria Lins de Medeiros*

Option Two: Do the group story game. Each person can contribute one, two or three sentences — no more — and then the next person continues the story. In the first group story game ask students to make up something about someone who uses negative or self-doubting self-talk. Allow them to continue to go around until everyone who wishes to do so has contributed to the story. (Have a good time! The story can be ridiculous and create a lot of laughter.)

Now do a group story game asking the young people to use only positive or loving and encouraging self-talk.

Expressive Activity

Eight to Nine Activity: Paint/color kindness, or paint/color the value of caring and kindness on one-half of a piece of paper and its anti-value, meanness, on the other half. Or draw a picture about one of the stories you created.

Ten to Fourteen Activity: Write a thought and feeling chain of positive self-talk versus negative self-talk. Starting from a mid-point on the paper, the positive chain can create an upward spiral and the negative chain a downward spiral. If you wish, ask them to keep this and continue to add to it during the time you are working on love and caring.

Close with the I am Lovable and Capable Relaxation/Focusing Exercise.

LOVE LESSON 9
Love Is Understanding

Begin with a song.
Discuss the following Reflection Point:
- ♦ Love means I can be kind, caring, and understanding.

Mention to students that in an earlier lesson, they practiced listening. Today, you want them to think of a time someone really listened to them.
Ask:
- How did they show they were listening?
- What was their attitude?
- What did that feel like?

Activity

Ask the students to form pairs with someone they do not know very well. One student is to share something he or she enjoyed doing when younger, or something that interested the student. The other student is to listen. They then exchange roles. Each person can share what he or she discovered about the other person to the class or a small group.

Homework: Listen to someone in your family and stay full of love as you listen. Listen to an adult one day and to a sister or brother another day.

— *Contributed by Marcia Maria Lins de Medeiros*

Close with the Sending Love Relaxation/Focusing exercise.

LOVE LESSON 10

Conflict Resolution and the Effect of a Caring Attitude

Begin the lesson with a song on Love.

Then refer to the content of Peace I Lesson 9 by putting up the poster or drawing on the board the diagram used during the lesson on feeling valued, hurt, or angry.

Ask:
- Do you remember this diagram? Who can tell me about it?
- Can you think of some examples when you've seen this happen?

Discuss the following Reflection Points in relationship to the diagram:
- When I am full of love, anger runs away.
- When my words give flowers instead of thorns, I create a better world.
- When we feel strong inside, it's easy to be loving.

Activity

Assign small groups of students to create a short skit about a conflict relevant at school or in the neighborhood. Ask them to introduce a "freeze-and-replay" element into the skit — in which the actors return to the actions and words in the play when the conflict started and when a caring or loving attitude would have affected the outcome. They are then to inject that loving attitude into the replay. Allow them to do their skits/sketches for the entire group.

Note to Educator: If the students enjoy doing this, the technique can be used when something is going amiss on the playground or in the classroom. The teacher can say: "Freeze — let's have a replay. What was the starting point?" This is an interesting element to include when doing conflict resolution.

Close with a relaxation/focusing exercise of your choice.

LOVE LESSON 11

Love is Caring, Love is Kindness

Begin with a song.

Discuss/Share

Discuss the following Reflection Point: Love is caring, love is sharing.

Ask:
- What helps people feel cared about in our classroom?
- What helps people feel included or that they belong?
- How do you think people feel when they feel left out?
- How does it feel when everyone in the class is valued and safe?
- Is there anything you would like to suggest that would make our classroom a kinder place? (Follow-up on their ideas as appropriate.)
- What are kind things we could do in our school, in the community or at home?

➢ **For students involved with social media, ask:** "What are kindness guidelines you would like everyone your age to use on social media?" (Actively listen to their experiences and allow them to discuss what is currently happening locally.) What would you advise students to do when they are reacting to something mean that someone did and are tempted to respond with meanness?

➢ **For younger students, not involved with social media, read** "Enemy Pie" by Derek Munson. The Joy of Reading Project's creators kindly gave permission to post the story on the international LVE site, www.livingvalues.net. You will find it under For Schools /Children Ages 8–14 / Download Free Stories /Love 8–12. After reading the story, ask the students: "What secret did the Dad in the story know?" "What was the secret ingredient that got rid of enemies?"

Activities

Social Media Kindness Guidelines Activity: Invite the students to form small groups and discuss what kindness guidelines they recommend for people their age. Allow them to create posters and present their views to the class.

Helping Others Activity: Invite the students to select something to do. You may wish to have them do this as an individual project, such as making cards for their parents on special days, making cards for a child who has moved, sharing a meal or dessert, help someone. Or, you could invite small groups to discuss other activities. For example, several students who are friends could befriend a new student in their class, showing him or her around, and playing or spending time with him or her at break. Perhaps there are students who need tutoring. The class may wish to select a Secret Friend for the remainder of the week.

Secret Friend Activity: Each student can write his or her name on a small scrap of paper and put it in a box. Allow each student to choose one name from the box, being careful not to select his or her own name. During the week, each student is to note down positive behaviors and qualities about the student whose name they have chosen.

At the end of the week, each student can make a card (younger students may wish to make a picture of the other student) and write down some of his or her positive notes. If a respectful atmosphere already exists within the class, allow each student to share what is written. The students in the class can guess for whom it is written.

– *Contributed by Pilar Quera Colomina and Sabine Levy*

Close with a relaxation/focusing exercise.

LOVE LESSON 12
A Trustworthy Friend

Begin with a song.

Discuss/Share

Discuss the following Reflection Point: Love is being a trustworthy friend.
Ask:
- What does that mean?
- What do we want in a friend?
- What makes a friend trustworthy?
- What does someone do that makes us think we cannot trust that person?
- How do you show that you are a trustworthy friend?

Bring up another Reflection Point:
♦ Love for others means I want what is good for them.
Ask:
- What does that mean?
- How do you show your friends you care and want what is good for them?

Some teachers may want to link the above two Reflection Points. That will depend on your students and whether you feel they need to hear the following. Concept: Some students have a common misperception that part of being trustworthy is to hide information from adults when a friend is in serious trouble. Friends who are trustworthy also want what is good for their friend. That means if a friend is in serious trouble, one should take action to help. An example of this is telling the teacher or a parent that someone is thinking of hurting himself or herself. Ask: "Can you think of any other examples when a friend should take action to help?"

Point. When we love someone, we want that person to be safe.

Creative Activity

Create a slogan on the value of Love. Groups of three students can work together to make banners. Hang them on the walls. Or, create a dance on universal love or create songs on love and caring.

Close with a relaxation/focusing exercise.

LOVE LESSON 13
Creating A Story

Begin with a song.

Activity

Step 1. Ask the students to write a story entitled "A Day in the Life of a Child in a World Full of Love." What is the child's morning like at home, his or her day at school, while with friends? What do people say to this child during the day?

Step 2. After the stories are written, students can read them aloud for a couple days. As they read, other students can record what people said to each other in their loving worlds. Create a list to post on the wall. The teacher may want to add a few.

Step 3. Say, "I would like you to think about which statements you would like to hear at home, and which statements you would like to hear at school."

Step 4. Give students six dots or permission to make six marks by the remarks they would most like to hear at school and invite them to put those dots or marks on the list.

Step 5. Create small groups of three to write one or two of the preferred comments on long slips or pieces of paper and post them around the room. Invite them to use the statements they have created.

Close with a relaxation/focusing exercise.

Follow-up: During the next week or two, notice when the students are using some of the statements they have put on the walls. Ask how they feel about that.

LOVE LESSON 14
A Mural

Begin with a song.

Activity

Tell the students they can make a quick mural as a group. Divide the class into teams of students. One team can be responsible for the sky, another for the ground and trees, another for buildings, another for animals, and another for people. When the teams are ready, being to very slowly read the Imagining a Loving World exercise again, inserting a little more dialogue on the beauty of the sky, meadows, trees, buildings, and animals. Tell them to pretend they are in that world of kindness and caring while they are painting.

— *Contributed by Diana Hsu*

Close with a relaxation/focusing exercise.

Additional Love and Caring Lessons

LOVE LESSON 15
Project

The class may wish to do a project of its own. Ask the students what they wish to do. What are the needs in the community? Would they want to rotate being tutors to younger students for 20 minutes a day? Would they like to create slogans on caring or kindness and making a difference in the community? Are there ways they can grow their circle of compassion?

Begin each session with a song and close with a relaxation/focusing exercise of their choice.

LOVE LESSON 16
Show and Tell

Begin with a song.

Activity

Step 1. The teacher brings something from home that they love and shares it with the class.

Step 2. Invite the children to bring, with permission, something small and non-living from home that they love.

Step 3. The children share their individual things that they love.

Reflection: We all love different things. Let's remember to value them all.

— *Contributed by Batool Arjomand*

Close with a relaxation/focusing exercise or moving around the room to music and stopping when the music stops to share the thing they brought with one other person, until they have shared with three others.

LOVE LESSON 17
Kinds of Love

Begin with a song.

Discuss/Share

- What do you have love for? (love for family, the self, friends, girl/boyfriends, nature, animals, possessions, playing, sports, humanity, your own country, the world, peace, etc.)
- What is love?
- Let's see if we can name some different kinds of love. (self-love, brotherly love, platonic love, romantic love, love for the family, universal love, love for nature, love for humanity, etc.)

Discuss the following Reflection Point: I can have love for myself, love for my family, love for others, love for my country, love for my goals, and love for the world — all at the same time.

Ask: "Is that possible?"

Eight to Ten Activity: The teacher can relate one of the kinds of love above to an aspect the students are studying — perhaps a story, poem, or social studies unit.

Eleven to Twelve Activity: Take up the aspect of "love for goals."

Step 1. Ask the students what their goals are — in school currently or perhaps for their family or ask what goals they hope to achieve when they are older.

Step 2. Ask what they can do now that will affect obtaining those goals in the future

Step 3. Ask them to write down two things they can do this week toward achieving those goals.

Note to Educator: Do the above activity if the following activity is not appropriate for students of this age in your particular culture.

Thirteen to Fourteen Activity: Relate "romantic love" and "platonic love" to works recently studied in literature, or refer to classics, or literature, or oral stories from the culture of the students.

If the teacher is comfortable doing so, and it is appropriate for the culture, ask the students what they think the rules of platonic love should be now. What do they think the rules of romantic love should be? What should people never do? (This is an opportunity to confirm that any violence toward a boyfriend or girlfriend is wrong.) How old do they think people should be when they get married? (Students usually say an age which is older than one would expect!) What are the advantages of waiting to get married? (Students have more time for school; with a better education they can choose an occupation they enjoy; they can more easily provide for their families, etc.)

Close with a relaxation/focusing exercise.

LOVE LESSON 18
Drug Sellers Pretend to Be Nice at First

Begin the session with a song about peace or love.

Note to Educator: The following story was adapted from "The Street-Children Family" stories in *Living Values Activities for Street Children Ages 11–14*. It has been adapted in such a way that the characters in the story could be living in homes. The first story in this book on drug prevention is in Love Lesson 6. The below story continues with Joe, Marion and Nelson the next morning.

Share a Story: Drug Sellers Use Kids Like Slaves

Joe woke up not feeling like himself. His head hurt and his legs and arms felt really tired. He remembered the day before with a sinking feeling. He had been fooled into sniffing glue. Marion and Nelson had been so upset. He peeked a look at his big sister and saw that Fred had brought them breakfast.

"Are you still angry at me?" he whispered.

"Why do you think I'm angry?" asked Marion.

"Because I sniffed glue."

"I was scared and disappointed," said Marion. "But Nelson and I are partly to blame. We should have told you before about drugs — and how mean people try to get kids to take drugs."

"I promise never to take drugs again," said Joe.

"That would be terrific," smiled Marion.

"Joe," she said, "come on. Let's get cleaned up and eat breakfast. We need to leave for school pretty soon."

On the way to school, Marion said, "You have to be very careful if anyone offers you drugs. Adults who sell drugs hook teenagers and younger kids on drugs and then get them to sell drugs. Yesterday kids just a little older than you gave you drugs. We sometimes think that all kids are okay — but when kids give you drugs it is because they are hooked on drugs. They want you to get hooked so you will buy them. Then they will have money to buy drugs for themselves. Drug sellers — whether they are kids or adults — pretend to be nice at first, but it's only until you are hooked on the drugs!"

"What do you mean, 'hooked on drugs'?"

"After you take drugs a few times it's very, very hard to stop taking them because your body craves them. That's called 'hooked on drugs'," explained Marion. "Drug sellers are very selfish. They pretend to be nice by offering you drugs free. Then once you are hooked, they charge you money. They won't give you drugs for free. They will charge you money and make fun of you when you don't have it. Some kids start to steal in order to get money for drugs and get themselves into more trouble."

"Nelson told me never to steal," said Joe.

"That's right," said Marion. "Listen for a minute and think. Children who sell drugs can be controlled by adults who supply them. The adults who sell drugs are the worst — because they know they are destroying the lives of children. The adult drug sellers make money on the teen drug sellers and they use children drug sellers like slaves."

"The adults trick the children and make them like slaves?" asked Joe.

"Yes, exactly," said Marion. "And sometimes people who sell drugs say they will give you the drug free if you bring your friends. If you care for your friends, you would never ask them to take drugs," said Marion.

"I care for my friends," said Joe.

"I know you do," said Marion. "You're a good friend. Drug sellers are selfish and mean. I feel so sorry for the kids that they use like slaves."

"Hey," said Mohammed, "drug dealers are in it for the money, not to help people. You think people who know they are ruining your life are going to treat you nice?"

Marion nodded in agreement. She added softly. "Peoples' brains get all weird with glue and they get violent. If mean people have you under their control you are in big trouble. Imagine how you would feel if mean people started pushing around the glass ball you were in?"

"I would get hurt if someone pushed a glass ball with me in it!" said Nelson. "I'm not going to be anyone's slave!"

"You're free when you're drug-free," said Marion. "People who take drugs get dumber and dumber. Children without drugs get smarter and smarter."

"I want to be smart," said Joe. "Like you and Mo and Nelson and Fred."

"You are smart," said Marion. But sometimes people take advantage of others so we have to use our mind and stay smart all the time. We have to know who our real friends are — which people are safe and want the best for you, and who love and care for you. Drug dealers are never real friends. Got it?" asked Marion, holding up her hand for a high five.

"Got it!" said Joe with a smile.

Marion gave him a big smile and a high five.

Discuss

Questions for students 8 to 10:

- Why do drug sellers pretend to be nice? (To get kids to try drugs.)
- What does 'hooked on drugs' mean? (After you take drugs a few times it's very hard to stop taking them because your body craves them. That's called 'hooked on drugs.')
- Do the older drug sellers usually try and have teenagers and then even younger children sell drugs? (Yes.) Why do you think they do that?
- Marion said in the story, "If you care for your friends, you would never ask them to take drugs." Do you think that is true? Why?

Questions for all:

- Usually people take drugs when they feel bad and don't know how to stop feeling bad. Can you think of things they could do instead?
- What can you do to feel better when you feel sad or upset?

- What you do think drug sellers need to learn? What would you like to tell them?

Activity

Divide students into groups to create dramas/skits about drug dealers and their interactions with children and/or teens. They may wish to incorporate their own messages from the above activity. Allow them to present their drama.

If appropriate to your situation, create the opportunity for some of the skits to be shown to other children or to the community. If this is to be done, you might wish to take time during another lesson to create props, practice and advertise the event with posters made by the students. Encourage their "voice" against drug dealers and harmful drugs. Perhaps they could also create slogans about caring for others at their show.

Close with a relaxation/focusing exercise of your choice.

Unit Four: Tolerance

Tolerance Lessons

The Oxford Dictionary defines tolerance as "The ability or willingness to tolerate the existence of opinions or behavior that one dislikes or disagrees with." The Random House College Dictionary, defines tolerance as "a fair and objective attitude toward those whose opinions, practices, race, religion, nationality, or the like, differ from one's own; freedom from bigotry." What we are aiming for in this values unit includes this meaning and adds the broader dimension of actively respecting and appreciating other cultures.

Tolerance is used by the United Nations and in political arenas as the name of the value which allows people of different cultures to coexist with mutual understanding, dignity and respect. November 16 is celebrated by the United Nations and many Member States as the International Day of Tolerance. "The United Nations is committed to strengthening tolerance by fostering mutual understanding among cultures and peoples. This imperative lies at the core of the United Nations Charter, as well as the Universal Declaration of Human Rights, and is more important than ever in this era of rising and violent extremism and widening conflicts that are characterized by a fundamental disregard for human life."

On November 16, 1995, "UNESCO's Member States adopted a Declaration of Principles on Tolerance. Among other things, the Declaration affirms that tolerance is neither indulgence nor indifference. It is respect and appreciation of the rich variety of our world's cultures, our forms of expression and ways of being human. Tolerance recognizes the universal human rights and fundamental freedoms of others. People are naturally diverse; only tolerance can ensure the survival of mixed communities in every region of the globe." (Source: United Nations website)

Your school may wish to use the word Tolerance. However, some educators have shared that students relate more easily to the word Appreciation. Please feel free to use either word for this value.

While in this unit on tolerance the above is the primary focus, a couple of lessons also take up another meaning: the ability to endure a hardship, or something unpleasant or difficult.

Continue to play a song daily if you and the students are enjoying this. When studying different cultures, perhaps bring in some of that culture's songs and music at the beginning of the lesson. Perhaps sing or listen to songs that speak of the world's peoples as family. For example, "One Family" by Red Grammer speaks of the human world family as "sisters and brothers, a coat of many colors."

Do one of the Relaxation/Focusing exercises every day or every several days, as suitable for your class. The students may enjoy making up their own.

Tolerance Reflection Points

- Peace is the goal, tolerance is the method.
- Tolerance is being open and receptive to the beauty of differences.
- Tolerance is respecting and appreciating the culture of others.
- Tolerance is mutual respect through mutual understanding.
- The seeds of intolerance are fear and ignorance.
- The seed of tolerance, love, is watered by compassion and care.
- Those who know how to appreciate the good in people and situations have tolerance.
- Tolerance is an act of humanity, which we must nurture and enact each in ow lives every day, to rejoice in the diversity that makes us strong and the values that bring us together. —UNESCO Director-General Audrey Azoulay
- Tolerance recognizes individuality and diversity while removing divisive masks and defusing tension created by ignorance. (For 12- to 14-year-old students only.)
- Tolerance is the ability to face difficult situations.
- To tolerate life's inconveniences is to let go, be light, make others light, and move on.

Tolerance Unit Goals and Objectives

Goal: To increase tolerance through understanding others.
Objectives:
- To understand that each one of us is different, and to do the "move like you" exercise with another student.

- To discuss feelings that arise when a person is discriminated against.
- To interview and listen to others.
- To express their stories if they are refugees, or to develop more empathy and understanding of the plight of refugees by hearing stories of refugees and/or writing a story about migrating to a pretend country.

Goal: To increase knowledge and appreciation of different cultures.
Objectives:
- To understand that every culture and race is valuable, as is every ray of the rainbow.
- To participate in discussions about the Tolerance Reflection Points and be able to talk about two or more of them.
- To learn about two or more cultures other than their own, through hearing stories, learning songs, and participating in some form of artistic expression of that culture.

Goal: To develop socially conscious skills for increased social cohesion.
Objectives:
- To understand that the seeds of intolerance are fear and ignorance.
- To identify some of the divisive social practices that create intolerance such as name calling, thinking they are better, blaming others for your problems, etc.
- To write and discuss their advice about how people should treat other people.
- To become more aware of acts of tolerance and intolerance by collecting current or past news stories; to make a class collage of acts of tolerance and to locate on a map acts of intolerance.
- To become more aware of intolerant attitudes, if they exist in the class, school or community, and work towards a positive resolution of the problems.
- To be able to generate at least two "benevolently assertive responses" to discriminatory statements during a class exercise.
- To become aware of another meaning of tolerance, meaning to tolerate difficulties, and discuss "self-talk" that is helpful.

TOLERANCE LESSON 1
Divisive or Inclusive?

Educator Preparation: Write the following Reflection Points on the board.
- Tolerance is being open and receptive to the beauty of differences.
- Tolerance is respecting and appreciating the culture of others.
- Tolerance is mutual respect through mutual understanding.

Begin with a song about love, peace, unity or inclusion.

Introduce: "In the next few weeks, we will be learning about tolerance. In the dictionary, tolerance is defined as "a fair and objective attitude toward those whose opinions, practices, race, religion, nationality, or the like, differ from one's own; freedom from bigotry," that is, freedom from discrimination. Tolerance as a value is even more beautiful, for it is being open to understanding, respecting and appreciating other cultures, races and nationalities."

Ask:
- Do you remember the Baking a Peace Cake activity when we were studying peace? Many of the cakes had the ingredients of peace, respect, and love. Tolerance is based on those ingredients.
- What do you think would happen in the world if everyone respected the religion of everyone else?
- What do you think would happen in the world if everyone respected the culture of everyone else?

Say, "I'm going to read you a story about some imaginary people who did not have tolerance." Read "The Shorties and the Tallies", based on a story by John McConnel.

Share a Story: The Shorties and the Tallies

There was once a land where all the people were either short and fat, or tall and thin. There was no one in between. The "Shorties" and "Tallies," as they were called, did not like each another. Each thought they were better than the other. When the Shorties were talking among themselves about the arrogance of the Tallies, they would call them "beanpoles." The Tallies would talk to each other about how stupid the "shrimps" were.

Living Values Education Activities for Children Ages 8–14, Book 1

The "beanpoles" and "shrimps" were always arguing and fighting, and there was no peace in the land.

The Shorties and the Tallies did not know each other very well. They never tried to be friends. Indeed, they both refused to have anything to do with the other. They refused to live next door to one another, used different shops, and their children even went to different schools. Separate businesses and even churches and temples were built to meet the needs of the Shorties and Tallies. Demand grew for the land to be divided in two, and there was talk of war as the "beanpoles" blamed the "shrimps" for problems in the land. Each side rushed to buy guns.

The ruler of the land did not help. Most of the time he was interested in accumulating more wealth for himself. Sometimes he even blamed the Tallies for the problems of the land. As intolerance increased, the children were told more and more by adults that the other group was not good. The children of the Shorties were told to not make friends with the "beanpoles," and the children of the Tallies were told not to make friends with the "shrimps."

Then one day a strange thing happened. All the people of the land went blind. Not even one person could see anything. Everyone's world was turned upside down in more ways than one. The people stumbled around, trying to find their way from the shops and the churches and temples to their homes. They were bumping into one another and tripping over each other. Little children, teenagers, and adults all needed help, and they helped each other. Adults conversed with anyone they bumped into to ask for help in finding their way. Little children were taken care of by older children, and mothers of both Shorties and Tallies helped each other find their children.

At first, the Shorties did not know they were sometimes being helped by "beanpoles," and Tallies did not realize they were being helped by "shrimps." They welcomed the understanding voices and the generous help. But as they helped each other with their hands, they began to realize that some of those kind hands were thin and long, and other kind hands were short and plump.

"Humph!" one Shortie named Miriam said to herself, "I bet that's the only nice beanpole out there." But as Miriam tried to find her way to the store to buy food, she was again helped by another Tallie!

Ali, one of the Tallies, was also surprised. "Those shrimps aren't all so mean," he thought to himself one day when a Shortie helped him find his little brother.

As one long week and another week passed, each person began to realize that the shape and size of each other's body no longer mattered. They began to judge each person they met by his or her behavior instead of the physical. What was important was whether they were kind and gentle or mean-spirited. They began to appreciate their new friends and understand that a person's character is much more important than the way he or she looked — and that good qualities can be found in everyone.

With this realization, the hearts of the short fat people, and the tall thin people began to melt. They were kinder to everyone they met. As they began to grow fond of their new friends, their sight returned just as suddenly as it had disappeared! They laughed with each other in their joy of seeing, and they promised never to be deceived by their eyes again.

Discuss/Share

Ask:

- What were some of the things the Shorties and Tallies did to create intolerance?

➢ Tell the students that you will read the story again and you want them to call out "dividing" or "divisive" when you read a way they created conflict or were discriminatory, such as thinking they were better, name calling, separate schools, blaming others for their problems, etc. With older students, ask them to read the story and stop when they find a divisive practice, then pass the book for another student to read, and so on.

➢ Create a list on the board of all the divisive practices that help create intolerance.

Ask:

- What are other things that people do that are discriminatory?
- Have you seen that happen?
- Has that happened to you?
- How do you feel when that happens? Or: How do you think people feel when that happens?
- When people are treated unfairly, how do they feel?
- What would you like people to do instead of being discriminatory or believing that they are better than others?

➢ Look at each item on the "divisive list" and ask students what inclusive practices would help create tolerance. For example, instead of separate schools the children could go to the same school.

Discuss the story work in relation to the following Reflection Points:
- ♦ Tolerance is mutual respect through mutual understanding.
- ♦ The seeds of intolerance are fear and ignorance.

Ask:
- Why do you think people create discrimination and mistrust? What are they afraid of? Or, is it something they learned from adults and so just do it automatically?
- *For Ages 12 to 14:* What is the history of intolerance in our country?
- What would the world be like if everyone had tolerance, that is, if everyone appreciated all other races, cultures and religions?

Artistic Expression Activity

Invite the students to draw or paint the feelings of appreciation and tolerance. Older students may be invited to do that or to draw or paint the positive feelings on one side of a piece of paper and feelings that result from intolerant practices on the other half of a piece of paper.

Close with the Flowers of the Garden Relaxation/Focusing Exercise.

TOLERANCE LESSON 2
Real Stories

Begin with a song.

Share a Story

Read to the students or they can read a story about real people who experienced intolerance. For younger students, one such story is "Molly's Pilgrim" by Barbara Cohen. Older students could read parts of Nelson Mandela's "Walk to Freedom" or another work from your language arts' Tolerance lesson curriculum. You may wish to choose a piece by one of your country's authors.

Activity

Talk with students about their feelings regarding the story they have read. Ask them to write a few lines and illustrate their thoughts or write a short personal essay.

Close with a relaxation/focusing exercise.

TOLERANCE LESSON 3
Moving Like You

Begin with a song.

Activity

Step 1. Tell members of the class that you will be asking them to pair up with someone they do not normally play or work with and to decide who is going to be A and B. This is a silent exercise to discover what it is like to pretend to be somebody else.

Explain that the A's are going to go for a walk for ten minutes (the A's keep time). The B's are going to follow them and copy everything they do — from the length, speed, and rhythm of their stride and the way they place their feet to the way they hold their hands and swing their arms. They will look and listen to whatever the A's look at and listen to. In other words, B is going to spend ten minutes discovering what it is like to be A.

Step 2. Invite them to walk as explained above. After ten minutes they can stop and talk, and B can tell A what he or she discovered — what changed when pretending to be A.

Step 3. Reverse roles and walk for another ten minutes. Follow this with sharing. repeat the above.

Step 4. When you all return, invite them to share their discoveries and put them up on the board.

— *Contributed by Diana Beaver*

If there is time, you may wish to start the next lesson.
Close with a relaxation/focusing exercise.

TOLERANCE LESSONS 4 to 8
A Rainbow of Cultures

Begin with a song.

Close each day's lesson with a relaxation/focusing exercise. You or the students may wish to play music from the cultures you are studying, and perhaps use some of the values cherished by that culture during the relaxation/focusing exercise. A small group of students could be responsible for creating different relaxation/focusing exercises.

Living Values Education Activities for Children Ages 8–14, Book 1

Discuss one of the following Reflection Points each day prior to doing the following activities:
- Peace is the goal, tolerance is the method.
- Tolerance is respecting and appreciating the culture of others.
- Tolerance is being open and receptive to the beauty of differences.
- Tolerance is mutual respect through mutual understanding.
- Those who know how to appreciate the good in people and situations have tolerance.
- Those who know how to appreciate the good in people and situations have tolerance.
- Tolerance is an act of humanity, which we must nurture and enact each in own lives every day, to rejoice in the diversity that makes us strong and the values that bring us together. — UNESCO Director-General Audrey Azoulay

Activities
Making a Rainbow Activity — Lesson 4

Explain Concept: Compare the variety of races, cultures and religions to a rainbow. The rainbow would not be nearly as beautiful if it were missing one or two colors — in fact, it would not be a rainbow with only one color. The human family is like a rainbow; it comes with a wonderful variety of colors. Each culture and tradition have something important to contribute.

Make a rainbow: As a class, stay in a space of respect, caring and fun as you make a large rainbow on the wall. This may be made of paper. If this is not possible, allow the students to make individual rainbows on paper while creating a line drawing on the board.

Say, "Let's look at different cultures throughout the world. Let's start at the top of the globe. What are the cultures furthest north?" (Nordic culture or Eskimos.)
- ➤ Begin to go south on the globe, having the students come up with different cultures as you write down in broad terms the major cultures, for example: Nordic, Indigenous Cultures, Slavic/Russian, European, Arabic, Asian, African, Hispanic/Latin American, putting the northern most cultures at the top of one slice of the rainbow and moving downward. It is fine to have more than one culture on each line. Try to put similar cultures together.

> Now start with the major religions of each culture and again begin at the top of the globe and move downward, filling in another vertical slice of the rainbow.

NOTE TO EDUCATOR

Think about which cultures you would like the students to explore. Perhaps the first year, you may wish to explore a couple of the cultures that exist in the class, school or area in order to create more tolerance. If you have students that are recent immigrants, deepen their welcome by learning about their culture. Another year, choose different cultures that they may not encounter frequently.

Learn about Different Cultures through Stories or Guest Speakers — Lesson 4 to 7

Do lessons on informative stories about the two or more cultures, selecting fiction or non-fiction stories appropriate to the ages of the students, or study and research about the culture.

Invite teens or adults from the chosen cultures to come and talk with the students. They may be willing to bring in a traditional treat, or share a song, poem, or piece of art from that culture. Perhaps one or two of the guests can teach you a dance.

Discuss/Share

Discuss the information afterwards. Put the culture you learned about in a different ray of the rainbow.

Ask:
- What did you learn about that culture that you didn't know before?
- What values are important to this culture?
- How do they show that?

Option: Learn about Traditional Dress or Customs

Make or draw figures in traditional dress of the cultures you are studying. Place them around the rainbow. Older students could make symbols from that culture, describe relevant characteristics, or write down significant events in the history of that culture.

Expressive Activity — Lesson 8

Ask the students to stand in a circle and share just a couple of sentences about what they discovered and really appreciate about a culture different than their own.

Invite the students to form small groups and make up a poem or a song about the human world family as a rainbow or about the different cultures and the theme of Tolerance/Appreciation.

Homework: During these lessons begin to watch the news and/or find pictures and articles in the newspaper or on-line about examples of intolerance and tolerance.

NOTE TO EDUCATOR

The teacher is responsible for providing a tolerant atmosphere in which the students can thrive. Be attentive to all forms of exclusion, selfishness, and meanness that mask fear and ignorance. Establish the spirit of tolerance through dialogue and understanding.

Please help students put an end to intolerance by encouraging them to appreciate the beauty of diversity and the richness it brings. Emphasize that listening to others is the first step towards tolerance. Help them listen, be tolerant, and have the aim of understanding and achieving a positive and accurate solution. Continue to reinforce respect while helping them understand others.

When conflicts arise that have a hint of intolerance, discuss them. Perhaps ask:
- What are little things that people do that indicate prejudice or intolerance? (You can't play. It's my ball. She's not good enough to _____, etc.)
- What can we do to change that?

Make the point that tolerance is the ability to face situations and offer creative solutions.   — *Contributed by Pilar Quera Colomina and Sabine Levy*

TOLERANCE LESSON 9

A Collage of Tolerance, A Map of Intolerance

Begin with a song.

Activity

Ask the students to continue to watch the news and/or find pictures and articles in the newspaper or on-line about examples of tolerance and intolerance. Ask them to observe situations of tolerance and intolerance around them.

During the time they report their findings, issues for discussion will come up. Positively comment on the situations of tolerance and notice together what words or actions contribute to the generation of tolerance. When situations of intolerance come up, this is an opportunity for the class to generate ways to deal with the situation(s) in a manner that promotes harmony.

A collage on tolerance and a map on intolerance can be developed as students continue to bring in information. Their drawings, poems, and pictures can be added to a collage on the wall during the weeks they are studying tolerance. Place pins or dots on a map for instances of intolerance.

— *Contributed by Pilar Quera Colomina and Sabine Levy*

Close with a relaxation/focusing exercise.

TOLERANCE LESSON 10
Discrimination

Begin with a song.

Share a Story

Eight to Ten Story: Read a story with a little discrimination, but a positive outcome, such as "One Green Apple" by Eve Bunting. In this story, a Muslim girl feels different with her headscarf when she goes to school in her new country. The Joy of Reading Project kindly gave their permission to post this story on the international LVE site, www.livingvalues.net. You will find it under For Schools /Children Ages 8–14 / Download Free Stories / Tolerance 8–10.

Eleven to Fourteen Story: Read a story or some history about discrimination. Perhaps pick a story from your own country, or you may wish to read about Nelson Mandela or Mahatma Gandhi.

Discuss/Share

Ask students about the lack of tolerance of differences they have noticed at school or in society. Ask students if they can think of an example of intolerance. If they cannot, mention, in age-appropriate terms, one that they might be aware of, such as:

- Are some people tolerated less than others?
- Are some discriminated against? On what basis?

- What are different ways people discriminate against others, that is, act like they are less than? (This may include racial jokes, insults to someone's culture or stereotyping, such as all _____ people are dumb.)
- Have you ever been discriminated against?
- How did it feel?
- What attitude would you like everyone to have toward each other?
- If someone is very popular, will people be more likely to tolerate that person?
- What kinds of things can we say to ourselves so we can have more tolerance of others?

Eight to Nine Activity: Write a few sentences about how people feel when they have been discriminated against and draw a picture. Then, write two or three sentences of advice about how they would like all people to act. The students could read their advice in small groups, and each group could then make a slogan. Draw the slogans on posters or long pieces of paper and place them on the walls.

Ten to Fourteen Activity:

Step 1. Ask students to write a short personal essay about feeling discriminated against or being treated unfairly. Ask each student to think of his or her advice about how people should treat each other. The teacher may wish to instruct students to focus their advice, that is, if the students are studying the structure of the government, what would their advice be to the leaders of the country? Or, what would their advice be to other students of the world, parents, teachers, or adults?

Step 2: Divide students into small groups to share their advice.

Step 3. Invite each group to make a slogan. Draw the slogans on posters or long pieces of paper.

Step 4. Place the slogans on the walls.

Close with a relaxation/focusing exercise.

TOLERANCE LESSON 11
A Pretend Immigration

Begin with a song.

Activity

Ask the students to make up a story about immigrating to a pretend country. Ask them to talk about how they want to be treated and how they want their parents to be treated. Younger students may wish to illustrate their story with a drawing. Older students can make images of tolerance and add them to the collage.

— *Contributed by Marcia Maria Lins de Medeiros*

Note to Educator and Optional Additional Activities: While some students are refugees themselves, others may be in need to developing more empathy in regard to the plight of refugees. In the former instance, invite the students to share their stories and make drawings of some of their memories. Please ensure there is a caring and safe classroom atmosphere and use active listening and validation as they share. Allow them time to do this, perhaps several periods.

If sensitization is needed, provide the opportunity for them to learn more about the incredibly difficult struggles of many refugees. On the livingvalues.net site, the story "Brothers in Hope — The story of the lost boys of Sudan" by Mary Williams is suitable for students 12 and older. The Joy of Reading Project kindly gave their permission to post this story. You will find it under For Schools /Children Ages 8–14 / Download Free Stories / Tolerance 12-YA.

Close with a relaxation/focusing exercise.

TOLERANCE LESSON 12
Disarming Prejudice

Begin with a song.

Discuss/Share

Ask the students if they have heard mean or prejudiced things said in the past. If the answer is "yes", ask them if they would like to think about ways to change that in the future. Then, ask:
- What prejudiced or mean things have you heard people say at school? (List those quickly on the board.)
- What usually happens when that type of thing is said?

Say, "Sometimes when someone says something aggressive, feelings are hurt, and things get even worse. Sometimes when one is aggressive, the other person says or does something aggressive back."

If they talk about the insulted party going away and saying nothing, say, "Sometimes when someone says something aggressive, the other person goes away. The other's response appears passive."
Ask:
- But how does he/she feel inside? (Acknowledge their responses.)
- Do you remember the benevolent-assertive response from the Peace I Unit? When someone says something mean, there are generally three types of responses: aggressive, passive responses or assertive.

"You have been learning about assertive responses already. When someone does something mean and you say, 'I don't want you to do that; I want you to stop,' that is an assertive response. You are being assertive during conflict resolution when you say to someone, with respect, 'I don't like it when you _____, and I want you to _____.'

Say, "Sometimes people say mean things, and we just want to say something back." Ask:
- What happens if we say something back which is aggressive? (Acknowledge their responses: people become even angrier; there is more resentment; more fights; and retaliation begins.)
- What happens when we are passive? (Some may say: People have no respect for you and treat you worse; you feel like you have no courage.)

Say, "I want you to put on your thinking caps and think of assertive responses that could be said to these mean, prejudiced remarks we have listed on the board. But, I want you not only to think of something that is not aggressive, and something that is not passive, I want you to think of something benevolently assertive!"

Activity

Step 1. Divide students into groups of three or four and ask them to generate remarks that could be said in response — remarks that offer a more tolerant view that could be considered assertive yet benevolent — not aggressive, but not wishy-washy either. Examples are, "It wouldn't be such an interesting world if we were all clones," "I admire her _____," "I like your ability to _____ and I like his ability to _____." or "What would you do if you were in her place?" Ask students to make a list of the best supportive comebacks.

Living Values Education Activities for Children Ages 8–14, Book 1

Step 2. Ask each group to role play for the entire group a few of their favorite responses. Encourage them to stay in self-respect as they repeat their remarks. Lead the applause.

Step 3: Discuss the following Reflection Point: The seed of tolerance, love, is watered by compassion and care.

Close with a relaxation/focusing exercise.

TOLERANCE LESSON 13
The Key

Begin with a song.
Discuss the Reflection Point:
- ♦ Those who know how to appreciate the good in people and situations have tolerance.

Activity

Step 1. Generate and practice benevolently assertive responses or other supportive comebacks for 10 minutes or more, practicing the skill learned in the last lesson. The teacher or students can say comments they heard on the playground. Others can offer replies which are assertive and full of self-respect. Practicing these until they are comfortable makes them more likely to be used.

Step 2. Role play a couple of scenes and recognize students for doing a good job.

Step 3. Ask each student to write a list of things that help create tolerance. (Younger students can list four, older students eight.)

Step 4. Ask students to then discuss their lists in groups of three or four and come up with three or four things they feel are most important for creating an atmosphere or appreciation or tolerance. What are the values under those words, attitudes or actions?

Step 5. Invite each group to present their list.

Close with a relaxation/focusing exercise.

TOLERANCE LESSON 14
Tolerating Difficulties

Begin with a song.

156

Explain that Tolerance has other meanings, such as to endure. The Reflection Points for this kind of tolerance are:

- Tolerance is the ability to face difficult situations.
- To tolerate life's inconveniences is to let go, be light, make others light, and move on.

In this form, tolerance is facing difficult situations by seeing them from a different perspective: as molehills, not mountains. Adopting that perspective, of course, would depend on the nature of the situation. Express to the students that sometimes what appears as a formidable challenge — "a mountain" — may, in retrospect, have only been "a molehill". It's a matter of seeing the circumstance in the overall scheme of things.

Share a Story

Eight to Eleven Story: "The Royal Bee" by Frances Park, Ginger Park and Christopher Zhong-Yuan Zhang is a based on a true story which took place in Korea. The Joy of Reading Project kindly gave their permission to post this story on the international LVE site, www.livingvalues.net. You will find it under For Schools /Children Ages 8–14 / Download Free Stories / Tolerance 8–11. In this story, the protagonist has one type of tolerance, and the teacher has another. Discuss: Who has which? What was the boy willing to endure?

Twelve to Fourteen Content: Select a biography of someone who has demonstrated exceptional tolerance in her or his life. Read aloud passages that illustrate the value of tolerance. Or, the students could write a short story or personal essay on something they have tolerated.

Discuss/Share

Ask the students to share "self-talk" or methods that help them face or accommodate difficulties. Positively reinforce their sharing. Perhaps ask them to share what things are difficult now and what might help them cope with it by positive or encouraging self-talk.

Close with a relaxation/focusing exercise.

Additional Tolerance Lessons and Activities

TOLERANCE LESSON 15
An Ending Note

Possible Activities

Cultural Celebration: If you would like a celebratory finish to the Tolerance Unit, help the students plan a celebration of different cultures, with song, dance and food from a variety of cultures. You may wish to have this as a classroom activity, a school-wide activity or an assembly. If greater cultural appreciation and integration is needed in your community, please involve community members to involve more parents and families.

Special Project: If there is discrimination in the community, ask the students what they think they can do about it as a class. Perhaps they would like to create a skit/drama about students who have prejudice learning to appreciate each other's culture, race or religion. Perhaps other students in the class can provide music and poems. Share it at an assembly in your school and perhaps in other schools. When creating the skit, ask them to review some of their suggestions for tolerance/appreciation and some of their benevolent assertive response. Perhaps some of these can become part of the skit, or slogans that the students share. As a follow-up, ask: "Would you like to share some of these slogans with others in our school or community?" "How could we do that?" Students 12 and older may be able to share their slogans on social media.

TOLERANCE LESSON 16
Walking in Your Shoes

Begin with a song.

During history, social studies, or literature, ask students to identify a character who is different than they. To develop understanding, ask them to write a short story as if they were that person, explaining the beliefs and reasons behind that character's actions.

Close with a relaxation/focusing exercise.

Activities

Pen Pals

Having Pen Pals is a wonderful method for students to truly understand that other people around the world are much the same as they are.

ToGether — Children from different cultures singing, dancing and creating together

"ToGether" was a joint effort of OneMelodie (a non-profit organization for Social Education in Utrecht), the LVE School De Vrije Ruimte in The Hague, and LVE The Netherlands. Over the course of a year, they brought together two equally-sized groups of children ages 6 to 12 of different cultures and backgrounds who would normally never have the chance to meet and play with one another. One group of children came from a neighborhood in Utrecht, home to refugee and immigrant families originating from Sudan, Senegal, Ghana and Morocco. The other group was of native Dutch children. The children prepared meals together, made paintings, played games, danced and sang, sewed and made all kinds of crafts. In addition, they made a CD of Dutch songs in a professional studio. Two values, cooperation and happiness, took a central position and were practiced in all activities.

Suggestion: Find opportunities for the students to engage with students of another culture.

Unit Five: Honesty

Honesty Lessons

The importance of honesty and integrity is becoming ever more apparent as dishonesty and corruption grow in many lands across the world. This unit brings forth the easiness and building of trust and good relationships through honesty, and contrasts the effects of honesty and dishonesty in individuals, friends and families, as well as the effects of dishonesty and corruption in businesses, society and the world. The lessons offer educators activities to go as deep into the subject as they wish, in accordance with the age and interest of their students. Thank you for your willingness to help students understand the impoverishment that dishonesty brings, and the beauty and benefit for all inherent in honesty and fairness.

Continue to play a song daily. Do one of the Relaxation/Focusing Exercises every day or every several days, as suitable for your class. The students may enjoy making up their own exercises.

Honesty Reflection Points

- Honesty is telling the truth.
- Integrity is part of honesty, it means doing what is right.
- Integrity is part of honesty, it means being fair.
- Integrity is part of honesty, it means keeping your word, keeping your promises.
- Integrity is part of honesty, it means being true to yourself and your values.
- When I am honest, I feel clear inside.
- A person who is honest and true is worthy of trust.
- Honesty and kindness build trust.
- There is a deep relationship between honesty and friendship.
- Honest thoughts, words, and actions create harmony.
- Honesty is to use well what has been entrusted to you.

- Honesty allows me to be free of worries.
- When I am honest, I can learn and help others learn to be giving.
- Greed is usually at the root of corruption.
- There is enough for man's need, but not enough for man's greed.
- When we are aware we are interconnected, we recognize the importance of honesty.

Honesty Unit Goals and Objectives

Goal: To increase knowledge about honesty.
Objectives:
- To participate in discussions about the Honesty Reflection Points and be able to talk about three or more.
- To learn about integrity as part of honesty: it is doing what is right, keeping your promises, being fair, and being true to yourself and your own values.
- To express and/or hear others express their feelings about when people are honest and keep their promises.
- To understand the relationship between honesty and trust.

Goal: To develop awareness about the effects of dishonesty and corruption.
Objectives:
- To express or hear others express their feelings about when people are dishonest, don't keep their promises and are unfair.
- To create and then participate in a skit on the theme of honesty and dishonesty, placed within a period of history the students have been studying, or in a local context for younger students, and to discuss the effects on the people of that time economically and socially.
- To understand different ways in which people can be corrupt.
- To Mind Map the effects of honesty or dishonesty/corruption.
- To participate in lessons and discussions about why people lie, how we feel when we lie, how we feel about others when they lie, and how others feel about us when we lie.
- For older students to examine the effects of dishonesty and corruption in a real-world event.

Goal: To learn social skills that can help one be honest.

Objectives:

- To participate in lessons about "one minute of courage."
- To discuss and practice communication skills when we have done something we regret.
- To make up Honesty Situation Cards and act out honest and dishonest responses and the consequences.

Goal: To value being honest.

Objectives:

- To enjoy "The Emperor and the Flower Seed" story and be asked to think of a time when they were loved for their honesty.
- To understand that when I am honest, I will be clearer and happier inside.
- To write three guidelines for being a good friend.

HONESTY LESSON 1

Honesty and Trust

Begin with a song.

Introduction: "Today we will begin to explore the value of honesty."

Discuss/Share

Ask:

- What does honesty mean to you?
- What are different ways people show their honesty?
- Do you like it when people tell you the truth?
- Do you like it when people keep their promises?
- How do you feel when they break their promises?
- If they break their promises more than once, do you trust them to keep their promise the next time?
- Do you like it when people are fair?
- Do you trust people who are honest? Why?
- Do you trust people who lie to you or try to cheat you? Why not?

Honesty Reflection Points:
- Honesty is telling the truth.
- Honesty is being true to yourself and your values.
- A person who is honest and true is worthy of trust.

Read "The Emperor and the Flower Seeds" or another story in which honesty is rewarded. There are many versions of the ancient tale below; the original author is unknown.

Share a Story: The Emperor and the Flower Seeds

Long ago there lived an Emperor who loved nature. Anything he planted burst into bloom. Up came flowers, bushes, and even big fruit trees, as if by magic! Of everything in nature, he loved flowers most of all, and he tended his own garden every day. But the Emperor was very old, and he needed to choose a successor to the throne. Who would his successor be? And how would the Emperor decide? As the Emperor loved flowers so much, he decided that flowers would help him choose.

The next day, a proclamation was issued: "All men, women, boys, and girls throughout the land are to come to the palace." The news created great excitement throughout the land.

In a village not far away, there lived a young girl named Serena. Serena had always wanted to visit the palace and see the Emperor, and so she decided to go. She was glad she went. How magnificent the palace was! It was made from gold and was studded with jewels of every color and type — diamonds, rubies, emeralds, opals, and amethysts. How the palace gleamed and sparkled! Serena felt that she had always known this place. She walked through the palace doors into the Great Hall where she was overwhelmed by all the people. It was so noisy. "The whole kingdom must be here!" she said to herself.

There then boomed the sound of at least 100 trumpets announcing the arrival of the Emperor. All fell silent. The Emperor entered, clutching what looked like a small box. How fine he looked — so noble and elegant! He circled the Great Hall, greeting each and every person and presenting something to each one. Serena was curious about the small box. "What was inside?" she wondered. "What was he giving to everyone?"

At last, the Emperor reached Serena. She curtsied and then watched as the Emperor reached into the small box and presented her with a flower seed. When Serena received the seed, she became the happiest girl of all.

Then the sound of trumpets filled the Great Hall once more, and all became silent. The Emperor announced: "Whoever can show me the most beautiful flowers in a year's time will succeed me to the throne!"

Serena left for home filled with wonder over the palace and the Emperor, clutching the flower seed carefully in her hand. She was certain she could grow the most beautiful flower. She filled a flower pot with rich soil, planted the seed carefully, and watered it every day. She couldn't wait to see it sprout, grow, and blossom into a magnificent flower!

Days passed, but nothing grew in the pot. Serena was worried. She transferred the seed into a bigger pot, filled it with the best quality richest soil she could find, and watered it twice a day, every day. Days, weeks, and months passed, but still nothing happened. By and by the whole year passed. Finally Spring came, and it was time to return once more to the palace. Serena was heartbroken that she had no flower to show the Emperor — not even a little sprout. She thought that everyone would laugh at her because all she had to show for the whole year's effort was a pot of lifeless soil! How could she face the Emperor with nothing?

Her friend stopped by on his way to the palace, holding a great big flower. "Serena! You're not going to the Emperor with an empty pot, are you?" said the friend. "Couldn't you grow a great big flower like mine?"

Serena's father, having overheard this, put his arm around Serena and consoled her. "It is up to you whether you go or not," said her father. "You did your best, Serena, and your best is good enough to present to the Emperor."

Even though she felt reluctant to go, Serena also knew she must not disrespect the Emperor's wishes. Besides, she also wanted to see the Emperor and the palace again! And so, Serena traveled once more to the palace, holding the pot of soil in her hands.

The Emperor was happy to see the Great Hall filled with his subjects, all proudly displaying their beautiful flowers, all eagerly hoping to be chosen. How beautiful all the flowers were! Flowers were of every shape, size, and color. The Emperor examined each flower carefully and thoroughly, one by one. Serena, who was hiding in a corner with her head bowed down, wondered how he could choose, since they were all so lovely. Finally, the Emperor came to Serena. Serena dared not look at the Emperor. "Why did you bring an empty pot?" the Emperor asked Serena.

"Your Majesty," said Serena. "I planted the seed you gave me and I watered it every day, but it didn't sprout. I put it in a better pot with better soil, but still it didn't sprout. I tended it all year long, but nothing grew. So today I brought an empty pot without a flower. It was the best I could do."

When the Emperor heard those words, a smile spread slowly over his face, and he took Serena by the hand. Serena was frightened. She wondered if she were in some sort of trouble.

The Emperor led her to the front of the Great Hall, and turning to the crowd, he exclaimed: "I have found my successor — the person worthy of ruling after me!"

Serena was puzzled. "But your Majesty," she said, "I have no flower, just this pot of lifeless earth."

"Yes, I expected that," said the Emperor. "From where everyone else got their seeds, I do not know. The seeds I gave everyone last year had all been roasted. It would have been impossible for any of them to grow. Serena, I admire your great courage and honesty to appear before me with the truth. I reward you with my entire kingdom. You will be the next Empress."

Discuss

Begin with the comments about the story, such as "Serena was loved for her honesty. She was true to herself and her values."

Ask:

- Why do you think the king wanted a successor with honesty?
- If you were old and had lots of money, why would you want people around you to be honest? Why or why not?
- Do you want honest or dishonest friends now? Why?

Share the Reflection Point: "A person who is honest and true is worthy of trust."

Activity

Eight and Nine Activity: Ask the students to draw a picture of one aspect of the tale or make a few props and act out the story.

Ten to Fourteen Activity: Ask older students to discuss in groups of five or six why they would want an honest successor if they were a king or queen. Would they also want honest advisors and subjects? Why or why not? What would some of the consequences be? Present their findings to the entire class in the form of a humorous dialogue or short skit/drama.

Close with a relaxation/focusing exercise of your choice.

Living Values Education Activities for Children Ages 8–14, Book 1

HONESTY LESSON 2

Thinking about Corruption — Reflecting on Integrity

Begin with a song.

Discuss/Share

Say, "A really honest person is automatically considered to have a value called integrity. Integrity is part of honesty, it means doing what is right, doing what is fair."

Discuss the following Reflection Points:
- Integrity is part of honesty, it means doing what is right.
- Integrity is part of honesty, it means being fair.
- Integrity is part of honesty, it means keeping your word, keeping your promises.
- Integrity is part of honesty, it means being true to yourself and your values.

Say, "Some of the people in the world have integrity and others are dishonest. Someone can be honest most of the time, but occasionally tell little lies. Some people are dishonest and lie whenever they find it convenient. But when people are so dishonest that they try to cheat others, they are being corrupt.

- Let's say one of you wanted to be class president. What would be an honest way to try to get votes of your classmates? (To tell them why you want to be president and what you will work for if you are president, etc.)
- What would be an unfair or corrupt way of trying to get the votes of your classmates? (To tell them you will give them money if they vote for you.)
- If you were making something to sell so you could make money, would it be fair if your friend's big brother told you that you could only sell the things you made if you gave him one-third of your money? (No. That would be unfair, that is, corrupt. That would be taking something that is rightfully yours.)
- Would it be unfair or corrupt if someone told you she was selling you a certain bicycle and then gave you one worth only half that much?
- If someone had integrity would she sell you exactly what she told you she was going to sell you? Or would she try to trick you into paying more?
- What are other examples of corruption?
- What are other examples of integrity?

Reflective Activity

I'd like you to relax for a few minutes and reflect on people you know who are honest . . . people who are fair and do what they say . . . people with integrity.

- ❖ Please close your eyes and think about how you feel when you are with someone that makes a promise, and you know they will keep their promise. (Pause for 10 seconds.)
- ❖ How do you feel when you are with someone who tells you something and you know it is true? (Pause for about 15 seconds.)
- ❖ Think of some of the people in your life who always are fair and honest with you and everyone else. . . . What other values do they have? (Pause for 20 to 30 seconds.)
- ❖ Think of a few times when you were really fair with a friend or a brother or sister. . . . How did you feel?
- ❖ Now please imagine a world where everyone is honest and fair . . . where everyone is true to themselves and to their values. . . . Imagine such a world . . . and interacting with people in that world. (Pause for two minutes.)
- ❖ Now please think of two or three of your most important values. . . .
- ❖ What does it mean to be true to yourself? . . . (Pause.)
- ❖ What makes it easy to be true to yourself? . . . . (Pause for one minute.)

Share: Ask the students to share their thoughts and feelings about a world where everyone is honest and fair, true to themselves and their values. What would it be like?

Reflective Writing: Invite the students to write some of their thoughts about what it means to be true to themselves and what makes it easy to be true to themselves.

Close with relaxing music as if you were doing a relaxation/focusing exercise. However, instead invite the students who wish to do so to share one word, phrase or sentence from their reflection as the music plays.

HONESTY LESSON 3
Mind Mapping Honesty and Dishonesty

Begin with a song.

Activity

"Today, let's explore the differences between a world with all honest people and a world with many dishonest or corrupt people through mind mapping."

Mind Map: Begin by drawing a large circle on a white board, putting Honesty on the right side and Dishonesty/Corruption on the left side. If you are not familiar with Mind Mapping, you will find information in the Appendix (Item 1). Start with a branch for Self on the Honesty side of the circle, asking them what happens when there is Honesty in the Self and writing in brief their responses. Then ask them what happens when there is a lack of honesty in the Self. The students are to supply all the answers. Also do branches for Families and Friends. For Businesses and Government, please contrast honesty and corruption.

Discuss the Reflection Points:
- Honest thoughts, words, and actions create harmony.
- Greed is usually at the root of corruption.
- There is enough for man's need, but not enough for man's greed.
- When we are aware we are interconnected, we recognize the importance of honesty.

Creative Activity

Divide the students into groups of five or six. Ask each group to create a song or poem about honesty versus dishonesty/corruption. It could be a rap song. Allow them to perform their creation for the group.

HONESTY LESSON 4
An Honest Heart Benefits Many

Begin with a song.

Activity

Step 1. Ask the students to from groups of six to eight. Ask them to portray a situation in which a leader is dishonest or corrupt and the same situation in which the leader is honest. The students could take the context from a unit the class has been studying, such as a stockbroker's office and investors, a feudal lord of medieval times, a current conflict in the world, or a theme from a social studies unit. Younger students might wish to make the skits of the owner of a pretend local store and his or her employees.

Step 2. Ask them to begin the skit with the dishonest or corrupt leader. Will the same leader change; will someone help his or her heart to change so that he or she is honest? Or, will a new person come in who is honest?

Step 3. Allow the different groups to put on their skits for the entire class.

Step 4. After the skits, ask the actors:
- How did you feel about working there when the leader was corrupt?
- How did you feel about working there when the leader was honest and kind?
- What was the effect on the people who were cheated?
- What was the effect of the dishonesty or greed on these people's lives?
- When the leader was fair what was the effect on people's lives?

Discuss the following Reflection Points:
- Honesty and kindness build trust.
- Honesty is to use well what has been entrusted to you.
- When I am honest, I can learn and help others learn to be giving.

Note to Educator: Sometimes the students want to enact their skit again. If they do, allow each actor to have a "shadow," a person who speaks the actor's true feelings and responds to questions from the class about thoughts of the actor. An actor can have more than one shadow when other students have different ideas to share.

Twelve to Fourteen Homework: Ask students to bring in a story on honesty or corruption from the media; it could be local, national or world news. Or, think about a historical example of corruption from a unit of history recently studied and be ready to discuss it during the next lesson.

Close with a relaxation/focusing exercise of your choice.

HONESTY LESSON 5 for Ages 12 to 14
Corruption Versus Honesty

Begin with a song.

Activity

Ask students to share the stories of honesty or corruption they have gathered, or discuss a historical example of corruption from a unit of history recently studied.

Living Values Education Activities for Children Ages 8–14, Book 1

Discuss the effects on the person, other people, and the effect on the general well-being of the country where the corruption occurs. Examine the short-term and long-term effects.

Ask:
- Would everyone in the country benefit if everyone were honest? Why or why not?
- What would happen to the safety level if everyone was paid well and had fair employers?

Activity

Ask students to form small groups. Ask them to choose one of the situations they have discussed and decide how honesty and a giving heart could resolve the situation. What understandings would people need to have?

Ask:
- What is your advice to the adults of the world?

Invite each group to share their resolution and their advice.
Close with a relaxation/focusing exercise of your choice.

HONESTY LESSON 6
Lying Versus One Minute of Courage

Begin with a song.

Share a Story

There are many classic tales of dishonesty. "Matilda" by Hilaire Belloc and "The Boy Who Cried Wolf" are about young people who came to misfortune because of lying. Teachers of older students may want to choose a real-life story about a person who was ruined because of lying. Tell a story about telling lies and have a discussion.

Say, "This story was a dramatic example of what happened with a lie. Today, let's talk more about lying and examine what happens when someone tells a lie."

Discuss/Share
- How does it feel to be honest?
- Is honesty valued?
- How does it feel to be caught in a lie?

- Do you know an honest person?
- How do you feel about him or her?
- What are the consequences of lying or other kinds of dishonesty?
- What makes us dishonest?

— Contributed by Linda Heppenstall

Say, "Yes, occasionally people who tell a lie get away with it. But why do they lie in the first place? Usually people lie because they are afraid of being embarrassed, or they may try to avoid being punished for having done something wrong. Then, when they're trying to cover the lie, things get very complicated because they have to remember what they said and what they did not say."

Ask:

- What happens when children lie to their parents?
- What else happens?

"Yes, that's right. The parents often get angry and disappointed, and the child gets in even more trouble. And although people may not look so clever sometimes, usually they can figure out the truth fairly well! And if we lie once, they may not trust us to tell the truth another time."

Ask:

- How much energy does it take to cover the lie versus telling the truth?
- What might happen to a researcher working for an important chemical company who lies about his or her research results?

It takes one minute of real courage to tell the truth."
Say, "Today's Reflection Points are:

- When I am honest, I feel clear inside.
- Honesty and kindness build trust.
- Honesty allows me to be free of worries.

Activity

Group Story Game: Each person is to speak one, two or three sentences — no more — and then the next person continues the story. In the first group story, ask students to make up something about someone who lies. Allow them to continue to go around until everyone who wishes to do so has contributed to the story.

Then tell the students that the character about whom they have made up a story has had a change of heart. He or she has become honest. Ask them to continue the story, using honesty to try and make everything right. Ask them what the character learned.

Close with a relaxation/focusing exercise of your choice.

HONESTY LESSON 7
Films about Honesty

Begin with a song.

If possible, watch a film or discuss films students have recently seen where the protagonist has the courage to be honest and there is a positive outcome. For younger students, *Babe*, a story about a brave, honest pig is fun and can generate some interesting discussion. For students 11 to 14 you may wish to show, *How to Train Your Dragon*. This film is about a teen who is true to himself and finally honest about what is happening. With any film, please help the students look for all the values and qualities the protagonist displays.

Application: Help students evaluate their own efforts. Honest self-evaluation is important and useful in making progress.

— *Contributed by Pilar Quera Colomina*

Close with a relaxation/focusing exercise of your choice.

HONESTY LESSON 8
Trust

Begin with a song.

Discuss/Share

- How would you feel if a neighbor wanted you to wash his car and said he would give you ___, (Give an appropriate amount of money for the age of the students and the country.) but did not pay you when you finished?
- Was this man being honest? (No)
- What do you think the man should have done?
- How would you feel if a person said she would pay you for picking fruit from her orchard, but then only paid you half of what she said?

- Was this woman being honest?

Say, "Part of honesty is keeping our word. Our societies run much better when people keep their word."

Ask:

- Can you think of other examples of people not keeping their word?
- Can you think of examples of people breaking their promises?
- How do you feel when people break their promises?
- Do you feel you can trust someone who keeps his or her word?
- Do you want people to trust you?
- Why?

Discuss the Reflection Points.

♦ Honesty and kindness build trust.

♦ There is a deep relationship between honesty and friendship.

Say, "It's important to be honest because our relationships are then built on trust. When people are honest and trustworthy, we know we can depend on them."

"In the same way that it sometimes takes courage to tell the truth — like when we did something we weren't supposed to, or when we didn't do something we were supposed to — it also takes courage to apologize for not keeping a promise."

Ask:

- If someone did not keep his or her promise to you, what would you like her or him to say?
- If you did not keep your promise to someone, what could you say? Please start your sentence with "I" and share your feelings.

With older students, ask them to use the previously presented communication skill of: "I feel/felt _____ when _____ because _____." For example, "I felt bad when I was late because I let you down and I really value your friendship."

Practice in small groups: In groups of three, think of three different situations and practice using the above skill.

Close with a relaxation/focusing exercise of your choice.

HONESTY LESSON 9
Pressure to Be Dishonest

Begin with a song.

Read the story, "The Miner and the Prince", by Lamia El Dajani.

Share a Story: The Miner and the Prince

Ali was a miner who used to live with his family in a small house near the jungle. One day, Ali had an accident in the mine. His injuries prevented him from working in the mine. Life then became hard for him and his family. After his injuries began to heal, he started going to the jungle to find a way to feed himself and his family.

One day, Ali was in the jungle sitting below a tree, when suddenly he heard the sound of horses running very fast. He saw the Prince riding a horse and behind him a group of soldiers on their horses. They were chasing a deer. As they disappeared and the forest became quiet again, he saw something on the path. He picked up the object and found it was a very fine leather wallet. The Prince's name was embossed in gold on the front of the wallet. He slowly opened the wallet and saw a large amount of money. Ali remained where he was in the jungle, waiting for the Prince and his soldiers to return so he could give back the wallet. Gradually it grew dark. When the moon rose and there was still no sign of the Prince, Ali decided to return home.

Ali's wife hurried to meet him, worried that he was coming home so late. He excitedly told her what happened and showed her the wallet. She too became very excited and happily said, "This is a gift from God to us."

Ali was surprised. He protested, saying, "This money is not for us. It belongs to the Prince. I found it so I must return it."

His wife became furious and replied, "The Prince has a lot of money! We are in sore need. We should keep the money for ourselves." She added, more softly, "Especially since we did not steal the money. We found it in the jungle."

Ali decided not to argue with his wife. He put the wallet in the cupboard and sat with his family and listened as they continued to fuss about the event.

The next day, Ali woke up very early in the morning and slipped from the house before the rest of the family woke up. He took special care not to awaken his wife. He took the bus to the city and searched for the palace. When he reached the palace, the guards stopped him at the gate and prevented him from entering. He had no appointment to meet the Prince. They asked him why he wanted to meet the Prince, but he refused to tell them the reason. He just said that he needed to meet the Prince immediately about an important matter.

"I must meet with the Prince. I will not leave without seeing him," he said. They pushed him away, but he insisted on seeing the Prince. As the guards began to shout, suddenly the car of the Prince approached the gate. Ali threw himself on the car and called out to the Prince. The Prince opened the window of the car and asked what he wanted. Ali handed the Prince his wallet.

The Prince, looking very surprised, asked Ali where he found it. Ali told him the story of the previous day in the jungle. The Prince then opened his wallet. One could see that he was astonished to find the money untouched. The Prince asked Ali, "Why didn't you take the money?"

Ali replied, "I cannot take something that does not belong to me."

A gleam of respect appeared in the Prince's eye. The Prince took a large amount of money from the wallet, and with a nod of thanks, gave it to Ali.

Discuss the story and its implications. Then say, "Sometimes there is pressure to be dishonest."
Ask:

- Can you think of any examples?

Say, "Sometimes it is difficult to resist that pressure."
Ask:

- What things can you think of that would help you resist the pressure to _____. (Insert one of the examples the students gave you. It might be about lying, cheating, or stealing, etc.)
- What kinds of things could you say to yourself or to a friend if there is a temptation to be dishonest?
- Would it help you resist the temptation if you looked at the consequences? What could happen as a result? (Teachers might want to question further about consequences, such as the feelings over time of the one who has cheated, the effect on relationships with friends, trust and loss of trust, hurt or harm to others, belief in the self, etc.)

Eight to Nine Activity: Draw your favorite scene from "The Miner and the Prince", and below the picture write why you like that scene.

Living Values Education Activities for Children Ages 8-14, Book 1

Ten to Fourteen Activity: Organize students into groups of five to seven. Ask each group to make up two or three Situation Cards on honesty and dishonesty. It might be a situation about lying, cheating or stealing. Instruct each group to act out a situation, acting out the dishonest and honest responses and the consequences. The "actors" may freeze the skit at times to share their thoughts in an aside to the audience.

Honesty Situation Card

Situation:

Act it out:
1. Lie about the situation and act out what consequences develop.
2. Be honest about the situation and act out what happens.

The characters are to occasionally freeze their actions so they can tell the audience what their thoughts and emotions are.

As the educator, you know the students and the local situation. If you feel it would be helpful to the students to consider another consequence, say, "I'm putting on my Director hat," and ask for a volunteer to play the part of a policeman, friend, victim, parent, etc. For example, if one group of students seems to feel justified in doing a harmful prank, they may need to develop a little empathy. If so, ask for a volunteer to play the part of coming up and discovering what someone had done. Lead the applause for each role play.

Close with a relaxation/focusing exercise of your choice.

HONESTY LESSON 10
Lost and Found — and Consequence Maps

Begin with a song.

Discuss

- How would you feel if you lost your favorite game/toy/phone? (Use the name of an object appropriate for the age of the students.)
- How would you feel if someone found your game and returned it to you?

- How would you feel if you lost your lunch money (or something equivalent)?
- How would you feel if someone saw you drop it and returned it to you?
- How would you feel if someone stole your favorite game/toy/phone?
- How would you feel if we all worked very hard earning money for a special project and then someone stole all of our money?

Acknowledge their feelings and responses. Acknowledge that it is not nice for someone to do that.

Say, "Some people are not honest. They steal. Some people are very greedy. What do greedy people say? They say, 'It's all for me! It's all mine!' and they take what belongs to others."

Say, "Let's imagine that you saw a friend drop some money. You pick up the money quickly and run up to her to give it to her."

Ask:
- What does she say?
- How do you feel?

Say, "Let's imagine that you saw a friend drop some money. You pick up the money quickly and then run the other way."

Ask:
- How do you feel?
- How do you feel after one hour?
- How do you feel after one day?
- What might you say to yourself to justify your action?
- What does your heart say instead?
- What can you do to solve the problem?

Say, "An interesting thing about human beings is that when we do something good, we automatically feel happy inside. When we do something wrong, we may try to justify it to ourselves — but we still feel badly because we cannot really fool ourselves inside for very long. It takes courage to admit a wrongdoing, return the object, apologize and ask for their forgiveness."

Discuss the following Reflection Points:
- When I feel honest, I feel clear inside.

Living Values Education Activities for Children Ages 8–14, Book 1

- When I am honest, I can learn and help others learn to be giving.

Continue to discuss situations that are relevant to the students and their situation. Actively listen to any concerns or questions and take time to properly respond.

Activity

Make a consequence map together as a class with younger students and in small groups of four to six with older students.

Step 1. Decide on a dishonest action together that a person their age might consider.

Step 2. Write that action in the center of a piece of paper. Then draw a line downward with one possible thought and the emotion as a result of that thought.

Step 3. Question the students: What might the next thought be? And the next emotion? Draw another line downward for the possible consequences. What would be the consequence if your parents find out? How would they feel? What would be the consequence if the authorities found out? Draw a line from that consequence for consequences of that on your future, etc.

Step 4. Then upward from the circle in the middle, draw another circle with the alternative honest action.

Step 5. What would the thoughts and emotions be?

Step 6. Each group can decorate their consequence map with emojis and drawings. Close with a relaxation/focusing exercise of your choice.

HONESTY LESSON 11

In the Guise of Honesty . . .

Begin with a song.
Say, "Sometimes people can be mean or cruel under the guise of 'honesty'."
Ask:

- Can you think of some examples?
- Have you seen someone bully another person, saying something mean and pretending that they are "just being honest"?
- When is being "too honest" not really honesty, but a lack of love and respect for another person?
- What is the balance of love and "honesty"?
- Is an honest heart a heart full of love?

- How can you share something that needs to be said with a lot of love and honesty from the heart?

Activity

Gather in groups of three or four, or individually, and write poems or songs about sharing in an honest way with a friend, the value of an honest friend, or how relationships grow with kindness, honesty and _____.

Allow them to share their poems and songs.

Close with a relaxation/focusing exercise of your choice.

HONESTY LESSON 12
Honesty and Friendship

Begin with a song.

Discuss

Highlight the following Honesty Reflection Point: There is a deep relationship between honesty and friendship. Ask the students to think about a friend who always tells the truth and keeps his or her promises.

Ask:
- How do you feel about that person?
- How does that behavior affect your relationship?
- Have you experienced this Reflection Point: Honest thoughts, words, and actions create harmony?
- What makes a good friend?
- If you could write guidelines for being a good friend, what would you write?

Activity

Write guidelines for being a good friend — for yourself and for a friend. If the students are 12 and older, ask them to include social media guidelines.

Allow those who wish to share to do so. Is there a guideline that resonates with everyone? Invite them to gather in groups and make a few slogans to post around the class or the school.

Close with a relaxation/focusing exercise of your choice.

Living Values Education Activities for Children Ages 8–14, Book 1

Unit Six: Happiness

Happiness Lessons

I hope you enjoy this unit on happiness with your students. The lessons on happiness in this updated version also contain content on sadness, depression and dealing with our own feelings of sadness and hurt. As sadness is the opposite of happiness, this felt like the most appropriate place to put in this material. I felt this was necessary given the increasing suicide rates of young people. Several lessons are designed to help students explore how they are part of creating their own sadness and happiness as part of building social and emotion skills to create happiness for themselves and others. Thank you for being the keeper of a values-based atmosphere and providing a safe place for young people to be, share, explore and grow.

Happiness Reflection Points

- When I have love and peace inside, happiness just comes.
- Happiness is a state of peace in which there is no upheaval or violence.
- Give happiness and take happiness.
- When there is a feeling of hope, there is happiness.
- Good wishes for everyone give happiness inside.
- Happiness naturally comes with pure and selfless actions.
- Lasting happiness is a state of contentment within.
- When one is content with the self, happiness comes automatically.
- When my words "give flowers instead of thorns," I create a happier world.
- Happiness follows giving happiness, sorrow follows giving sorrow.

Happiness Goals and Objectives

Goal: To enjoy the experience of happiness.
Objectives:

- To enjoy the music of happy songs.
- To enjoy playing a game.
- To participate in an exercise of imagining a world of happiness.
- To paint or dance the feeling of happiness.

Goal: To increase knowledge about happiness and what creates happiness and sadness.

Objectives:
- To participate in discussions about Happiness Reflection Points and be able to talk about two or more of them.
- To reflect about when they are happy, and to write about their feelings.
- To think about words that create happiness and words that cause harm.
- To think about actions that contribute to the happiness of the self, others, and the world.
- To write down things they are grateful for.
- To reflect on lasting happiness versus happiness from material objects.
- To reflect on the relationship between happiness and trying to do our best.
- To reflect on their own self-talk and how to encourage the self more.
- To state discouraging thoughts and generate corresponding encouraging or empowering thoughts.

Goal: To increase knowledge about sadness and depression.

Objectives:
- To discuss sadness and feeling low as the opposite of happiness.
- To listen to a story about a parent being depressed and to understand that sometimes people experience being sad or depressed; to understand that depression is not catching; to understand that we are not responsible for a parent's depression.
- For students 10 to 14 to discuss suicide and how necessary it is to inform a responsible adult if someone they know shares that they want to kill themselves; to know it is important to tell that person how important they are and to ask them to promise not to kill themselves.
- To participate in a relaxation/focusing exercise on taking care of the self when I feel sad.

Goal: To explore skills for giving happiness.

Objectives:
- To do at least three actions at school that give happiness to others.
- To make up a story on giving happiness as part of a group.
- To do at least four actions at home that give happiness to members of their family.
- To think about the effects of excluding versus including others.
- To generate their own secret for giving happiness.
- To be part of a class project creating a happiness tree or giving tree.

HAPPINESS LESSON 1
Happiness

Play a happy song as the students enter.

Say, "This month we're going to explore the value of Happiness."

Discuss/Share

Discuss the following Reflection Points:
- When I have love and peace inside, happiness just comes.
- When one is content with the self, happiness comes automatically.
- Happiness is a state of peace in which there is no upheaval or violence.

As the teacher, share something that makes you happy. Then ask:
- What makes you happy?
- Can we create our own happiness? How?
- When do you feel most content?
- What kinds of things do you think to increase the feeling of happiness?
- What kinds of things can you do alone that make you feel happy?

List the students' ideas on the board. Help them identify differences in feelings — for example, feelings that are exciting versus feelings that are deeper and more long-term.

> Great. Now, think of three especially positive or happy moments. . . . Perhaps there was a special moment at home that stands out for you . . . or a moment

Living Values Education Activities for Children Ages 8–14, Book 1

while you were out in nature . . . or doing a sport . . . or being with a friend. . . or in this school. . . . Think of just three moments. . . . (Pause for a full two minutes.)

➢ Now, I would like you to write down the quality or value that you were experiencing during that moment of happiness.

Eight to Ten Activity: Make a zigzag happy book, or write sentences, "I feel happy when _____." — *Contributed by Linda Heppenstall*

Eleven to Fourteen Activity: Invite students to write about some of the happiest moments in their life and the values and qualities they were experiencing in those moments, or to write in their journal an entry on "I feel happy when . . ."

Close with the I Am Lovable and Capable Relaxation/Focusing Exercise.

HAPPINESS LESSON 2
Giving Happiness and Unhappiness

Begin with a song.

Share a Story

Read aloud or ask students to read tales about happiness. Think of your favorite childhood stories about happiness. The teacher may want to select folktales or old legends about happiness. Or, read the following stories.

Eight to Ten Story: Read "The Heart School" by Diana Hsu or "Finding the Magic." The former can be found in the Appendix (Item 7). "Finding the Magic" is the published version of the same story, developed further by Barbara Ramsey.

Eleven to Fourteen Story: Read "The Boy Who Grew Flowers" by Jen Wojtowicz. The Joy of Reading Project kindly gave their permission to post this story on the international LVE site, www.livingvalues.net. You will find it under For Schools /Children Ages 8-14 / Download Free Stories / Happiness 8-14.

Discuss the story afterwards, highlighting how giving and thoughtfulness generates happiness.

Discuss the following: It has been said that Aristotle did not include happiness in his original taxonomy of emotions, for happiness is a result of virtue.

Discuss/Share for Ages 8 to 10

Say, "In 'The Heart School' story, Marc learns that it is important not to get upset with himself or anyone else." Allow them to discuss the story, then ask:
- What caused Marc unhappiness at school? (Pushing and kicking others, speaking harsh and hurtful words, thinking "I can't do it" and being impatient.)
- What did the Bear tell Marc was the secret of being happy? (Be patient, say only kind words, help others, and always have good thoughts about yourself and others.)
- Are there other things that help us be happy and stay happy?
- What do you think about that?
- Are there other things that cause unhappiness/sorrow? What are those? (Take one of their responses at a time and follow it up with one of the following questions.)
- What would be the opposite of that? Would the opposite thing give happiness?

Discuss/Share for Ages 11 to 14

In "The Boy Who Grew Flowers" story, Rink was perceptive and thoughtful. Allow them to discuss the story, then ask:
- What do young people your age do to give happiness to each other? (Allow them to generate a long list.)
- When you give happiness to someone, how do you feel inside?
- What are things that give unhappiness or sorrow? (Allow them to generate a long list of the current reality of their setting.)
- When you give unhappiness or sorrow to someone, how do you feel inside?

Note to Educator: If one of the students shares that he or she feels happy after being hurtful or mean, respectfully actively listen to their responses, then conclude with: "It sounds like sometimes you are hurt inside so you want to hurt others." Then leave it be and see if their tendency to be kind increases over time. Be kind to them. If their tendency to hurt others does not improve within three months, refer them for counseling.

Ask:
- Which do you prefer — receiving happiness or sorrow?
- If you want to receive happiness, what do you need to give? (Yes, that's right, what comes around goes around.)

If students mention gossip or spreading negative comments or rumors as something that gives unhappiness, discuss the below antidote. If gossip is common, take time to allow them to discuss this in depth and role play positive responses.

Giving Sorrow: **Gossip** — either verbally or on social media

Antidote if gossiped about:
- ❖ Know that the person gossiping is insecure and being mean.
- ❖ Question yourself: Was your action toward the other person okay? If it was, don't worry. Discuss a saying by John Wooden: "Never worry about your reputation, only worry about your character."
- ❖ If your action was not okay toward the other person, think about what quality or value you would like to use in a similar situation if faced with a similar situation.

Proactive choice if someone gossips to you: Use benevolent assertion and have the courage to mention one or more of the qualities of the person being maligned.

Activities

Eight to Ten Activity: Ask the students if they would like to make individual Happy Boxes or one Happy Box for the class. Make the boxes. Ask the students to write cards for the Happy Box, putting on each card a practical suggestion that would make them happier. Some classes may wish to make individual boxes and take them home. Other classes may wish to have one box for the entire class.

Note to Educator: Many classes have discussion time during their "values time" at this point. You may wish to keep the Happy and Unhappy Boxes for your class if the students like them and appear to benefit from them. Either daily or weekly, take one card out of the Happy Box. Try this for at least four weeks. At least once a week, share your experiences and progress with each other, and also look for areas that need improvement. As the students discover new ways to be happy, ask them to write those down on new cards.

Eleven to Fourteen Activity:

Step 1. Divide students into small groups of four to six and ask them to generate rules of happiness.

Step 2. Ask each group to share their rules of happiness.

Step 3. Ask the entire group if they think it is possible to do this. As a class, invite them to choose three rules of happiness they would like to practice in the classroom.

Close with a relaxation/focusing exercises of their choice.

HAPPINESS LESSON 3
Words that Give Flowers and Pegasusses

Note to Educator: Three different names are in current use for the plural of pegasus, a winged horse. They are pegasi, pegasuses and pegasusses. The latter is approved by the Oxford English Dictionary.

Begin with a song.

Discuss/Share

Ask:

- What words give happiness?
- Think of words your family or friends say that make you happy. What are they?
- What do you like to hear?

Say, "Think about the following Reflection Point: When my words give flowers instead of thorns, I create a happier world."

Ask:

- What kinds of words are like thorns?
- Can words hurt people or cause harm? (Yes.)

"There is a child's poem: Sticks and stones will break my bones, but words will never hurt me. An adult changed this to: Sticks and stones will break my bones, but words hurt forever inside."

Ask:

- How do you feel when you hear someone hurt someone else's feelings?
- What kinds of words would you like to hear around you?
- What do you say that gives happiness to others?
- What words do you say to yourself that give you happiness?
- What are you grateful for?
- Reflect for a moment on things you are grateful for . . . perhaps for love from your family, good friends . . . perhaps food to eat every day.

- How do you feel when you are grateful for things?

Share a Reflective Story: Pegasusses

"Today I have a short tale about pegasusses. It is a participatory story, because I want you to use your imagination . . . One day, 24 (use the number of students in the classroom at the time) pegasusses come to our school. We go outside, and a pegasus comes up to each one of us. You can imagine our surprise to see pegasusses, and so many! These pegasusses are silvery white and have large wings. They look very strong. Each pegasus holds out one wing so we can each have help climbing onto its back. Once each one of us is safely seated on the pegasus' back, it starts to fly. Up we go! They fly to the place where they live — they must know that we've been studying these values and there was one on happiness today. The pegasusses decided to take us to a Land of Happiness. Well, when they start to land, we can see how beautiful it is . . . and, there are all these students your age! They come to welcome you. They are playing great music. And you join them in a picnic. . . . Delicious food! . . . And then you play games. . . . There are different kinds of games, so each one of you can join the one that you like to play. . . . Afterwards you sit on the grass and talk. One of students of this land tells you that in their world, they look at everyone like a beautiful flower. They see each one as more beautiful than the next. . . . As you sit there, you experience that everyone has love for you and for each and every other person there. . . . Then, one of the students leans a little closer to you and whispers, 'I'm going to tell you another secret about happiness.' . . . And then he or she tells you a secret of happiness. . . . Only you hear this particular secret of happiness. . . . What was whispered? . . . The pegasusses tell us that it's time to go, and they extend their wings again. The students wave goodbye to us as we fly off, and we wave goodbye to them. And, before you know it, we're back at school again and sitting here."

Discuss/Share

Allow a few minutes for students to share their thoughts and images. Invite those who wish to share their secret of happiness to do so. Tell the students that the child who whispered to you said: "The secret to being happy is 'Give happiness and take happiness, don't give sorrow and take sorrow.'" Ask: "What do you think that means?"

Activity

Write a story on "The Secrets of Happiness." Perhaps draw or paint a picture to accompany the story. Invite a few who wish to share their creation. There will be time for sharing in the next Living Values Education time.

Homework: Inform students that thinking about the things we are grateful for increases happiness. Ask them to write down three things they are grateful for tonight and every night for one week. Tell them that you will do this too!

Close with a relaxation/focusing exercise.

HAPPINESS LESSON 4
Happiness Is Sharing

Begin with a song.

Ask a few students who wish to share their "secrets of happiness" or ask the students to share one line from their gratitude homework.

Discuss the following Reflection Points:

- ♦ Happiness naturally comes with pure and selfless actions.
- ♦ Give happiness and take happiness.

Ask:

- What are pure and selfless actions?
- Can anyone think of examples? (This can be asked in relation to animals, the environment, family, friends, and strangers.)

Activities

Make something to give: Ask the students to make something to give to someone or think of something they can do for someone else. Examples are a friendly card for someone, a card for someone who is ill, a meal for the senior volunteers at your school, a poem for a friend, a happy heart card for a child you are tutoring in a younger class.

Game: If there is time during the week, perhaps simply play a game or do something that creates a mood of happiness. Sometimes giving happiness is spending time together and sharing something you all like to do. For instance, play a game that everyone loves, one that usually brings lots of laughter. Think of the games that you enjoyed as a child.

You may want to try an unusual version of musical chairs. Change the rules by allowing more than one person to sit in a chair. The students circle around the chairs when the music is playing, and then sit in the chairs when the music stops. Each time the music stops, another chair is removed. In this version, when the music stops and there are not enough chairs, instead of that child being out of the game, he or she simply sits on the lap of someone already seated on a chair. You may want to stop the game when there are four or five people seated on one chair! In many countries, it is important to play one round with girls, another with boys. There are many suitable games that are fun. Play one that you enjoy, too

Close with a relaxation/focusing exercise.

HAPPINESS LESSON 5

The Opposite of Happiness: Sadness and Depression

Begin with a song.

Discuss/Share

Actively listen to their responses.

- What do you feel like doing when you are happy?
- What is the opposite of being happy? (Sad, feeling low)
- Have you all felt sad?
- What do you feel like doing when you are sad?
- How can we make ourselves feel better when we are sad? (Reinforce concepts learned/presented previously, such as talking to the self in an encouraging and kind way, knowing that you are lovable and capable, talking with a friend, doing relaxation/focusing exercises and surrounding yourself with love, telling a safe adult about the difficulty, eating healthy foods, etc.)
- Another thing we can do when we are feeling sad if to lovingly accept our emotions. When we accept what we are feeling, we are accepting the self. If is important to love the self and to accept the self. Would it be okay if we practice that at the end of the lesson? Great.

Say, "Usually people say the opposite of feeling happy is feeling sad. Sometimes people call feeling sad, feeling "low". Everyone feels sad sometimes. We human beings are interesting. We all need to be loved. Sometimes children and adults can feel sad because they are afraid that they are not loved or respected. We all like to be loved and respected and we all like to be successful. Yes?"

"When people feel sad or low for a few weeks and don't feel like they want to do their usual activities in life, that is usually called being depressed."

Ask:

- Have you ever heard adults talk about depression or feeling depressed?

Share a Story

If you think it is appropriate for your students, read "Can I catch it like a cold? coping with a parent's depression" by the Centre for Addiction and Mental Health. The Joy of Reading Project kindly gave their permission to post this story on the international LVE site, www.livingvalues.net. You will find it under For Schools /Children Ages 8–14 / Download Free Stories / Happiness 8–14. Read just the story to the students. The information which follows the story is only for adults.

Invite the students to discuss the story, ask any questions and share whatever they wish. Actively listen and validate as appropriate.

Ask:

- How would you like people to treat when you are feeling sad?
- Would you like to receive friendly smiles?
- Would you like them to listen to you if you wanted to talk?
- If you don't want to talk, do you want them to tell you that you must talk? (No)
- Would you sometimes like a hug from a special friend?
- Would you want people to include you and just act normal around you? (Yes)
- Is there anything else you would like people to do?

Additional Questions for Ages 10 to 14: Sometimes we hear about people who commit suicide.

Ask:

- What is important to do if someone tells you they want to kill themselves? (Tell a responsible adult so that that person can get help right away.)
- What would you want to tell the person who is thinking of killing themselves? (Please list all of their comments on the board, acknowledging and actively listening to each suggestion.)
- Would anyone like to share anything else?

Yes, it is very important for people to know that they are important, they are good, they are special to you, they are loved — and that it is very, very, very, very important to not kill themselves. If anyone ever tells you that they want to kill themselves, please tell them how important they are, and ask them to promise not to kill themselves. Promise them that things will get better.

Ask:
- Can we change things for the better if we are alive? (Yes)

Say the following, if you can say it from your heart: "Each one of you is important. You are all powerful and wonderful, you are positive lights for the world."

Activity

Ask the students to write a journal entry, essay or poem on "When I am feeling sad, it helps me to feel better to . . ." Invite those who wish to share their poems, or a few ideas from their journal or essay.

Play some relaxing music and close with the relaxation/focusing exercise below. You may wish to play this special healing music published by ZenLifeRelax on YouTube. It is a Solfeggio frequency of 528Hz. https://www.youtube.com/watch?v=tnKBUdVh02s

Taking Care of Me When I Feel Sad Relaxation/Focusing Exercise

"Let the body be relaxed and still. Slow down within. . . . Breathe in deeply . . . and as you exhale, begin to relax. . . . Be aware of how you are feeling. . . . Breathe in deeply. . . and relax as you exhale. . . . Are your arms tight or your chest? . . . . Is there a feeling of sadness or hurt inside? . . . Allow yourself to feel where you are holding emotion in your body . . . perhaps in your throat . . . perhaps in your chest . . . perhaps in your stomach . . . perhaps in your gut. . . . Breathe in deeply . . . and exhale slowly. . . . Lovingly accept your emotions. . . . Be in the present . . . and lovingly accept how you feel. . . . Pay attention to that feeling . . . accept it with love . . . and it will quiet down a little. . . . Surround your sadness or hurt with the light of love. . . . Visualize the light of love surrounding that pain . . . and feel that love. . . . Breathe in love . . . and relax as you exhale hurt. . . . Let the mind be still . . . and absorb the light of love. . . . Perhaps that area of pain is getting smaller as you absorb the light of love. . . . Feel that light of love. . . . You are lovable and capable. . . . Breathe in love slowly and relax. . . . Know you are lovable and capable. . . . Exhale any sadness or hurt. . . . Breathe in love. . . . Think for a moment of what quality or value would help you now. . . . Imagine that quality or value taking the form of a jewel and let that jewel appear in front of you. . . . It may be a jewel of love . . . or courage . . . compassion for yourself . . . or others . . . patience . . . or fearlessness. . . .

You are a beautiful jewel. . . . You have the courage to be kind to yourself . . . and to live your truth. . . . Be still . . . quiet within . . . focused . . . absorb the light of love and peace. . . . Gradually begin to bring your attention back to this place . . . Wiggle your toes and move your legs . . . and bring your attention fully back to this place."

Close with a nurturing song of peace or love and invite everyone to stand up and move around the room with the song.

Note to Educator: An Additional Lesson on Depression and/or Suicide

If some of the students are concerned about depressed parents or friends, or the suicide of someone they know, perhaps take another period to allow them to draw a picture of what happened, discuss it, and ask any questions. You will need to lovingly and sincerely active listen to and/or validate their comments. Creating a safe and understanding space for them to share is important.

Perhaps read the story again. Definitely repeat part of the lesson above, that is: "Yes, it is very important for people to know that they are important, they are good, they are special to you, they are loved — and that it is very, very, very, very important to not kill themselves. If anyone ever tells you that they want to kill themselves, please tell them how important they are, and ask them to promise not to kill themselves. Promise them that things will get better."

Also, it is essential to tell a responsible adult so they can get help."

Ask:
- Can we change things for the better if we are alive? (Yes)

Promise them that you will work with them with whatever the concern is to make it better. Know what resources are available and ask the school or organization for help from the school counselor, psychologist or social worker if needed — or an outside organization.

Expressive Activity: Invite them to paint their feelings. Allow them to share their artistic creations.

Close with the Taking Care of Myself When I Feel Sad Relaxation/Focusing Exercise.

HAPPINESS LESSON 6
Encouraging or Discouraging Self Talk

Begin with a song.

Discuss/Share

"Today, let's think about the things we say to ourselves. Our self-talk can be positive or negative, encouraging or discouraging."

Ask:
- What do you say when you make a mistake?
- What tone of voice do you use when you say that?
- What do you say to yourself when you're afraid that you'll miss the ball during a ball game or fail a test?
- If you make a mistake, do you feel better if you call yourself "Stupid?
- Does it help if you get angry at yourself? (No.)
- Why do you think getting angry at yourself makes it worse? (One explanation: You are pouring negative energy on top of negative energy.)
- Does it help to get angry at someone else for your mistake? Is that fair?
- Does it help if you say, "It's okay to make a mistake, all I have to do is correct it"? There's no need to feel angry or sad — mistakes are simply things through which we learn.
- What happens to your feelings when you say, "I'll never be able to do it" or "I'll never make it"?
- Are the feelings different when you say, "This is a bit scary, but I'll do my best"?

➤ Make two columns on the board. For younger students, head one column with a sad face, the other with a happy face. For older students, head one column with the word "Discouraging/Disempowering" and the other with the word "Encouraging/Empowering".

➤ Ask students to tell you what they say to themselves that makes them feel sad or unhappy; and what they say or could say to themselves to make them feel glad or happy.

Then ask:
- Can anyone think of anything discouraging to say when working on an assignment?
- What can you say to yourself that is encouraging or empowering when working on an assignment?
- Can you think of something discouraging to say to yourself when you are getting ready to come to school?

- What can you say to yourself to create a happy feeling when you are getting ready to come to school?
- Which one makes you feel better?
- What can you say to create a happier feeling when you are working with others?
- What can you say to create a happier feeling when you are trying to understand something disappointing?
- What differences do you notice in the tone of voice you use with yourself when you say things to make you happy?

➢ Ask the students to call out Discouraging thoughts and write them down under the appropriate column. Then ask them to find an Encouraging thought to substitute and write that down in the appropriate column.

Activities

Ask for a volunteer to come up to the front of the room and share a discouraging thought. After the person shares, ask the students to call out encouraging or empowering thoughts to him or her. The volunteer is to then repeat a thought or two that he or she finds empowering. Enjoy continuing this with several volunteers.

Eight to Eleven Activity: Write a note to yourself, giving yourself advice about how you should talk to yourself.

Twelve to Fourteen Activity: Think about the Reflection Point: When there is a feeling of hope, there is happiness. Write a note to yourself, giving yourself advice about how you should talk to yourself. Consider situations when it is best to be encouraging, and tell yourself to persevere.

Invite the students who wish to do so to share some of their advice.

When working in a different subject area, the teacher might ask students about their inner dialogue. Continue to discuss this in a natural way, adding adaptive responses to the happy face list on the board.

Close with a relaxation/focusing exercise.

HAPPINESS LESSON 7
Three Wishes

Begin with a song.

One of the classes at West Kidlington School discussed the Reflection Point, Lasting happiness is a state of contentment within. The students talked about how happiness is temporary when sought from outside sources, that is, from wealth, material possessions, status, and relationships. They decided that lasting happiness is a state of contentment within that does not need to be fed by outside wants.

Ask:
- What happens when our happiness depends on getting money from someone? Can that happiness be constant?
- What happens when our happiness depends on getting a new possession (game, dress, etc.)? Can our happiness be constant?
- How do you feel when you do not get something you want?
- How can you remain happy when you do not get something you want?
- How long does your happiness last when you get something new?
- What kinds of thoughts and actions create lasting happiness?

Activity

You have just liberated a genie from a bottle you found. The genie gives you the right to ask for three wishes: one for yourself, one for your family, and one for the world. What are your three wishes? Create a drawing of your three wishes.

— *Activity contributed by Marcia Maria Lins de Medeiros*

Close with a relaxation/focusing exercise.

HAPPINESS LESSON 8
Happiness at Home

Begin with a song.

Discuss/Share

Ask the students to share any thoughts or questions they have from the last lesson. Ask them about their gratitude homework.

Ask:
- What do you do with your family that makes you happy?
- What other things make you happy about your family?
- What do your parents say that make you happy?
- What do your parents like to hear from you?

- How many of you have older brothers and sisters? What kinds of things did you like to do with them when you were little?
- Do you think your younger brothers and sisters would like to do that with you?
- What do you do to give happiness to your family?
- How can we contribute to the happiness of others?

Say, "Let's list all the things people your age can do to give happiness at home. List their responses on the board as they call out answers. Group them in different categories, such as, Words, Activities with Sisters and Brothers, and Actions.

Additional questions for Ages 12 to 14:
- What can you genuinely say to your parents that they would like to hear?
- If a person gave you several compliments, but you did not feel that person meant it, how would you feel?
- When a person gives you one compliment, but you feel that person really means it, how do you feel?
- Is it important to be genuine? Why?
- When you give a compliment and are genuine, how do you feel inside?

Needs and Wants Activity

Each student is to create a list of 12 things that give him or her happiness in life. As a class, discuss the difference between needs and wants. The students can discuss their choices in groups of three or four. Reduce the list to six items, then three items. Discuss it more to finally arrive at the one item on the list that gives the most happiness. The students can then write a letter of appreciation to the person connected with that item.

— Contributed by Ruth Liddle

Homework: Tell students their homework this week is to give happiness by doing three or four good deeds at home without telling anyone. As the week progresses, ask how their homework is going. (A lot of joy is created in the classroom with this activity.) The students may tell you that someone found out. Tell them that is okay, but to do another secret good deed.

Close with a relaxation/focusing exercise.

HAPPINESS LESSON 9

Quality

Begin with a song.

Concept: When you do your best, there is happiness. Quality thoughts lead to quality words. Quality words lead to quality actions.

Stimulus: Ask each student to choose a piece of work of which she or he is proud. Or, think about something which he or she does well.

Discuss

Talk about the importance of doing our best in work and at play.

Twelve to Fourteen Additional Discussion: Ask the students to discuss this in relation to the Reflection Point: When one is content with the self, happiness comes automatically.

Activity

Form small groups of students. Ask each student to go around the circle saying something he or she appreciates about each student.

— *Contributed by Linda Heppenstall*

HAPPINESS LESSON 10

Including and Excluding

Begin with a song.

Discuss/Share

- How do people feel when they are left out?
- I think almost everyone in the world has felt left out one time or another. Does it feel good?
- What can we do when we see that someone has been left out?
- How can we be inclusive rather than exclusive?
- Are you happy when others are successful? (If not, ask why. Then, ask if they can think of another way to think about the situation — so they can be happy for the successful person. Perhaps bring up self-respect points. Or think, "She is getting the success she worked for; I will get the success I am working for.")

— *Contributed by West Kidlington School*

Discuss the following Reflection Points:
- ♦ Good wishes for everyone give happiness inside.
- ♦ Happiness follows giving happiness, sorrow follows giving sorrow.

Activity

Group story game: Make up two stories, one in which everyone gives sorrow, and another in which everyone gives happiness. Start with the unhappy story first. Use the same beginning situation, and go around the room asking each student to add something to the story. Then, make up a story in which everyone gives happiness. Have a good time!

Close with a relaxation/focusing exercise.

HAPPINESS LESSON 11
A Happiness Tree or a Giving Tree

Begin with a song.
Please choose the tree you feel would most benefit your students.

Activity: Making a Tree of Happiness Qualities

Step 1. Create leaves/shapes/mini cards.

Step 2. Invite the students to draw/write, decorate their images for happiness on the leaves/shapes/mini cards.

Step 3. Find a tree in the school grounds or nearby. Hang the Happiness words and pictures on the tree.

Step 4. Choose a name for the tree. Sit around the tree and share your happiness pictures/words.

Step 5. Invite parents and the wider community to view the tree.

Reflection: Happiness is infectious. Spread it wherever you go. Wear a smile.

— *Contributed by Ioanna Vasileiadou*

Activity: Making a Giving Tree

Eight to Ten Activity: Instruct each student to make three certificates to hang on the tree, such as: Good for One Compliment, Certificate for Five Minutes Tutoring in Mathematics, Certificate for Pushing the Swing for Three Minutes, Good for One Game of Tether Ball, Good for Listening While You Practice Your Poem Three Times, Good for

Living Values Education Activities for Children Ages 8-14, Book 1

Showing the Latest Dance Move, etc. Each student could make up three certificates of something she or he has to offer. The certificates can be pinned to a paper tree posted on a bulletin board. The name of the person offering this service would be on the back of the certificate.

Perhaps for three days in a row — when the students are finished with their work — they can silently select one certificate. Some of the students may want to create a giving tree at home: Good for One Hug, etc.

Eleven to Fourteen Activity: Students may choose to make a small Giving Tree for their younger sisters and brothers or one for the entire family. If so, they can ask other members of the family to participate. Or, a group of students can decide to make a Giving Tree for a younger class of students. Or, the class can decide to contribute to a special project in the area.

Close with a relaxation/focusing exercise.

HAPPINESS LESSON 12
The Three Rings — Keeping Balance

Begin with a song.

Activity

Step 1. Collect 3 hoops of different sizes — large, medium and small size. Or, draw three circles — large, medium or small — on paper for the wall. Or, if outside, draw three large, medium and small circles on sand/earth.

Step 2. Ask: "What makes you happy?"
Write down your answers on individual Post It notes or the equivalent or draw on the soil/sand.

Step 3. Invite the students to pair up with a buddy or sit in small groups.
Ask:
- Which of your answers reflect, what I can do and do well?
- Which of your answers reflect, what can I give and share with others?
- Which of your answers reflect, what time I have for me?
- Which do you prefer? (The children will probably say all!)

Step 4. Invite the children to place each of their answers in the Display rings for all to view.

Step 5. Ask: "Is there an equal amount in each ring or more in some other rings?" Share.

Step 6. Ask: "Are you in balance for what you choose to do with time for yourself?" Accept all answers as okay, with a challenge to find more time for the self.

Reflection: It's good to be quiet and do things just for yourself as well as doing well and giving and sharing with others.

— Contributed by Batool Arjomand

HAPPINESS LESSON 13
Enact Happiness

Begin with a happy song.

Dance/Draw Happiness: Divide the students into two groups: those who want to create happiness through dance and those who want to create happiness through drawing or painting.

Optional Activity: Do a skit on happiness or play games.

End with a happy song or a relaxation/focusing exercise.

Additional Happiness Lessons and Activities

HAPPINESS LESSON 14
More Secrets of Happiness

Begin with a song.

Discuss/Share

Share the saying: Happiness begins with me. Ask: "What does this mean?"

Repeat the Pegasus Story (from Happiness Lesson 3), but add a line at the close of the story. After the student whispers a secret of happiness, insert the line: "And then, you share with your friend the secret of happiness you think is most important." Ask the students to illustrate or write their secrets of happiness: the one they were given and the one they shared.

Close with a relaxation/focusing exercise.

Activity Choices

Poem: Happiness is when _____.

Design a Happiness Badge.

Write an essay: Making Others Happy Brings Us Happiness, too.

– Contributed by Linda Heppenstall

The Happiness Walk

Community Project

Make a Happiness Walk with members of the community. This original idea from the Al Nowair Happiness Project was submitted by Batool Arjomand.

Reflection: Share happiness and give happiness away. Bring hope to those who are feeling sad.

Step 1. Find, write letters and get permission to use a community space to create a Happiness Walk.

Step 2. Invite members of the community to write/draw a Happiness quote/picture. Example: Write a simple message on a 'Post It' note.

Step 3. Invite them to add their writing drawing to the "Happiness Walk" trail. Examples: In a shopping mall, a covered bridge between 2 buildings or a parkland.

Step 4. Invite the press to share the imagery and happiness for others to enjoy.

Enjoy the walk with your class, and with family and friends.

Unit Seven: Responsibility

Responsibility is a value important for society, and for the wellbeing, productivity and happiness of the individual. It allows young people to build good habits and relationships, and grow toward their potential. In this values unit, responsibility is looked at from different angles, from the serious to the ridiculous, in an attempt to engage students in seeing the relevance and benefit of this value for the self, others and the world — and how they can make a positive difference.

Please feel free to add to the list of Reflections Points your favorite sayings from different cultures, legends or admired individuals.

Continue to play a song daily. Play songs that touch on responsibility, perhaps ones from your cultural heritage. Older students respond well to Circle of Life by Elton John or Conviction of the Heart by Kenny Loggins.

Do one of the Relaxation/Focusing Exercises every day or every several days, as suitable for your class. The students may enjoy making up their own.

Responsibility Reflection Points

- If we want peace, we have the responsibility to be peaceful.
- If we want a clean world, we have the responsibility to care for nature.
- Responsibility is doing your share.
- Responsibility is accepting what is required and carrying out the task to the best of your ability.
- Responsibility is carrying out duties with integrity.
- When one is responsible, there is the contentment of having made a contribution.
- As a responsible person, I have something worthwhile to offer — so do others.
- A responsible person knows how to be fair, seeing that each gets a share.
- With rights there are responsibilities.
- Responsibility is not only something that obliges us, but also something that allows us to achieve what we wish.

- Each person can perceive his or her own world and look for the balance of rights and responsibilities.
- Global responsibility requires respect for all human beings.
- Responsibility is using our resources to generate a positive change.

Responsibility Goals and Objectives

Goal: To feel good about being responsible.
Objectives:
- To enjoy being responsible during a trust walk.
- To enjoy songs that link responsibility to caring.
- To enjoy participating in a play about responsibility.
- To think about which value they wish to partner with responsibility to help others.

Goal: To increase knowledge about responsibility.
Objectives:
- To participate in discussions about the Responsibility Reflection Points and be able to talk about two or more of them.
- To make an "I Believe in . . ." booklet, exploring what they believe in, their rights, and their responsibilities.
- To explore the concept of "walking my talk."
- To participate in a discussion about responsibility for the self.
- To think about how they are responsible for themselves in many different ways.
- To participate in Mind Mapping the consequences of responsibility and irresponsibility.
- To discuss their contribution to their family, and to make a card or poem for a parent or write a personal journal page on showing responsibility.
- To discuss global responsibility and how they can make a positive difference in their daily life.

Goal: To develop skills for responsibility and participate responsibly in projects.
Objectives:
- To participate in a class responsibility project.
- To think about their goals as adults, and to develop at least two immediate, small, practical actions in relation to that goal.

- ❏ To participate in a class discussion on how to encourage the self to be more responsible when one has not been.
- ❏ To make an image of what they believe in, and to carry through on one new action toward that goal.

RESPONSIBILITY LESSON 1
Trust Walk — and Advice

Play a song as the students enter. Introduce the unit on the value of responsibility by asking the students what responsibility means.

Activity

Say, "Today, we will play with responsibility by having a trust walk." To do a trust walk, half the class wears blindfolds. One partner is responsible for carefully leading his or her blindfolded partner around, guiding physically as well as offering verbal information to manage uneven areas and to help the partner feel safe and comfortable. Do this for 10 minutes, then reverse roles.

Discuss/Share

Afterwards, give a few minutes for each pair to share their feelings with each other as the one trusting and the one responsible during the trust walk.

Ask the entire group:
- How did you feel when you felt your partner was responsible?
- How would you have felt if your partner were not responsible?
- Is there anything you would like everyone in the world to be responsible for? What might that be?

Group Story Game: Say, "Let's do the group story game. Each person can say one, two or three sentences — no more — and then the next person continues the story. In this group story, I want you to make up something about a person or an entire community of people who are not responsible." Ask one of the students to start. Allow them to continue to go around until everyone who wishes to do so has contributed to the story.

Then say, "The character (or the community) is now sleeping."

Living Values Education Activities for Children Ages 8-14, Book 1

Ask:
- What would you like to tell the character/people of the community? Please whisper to them what you think they need to know about responsibility.
- What other advice would you like to share so they get to know what they need to know?

"Well done! Now let's know that they heard you all . . . and let's continue with the story!" Lead the applause when they are done.

Close with a song or a relaxation/focusing exercise of their choice.

RESPONSIBILITY LESSON 2
Mind Mapping Responsibility and Irresponsibility

Begin with a song.

Discuss the following Reflection Points.
- Responsibility is doing your share.
- Responsibility is accepting what is required and carrying out the task to the best of your ability.
- As a responsible person, I have something worthwhile to offer — so do others.

Mind Mapping Activity

"Today, let's explore more differences between responsibility and irresponsibility through mind mapping."

Mind Map: Begin by drawing a large circle on a white board, putting Responsibility on the right side and Irresponsibility on the left side. If you are not familiar with Mind Mapping, you will find information in the Appendix (Item 1). Start with a branch for Self on the Responsibility side of the circle, asking them what happens when there is Responsibility in the Self and writing in brief their responses. Then ask them what happens when there is a lack of responsibility in the Self. The students are to supply all the answers. Also do branches for Families, Friends, Schools and the Neighborhood on both responsibility and irresponsibility. One student can be adding drawings and emojis to both sides of the mind map as you facilitate to illustrate the consequences.

Creative Activity

Divide the students into groups of four to six. Ask each group to create a song or poem about responsibility or responsibility versus irresponsibility. It could be a rap song. Allow them to perform their creation for the group.

RESPONSIBILITY LESSON 3 for Ages 8 and 9
Mini Plays of "Right" and "Wrong" Ways of Doing Things

Educator Preparation: Kindly note that Step 1 asks for teachers to create mini plays which show "right" and "wrong" ways of doing things.

Begin with a song.

Activity

Step 1: As teachers, create mini plays which show "right" and "wrong" ways of doing things. Prepare and act out two opposites. For example:

- Eating Healthy Food versus Eating Junk Food
- Coming to school on time versus Coming to school late
- Going to bed on time versus Going to bed late.
- Playing alone with an electronic game too much versus Being and sharing with others.
- (You may wish to include a responsible versus irresponsible teaching scenario as one of the mini plays!)

Step 2: Invite the children to view the play and choose the action they prefer.
Step 3: Enable the children to design and act out their own play.
Step 4: Let the children choose two or three they would like to share with the whole school in an assembly.

Reflection: We all can make responsible choices. What would you choose?

— *Contributed by Ioanna Vasileiadou and Velina Andreeva*

RESPONSIBILITY LESSON 3 for Ages 10 to 14
Responsibility Is "Walking My Talk"

Begin with a song.

Discuss/Share

Ask:

- Do you believe in peace? What do you believe in? (Write peace and their other ideas on the board.)
- Do you believe in caring for the environment?
- Do you believe in loyalty?
- Do you believe in being a good friend? Why?
- Do you believe in being a good student? Why?

Say, "Responsibility means that you try your best to do what you believe in. Let's look at some of the Reflection Points." Discuss:

- If we want peace, we have the responsibility to be peaceful.
- If we want a clean world, we have the responsibility to care for nature.
- Responsibility is carrying out duties with integrity.
- With rights there are responsibilities.
- Each person can perceive his or her own world and look for the balance of rights and responsibilities.

Concept: One responsibility we sometimes overlook is doing what we say. If we believe in certain principles or values, then what we do or how we act should support our beliefs and values. "For instance, if I believe in caring for the environment, but I throw the candy wrapper on the ground, then I am not 'walking my talk.'

> Say, "Let's consider one of these." Make a separate heading for Caring for the Environment on the board. Ask: "If you believe in this, what type of behavior would you have? What would you do? . . . Good answers. Let's consider another one."

Activity

Ask students to make an "I Believe in . . ." booklet. At the top of each page, write one sentence starting with "I believe in . . ."
Down a few lines, write, "I want the right to . . ."
Down a few lines, write "To have that right, my responsibilities are . . ." Each student is to complete each sentence.

Say, "Each of us can create our own life. We can claim many rights, but with those rights come responsibilities." Ask students to share one or more of their "I believe in . . ." statements.

Close with a relaxation/focusing exercise.

RESPONSIBILITY LESSON 4
I Want Responsibility's Partner Value to Be . . .

Begin with a song.

Activity

Inform the students that they will be doing another trust walk today. This time two members of the team are to guide, only with words, one student whose eyes are covered. Allow each student to take a turn with the blindfold for six minutes. Suggest that the more responsible the guides are, the more easily the blindfolded person will navigate the path. Are we using our best ability to give accurate directions?

Ask the students if they would like to partner the value of responsibility with another value for the trust walk. In addition to experiencing responsibility, would he or she like the directions to be given with love, with peace, with respect or with _____?

Allow each group to share their experiences in their group of three for a few minutes.

Discuss/Share

With the entire group, ask:
- What was your experience?
- What did you learn?
- What value did you choose to partner with responsibility?
- If you could make the world anyway you wanted it to be, and in this world all people were responsible, what value would you want to use to partner with responsibility?

Please reflect for a moment:
- What would happen if you wanted responsibility and love only for your family?
- What might happen if you wanted responsibility and love only for the people in your town or in your country?
- What might happen if you wanted responsibility and love for all of humanity?
- What would you pair with responsibility if you wanted all the children of the world to be able to reach their potential?

> Ask everyone to close their eyes and call out the values they feel are great partners to responsibility. When you have their list of partner values, choose the top few and allow them to form groups based on the one partner value.

Activity

Ask each group to create a mind map with pictures, or a picture or poster of what that world would be like. Invite each group to share their creation with the class.

Close with a relaxation/focusing exercise of their choice.

RESPONSIBILITY LESSON 5
Responsibilities in the Home

Begin with a song.

Discuss/Share

- What responsibilities do mothers have?
- What responsibilities do fathers have?
- What would happen if parents did not fulfill their responsibilities?
- What kind of parent would you like to be when you are an adult? What responsibilities will be important to you?
- What responsibilities do you have as a son or daughter?
- What contributions do you make to your family?
- What contributions do you feel proud of?
- Are there any other things you can think of that you could do to contribute to your family life?

Write the following Reflection Points on the board and discuss them with the students if you wish:

- Responsibility is accepting what is required and carrying out the task to the best of your ability.
- When one is responsible, there is the contentment of having made a contribution.

Note to Educator: The story, "TC Wants a Dog" by Ruth Liddle, may be a little young in tone for some of the older students. However, it is helpful in looking at how some young people don't do their chores at home. If your students have this tendency, the story would be appropriate to share. The story can be found in the Appendix, Item 8. However, if your students tend to be very responsible in doing their chores, kindly skip the story. If the case is the latter and your students are older, you may wish to share "Rickshaw Girl", listed at the end of this unit.

Share a Story

If you are reading "TC Wants a Dog," please say, "The first part of the story I am going to read you may remind you of something that goes on in countless homes around the world, perhaps even your own."

Read the story and discuss it afterwards. Ask younger students how TC proved he was responsible to his mother.

Ask:
- Does this story remind you of you sometimes? How?
- How does TC feel when he knew he should have taken care of his animals and he didn't?
- What are you responsible for at home?
- What could you say to yourself to help you fulfill your responsibilities?
- How do you show me, your teacher, you are responsible?
- How do you show your parents you are responsible?
- Sometimes most of us occasionally don't do things we know we should do. How do you feel when you do not do something you think you should do?
- What kinds of things do you feel a little bad about if you don't do?
- Is there anything you feel very bad about?
- Is it important to feel bad? (Answer: Say, "Sometimes feeling bad is the way people know that it would be better to act in a different way. We all make mistakes sometimes. We are all human. But, feeling bad a lot does not help us do the positive things we really want to do.")

Say, "Feeling sad or ashamed about something is natural, but is not good to remain feeling like that. Instead:
1. Think about what you wish you would have done.
2. Identify the value or quality you need for that.
3. Imagine that quality and feel it in your mind.
4. Talk kindly to yourself. Know that the next time that circumstance occurs, you will have the power to do what you want to do.

Living Values Education Activities for Children Ages 8-14, Book 1

Activity Options

Eight to Ten Activity: Write the four steps on the board. Engage the students in using real situations to apply the four steps they would like to change. Then please ask those students who wish to share, kind things that one can say to the self.

Eleven to Fourteen Activity: Write the four steps on the board. Ask the students to write in their journal, applying the four steps to a situation they would like to change. The teacher can ask the students to share, if they wish, kind things that one can say to the self.

Eight to Nine Activity: Invite the students to make a poem or write a card to their mother and/or father.

Ten to Fourteen Activity: Ask the students to reflect on the following questions and write a personal journal or a short essay on their reflections.

- What do you do that shows your mother you are responsible?
- What else could you do to show her your responsibility?
- What do you think might happen if you did that?
- What do you do that shows your father you are responsible?
- What else could you do to show him your responsibility?
- What do you think might happen if you did that?
- Is there anything you would like to be responsible for that would help your family?

Close with the Flowers of Respect Relaxation Exercise.

RESPONSIBILITY LESSON 6
Sharing Tasks

Begin with a song.

Say, "One basic definition of responsibility is doing your share. When you were little you may have heard a story about a hen who wanted to have bread, but did not have any wheat. So, she decided to plant some wheat. She asked someone to help, and he would not. At each step — when it came to watering the wheat, cutting it down, grinding the wheat, building a fire, and making the bread — she continued to ask people if they wanted to help. Each time, no one did. But, when it came to eating the bread, what happened? . . . That's right — everyone wanted to eat it! And she said, 'When I asked

Living Values Education Activities for Children Ages 8–14, Book 1

you to help me plant, water, and harvest, grind, and bake . . . you said no, no, no, no, and no. And so, I made it myself and I'll eat it myself!'"

Say, "As humans, we are very fortunate — we can create things — we do create our world. To be responsible, we have to do our share of a task. So, what would you like to create? (Offer possible options in your setting. Offer something to do that is enjoyable.) Shall we start with a meal? Shall we start with a flower or vegetable garden?"

Ask students to choose, and then ask them to list materials needed and the tasks that need to be done. Suggest that teams accept responsibility for different tasks. For example, if you decide to make a Mexican or a Moroccan meal (because that is the cultural unit you are studying), one small group can work on decorations, another group on obtaining ingredients, etc.

Activity

In addition to a class responsibility activity, create the opportunity for each student to take up a responsibility at school. Perhaps three pairs of students can be conflict resolution mediators at lunchtime for a week and another three pairs at recess. The next week, other students can take turns. Or, perhaps some students would like to tutor, etc. Ask the students about tasks they would like to be responsible for. Be open to talking about their experiences and helping them generate solutions to any problems.

Close with a relaxation/focusing exercise.

RESPONSIBILITY LESSON 7
The Right to Education — and My Responsibility

Begin with a song.

Share a Story: Running Shoes

Read "Running Shoes" by Frederick Lipp. The Joy of Reading Project kindly gave their permission to post this story on the international LVE site, www.livingvalues.net. You will find it under For Schools /Children Ages 8–14 / Download Free Stories / Responsibility 8-14. It is a story about a girl who is determined to go to school.

Discuss/Share

Discuss the story afterwards, noting that while almost all countries in the world have agreed that education is a right of all children, in some countries, poor children and girls are denied the right to go to school.

For older students, you may wish to mention Malala Yousafzai, who was a young girl when she was shot in 2012 for speaking out for the right of girls to attend school in Pakistan. Her story and that of Iqbal Masih are shared in the unit on Freedom.

Ask:
- If education is a right, what is my responsibility?
- How do you feel when you fulfill your responsibilities as a student?
- How do you feel, and what are the consequences when you do not fulfill your responsibilities?

Note to Educator: The situation for students varies greatly around the world. For some, there is little access to education while others have unlimited access but little motivation. The concept of it being part of a young person's responsibility to make effort to be a good student is appropriate when there is access. For those students an appropriate message is to study well and be an excellent student for then they can work as an adult at something they love doing. Working hard as a teen and young adult usually enables one to earn more and provide well for themselves and their family.

Eleven to Fourteen Question: "If you study well in middle school and high school (secondary school) what will you be able to do?" (Perhaps go to university?)

Discuss the following Reflection Point.
Responsibility is not only something that obliges us, but also something that allows us to achieve what we wish.

Eight to Nine Activity: Invite students to draw a picture of something they may wish to do when they are adults. Ask them to write two things they can do now that will help them to accomplish that goal. Help them make these actions specific, practical, and immediate — something they can do within the next day or two. They should be small, observable actions. In this way, students can see when they are making progress toward their goal.

Ten to Fourteen Activity:

Step 1. Ask each student to choose one subject he or she would like to improve in. On a scale of 1 to 10 — 10 being the highest mark — how do they rate themselves? Instruct the students to think about something they can do to improve in that subject to get nearer their goal. Their new behaviors should be specific, practical, and easily observable. In this way, students can see when they are making progress toward their goal.

Step 2. Invite the students to form small groups to share.

Step 3. Ask the students to write down three concrete things they can do.

Step 4. In three days, ask students to share in groups of three to review their progress, and encourage students to continue working toward their goal.

Close with a relaxation/focusing exercise.

RESPONSIBILITY LESSON 8
Global Responsibility and Making a Positive Difference

Begin with a song.

Discuss the following Reflection Points:

♦ Global responsibility requires respect toward all human beings.

♦ Responsibility is using our resources to generate a positive change.

♦ A responsible person knows how to be fair, seeing that each gets a share.

Ask:

- What would happen if everyone is the world respected all human beings?
- What do you think would happen if everyone was responsible and fair?
- If you could tell every person in the world that he or she had to be responsible, in what ways would you want people to be responsible?
- What would you want them to do?
- What would you want them not to do?
- What is our global responsibility?
- What is our societal responsibility?
- What is our moral responsibility?

Say, "Always know that you can make a positive difference. When we know that our actions affect others and are respectful, fair, kind and caring, we create safe and loving spaces for people. The more people do that the more we will create the world we want.

Reflective Activity

Play some relaxation music and ask the students to reflect on the following

statements and questions. Please give them time to reflect after each statement.
- ❖ Think of three people who are very important in the world.
- ❖ Think of three people who are famous.
- ❖ Now think of three people who are most important in your life. Who are they?
- ❖ It is not someone's money, position or fame that make them the most important to you. What is it that makes those people important to you?
- ❖ What responsibilities have your three most important people taken up in your life that makes them so important?
- ❖ What other qualities or values do they have that makes them your most important people?
- ❖ Think about their qualities or values that empowers them to make a positive difference for others.
- ❖ Now please think about why you are so special to them.
- ❖ Who are you important to?
- ❖ How do you make a positive difference?

Activity

Invite the students to form groups of three and share whatever they would like to share from the reflection. Then ask them to write about the qualities and values that empower people to make a positive difference in the world, and what would happen if everyone did that.

Close by playing some relaxation music and asking students to be in their relaxation/focusing silent space. Then ask those who wish to share to speak out one sentence, "We make a positive difference when _____."

RESPONSIBILITY LESSON 9
My Responsibilities

Begin with a song.

Discuss/Share
- What are you responsible for?
- Yes, all of you have responsibilities at home and school — and other things — but how are you responsible for yourself?
- You are responsible for breathing shallow breaths or deep breathes, aren't you?

Living Values Education Activities for Children Ages 8-14, Book 1

- You are responsible for taking care of your body. How much do you exercise? How much food you eat?
- What else?
- Are you responsible for what you think?
- Are you responsible for what you say?
- Are you responsible for your actions?
- Are you responsible for your own feelings?
- Are you responsible for making good choices or bad choices?

Facilitate a conversation based on the above. You may wish to steer it in a direction where you know there is a need. For example, perhaps many of the students are overweight and not exercising, drinking sodas or eating too much sugar. This can lead to one group researching healthy food habits or foods to avoid or how to get more exercise. It could lead to a discussion on emotions and how we are really responsible for our own feelings. Perhaps contrast that with blaming others.

Activity Options

Invite students to form small groups to discuss topics in which there was interest. They can research the topic, make a poster, and present their findings, thoughts and suggestions to the entire class. (You are likely to need more than one class for this.)

Or, ask students to make their own personal mind map of their responsibilities including the things they are responsible for. Ask them if there is anything they wish to refine or change. Ask: What thought about what you are doing would help all of this seem easy? An example of such a thought: I am growing in the direction I want.

Follow-up Activity: Is there a class project they would like to do? For example, perhaps they would like to improve their health with the Daily Mile. Many schools are allowing their students to do this. They benefit physically and socially. "The Daily Mile is a social activity, wherein the children run or jog — at their own pace — in the fresh air with friends. Children can occasionally walk to catch their breath, if necessary, but should aim to run or jog for the full 15 minutes." (https://thedailymile.co.uk/about/)

Close with a relaxation/focusing exercise of their choice.

RESPONSIBILITY LESSON 10
Taking Responsibility Makes Me a Good Friend

Begin with a song.

Say, "To be responsible means that you are trustworthy. We all want our family to be responsible for us. Parents are responsible for providing food and shelter — and love — and helping us grow up healthy and strong. What about a friend?"

Discuss

- Do you feel a friend has the responsibility to be trustworthy?
- What does that mean? How does a trustworthy friend act? What do they do and not do?
- How do you feel when people do not do what they say they will do or are irresponsible? For example, they say they will meet you and then don't?
- How would you feel if a friend gossiped about you or let you down?
- How do you feel is someone is not responsible for their own feelings and blames you?
- How do you feel when your friend is trustworthy?
- What can we say to people when they are irresponsible or let us down?

Activity

Ask the students to form groups of five. Each student in the group is to generate one situation in which he or she feels someone has let him or her down or has been irresponsible in some way and one situation in which he or she has been irresponsible or let someone down. They are to role play those situations, coming up with two solutions for each situation. Discuss the consequences of each. When students discuss real problems they are confronting, allow them to create Situation Cards and continue discussing, role playing, and generating positive, appropriate solutions.

Ask each group to make a slogan. Provide paper and paints and allow them to post them around the room.

Close with a relaxation/focusing exercise.

RESPONSIBILITY LESSON 11
A Play

Begin with a song.

Activity

Divide the students into groups of eight to ten and ask them to create a play demonstrating irresponsibility and/or responsibility. It can be a comedy or a drama. Allow them to share their skit/drama.

Close with a relaxation/focusing exercise.

RESPONSIBILITY LESSON 12
I Believe

Begin with a song.

Activity

Do the Peace Relaxation/Focusing Exercise with the students, and ask them to create an image of what they believe in. Below the image, each one is to write two new ways of being responsible or two things about responsibility that is most important/meaningful to them. Together make a collage on the wall.

Close with a song.

Additional Responsibility Lessons and Activities

RESPONSIBILITY LESSON 13
A Program

Begin with a song.

Make plans in a group for a special program for other students or the school on what you have learned about two values. Decide who will be responsible for each area of the program and carry it through. You may wish to include music, a play and your artistic creations.

RESPONSIBILITY LESSON 14 for Ages 11 to 14
Rickshaw Girl

Begin with a song.

Read the "Rickshaw Girl" by Mitali Perkins. The Joy of Reading Project kindly gave their permission to post this story on the international LVE site, www.livingvalues.net.

Living Values Education Activities for Children Ages 8–14, Book 1

You will find it under For Schools /Children Ages 8–14 / Download Free Stories / Responsibility 12–14. A story about a girl in Bangladesh, it touches on Naima's love and feelings of responsibility to help care for her family. Other themes in the story are poverty, gender inequality and the need for education. It is longer than most of the other stories on the site. Discuss the story with the students.

RESPONSIBILITY LESSON 15 for Ages 12 to 14
Would I like to be more committed?

Begin with a song.
Discuss the following Reflection Points:
- Responsibility is carrying out duties with integrity.
- As a responsible person, I have something worthwhile to offer — so do others.

Then, ask:
- As a person, what responsibilities do you have to others?
- To society?

Ask the students to make a list of all the responsible actions the class has been discussing during the unit on responsibility and to number each one. Ask each student to mark each act he or she believes in. Then, ask each student to look at the list and circle the number if he or she does that action in an automatic way. Compare the lists and see if you would like to be more committed in action to the things you believe in.

— *Contributed by Sabine Levy*

Activities

Community Project

There may be a need in the class, school or community with which the students can help. Planting flowers or vegetables could be quite helpful to many. For example, LVE rural schools in South Africa created gardens. The produce grown went to grandparents who were caring for their school-aged grandchildren whose parents had died of AIDS.

Civic Functioning for Ages 13 and 14

Explore responsibility through the regular curriculum, for example, learning about the different governing roles, public service, the functioning of associations, or the content of the Convention on the Rights of the Child.

Contributed by Pilar Quera Colomina and Sabine Levy

Living Values Education Activities for Children Ages 8–14, Book 1

Unit Eight: Simplicity and Caring for the Earth and Her Oceans

Simplicity and Caring for the Earth and Her Oceans Lessons

Each value is important, but the importance of simplicity and taking care of our Earth and her oceans at this point in time is paramount as human demands on the planet's resources increase and global climate change imperils human existence.

Simplicity as a value is addressed in a few ways: enjoying the simplicity and beauty of nature, valuing the simplicity and wisdom of indigenous cultures, simplicity as precursor of sustainable development and simplicity as a way to reduce our material demands on the planet.

In relation to caring for our Earth and her oceans, *Green Values Club* has been used in this unit. The nine short chapters in *Green Values Club* and subsequent lesson content contain specific scientific information about the harmful effects of human actions on the ocean, rivers, animals, air and ground — and on human beings themselves. I feel part of the process of helping students be more aware of the importance of taking care of the Earth is experiencing love and respect for nature and her creatures and learning about specific ways they can be a friend to the Earth.

Green Values Club weaves in the values of love and respect, camaraderie and helping others, and the understanding that each one of us can make a difference. Cognitive understanding of the effects of one action is amplified through an explanation of systems thinking and students charting effects with flow charts and mind maps. Educators can help empower students to take positive action and do service-learning projects through the activity ideas presented. Please add your own ideas and help them do what is most needed in the local community.

If you would like more activities on sustainable development, *Living Green Values Activities for Children and Young Adults* is available for free download on the international

LVE website. Lesson 17, "Environmental Projects and Service-Learning Activities" in the Young Adult section may be of interest.

Enjoy doing the activities with the students. We will be happy to post news of your projects, poems and songs in our newsletter or on the international website.

Thank you for helping take care of our Earth.

Simplicity and Caring for the Earth and Her Oceans Reflection Points

- Simplicity is natural. Simplicity is being natural.
- Simplicity is learning from the earth.
- Simplicity is beautiful.
- Simplicity is relaxing.
- Simplicity helps create sustainable development.
- Simplicity is staying in the present and not making things complicated.
- Simplicity is enjoying a plain mind and intellect.
- Simplicity teaches us economy — how to use our resources wisely, keeping future generations in mind.
- Simplicity is giving patience, friendship, and encouragement.
- Simplicity is appreciating the small things in life.
- Simplicity is freedom from material desires and emotional desires — permission to simply "be."
- Simplicity avoids waste, teaches economy, avoids value clashes complicated by greed, fear, peer pressure, and a false sense of identity.
- From simplicity grows generosity and sharing.
- Simplicity is putting others first with kindness, openness, pure intentions — without expectations and conditions.

Simplicity and Caring for the Earth and Her Oceans Goals and Objectives

Goal: To increase knowledge about and enjoy simplicity.
Objectives:
- To participate in discussions about the Simplicity Reflection Points and be able to talk about two or more.
- To express simplicity artistically.
- To enjoy observing simple things in nature during a walk.

- ❑ To discuss and write about the simple things they enjoy.
- ❑ To write a class play about rediscovering the simple things in life/nature.
- ❑ To participate in class discussions about the message behind selected advertisements and be able to generate an alternate "simplicity is natural" message in response.

Goal: To learn about the simple wisdom of indigenous cultures.
Objectives:
- ❑ To learn several ways in which indigenous cultures used resources wisely.
- ❑ To discuss the values within the cultural practices being studied.

Goal: To learn about the benefits of a healthy ocean and earth and scientific information about harmful effects of human actions on the ocean, rivers, animals, air, ground and human beings in order to build awareness of the importance of using earth-friendly practices which support sustainable development.
Objectives:
- ❑ To hear about the harm driftnets can cause marine animals.
- ❑ To learn that 50 to 70 percent of the oxygen we breathe comes from the ocean.
- ❑ To hear about a few of the benefits of kelp forests in the ocean.
- ❑ To understand how fertilizer-run-off and nitrogen pollution and pesticides kill the kelp and create dead zones in the ocean; to understand the meaning of dead zones and a few of the consequences.
- ❑ To learn about the negative effect of plastic and floating debris on marine mammals; to learn about the five huge ocean gyres of "toxic plastic soup".
- ❑ To think of solutions and consider positive earth-friendly actions they can do so as not to contribute to the "toxic plastic soup".
- ❑ To draw a large footprint on a piece of paper and inside write all the things that contribute to their carbon footprint; to think about the things they can do to reduce their carbon footprint.

Goal: To learn about simplicity and caring for the Earth and her oceans.
Objectives:
- ❑ To learn about simplicity as the precursor to sustainable development.
- ❑ To think of ways to conserve in the classroom, and to carry out at least two of those actions.

❑ To do one environment friendly project at the school or in the community.
❑ To use information being studied to carry out an environmental project in the community (for older students).

SIMPLICITY AND CARING
FOR THE EARTH AND HER OCEANS LESSON 1
Simple Art

Begin with a song. Perhaps play some beautiful flute music or music on an indigenous instrument. Or, if you have access, the students may enjoy the YouTube video of "The Circle of Life" by Elton John. The following version features Elton John singing it in his younger years and clips from the *Lion King*.
https://www.youtube.com/watch?v=IwH9YvhPN7c

Introduce the value of Simplicity and write the following Reflection Points on the board:

♦ Simplicity is natural. Simplicity is being natural.
♦ Simplicity is beautiful.

Activity

Explore works of art, historical pictures, or magazines for examples of simplicity versus something gaudily or excessively adorned. Make a collage or picture that reflects simplicity. While the students are working, play a beautiful piece of music with a simple melody or a recording of the sounds of nature.

Or, collect a few leaves and make a beautiful picture with those leaves. Paint them, draw them, or place them under a piece of paper and color on top of them.

Close with a relaxation/focusing exercises of your choice.

SIMPLICITY AND CARING
FOR THE EARTH AND HER OCEANS LESSON 2
Learning from Indigenous Cultures

Begin with music or a song.

Purpose: To learn about and appreciate the indigenous wisdom of your heritage and the heritage of others. In ancient traditions, natural simplicity, wisdom, and respect for the earth were inherent in almost every practice. The needs of the people and the methods to satisfy those needs were simple and without waste. Look at the natural simplicity in the lives of your country's indigenous peoples or other indigenous cultures.

Introductory Content: Many indigenous cultures in Africa, the Americas, Australia, Asia, and the Pacific islands showed respect for the earth and its resources in their gathering and hunting practices. For example, Native American Indian tribes were simple, economical, and wise in their use of plants and natural resources. Indians in the deserts of what is now California used each part of the ocotillo plant — the roots, leaves, and stem. They never overused resources and thus guaranteed there would be plenty. The Gwich'in Indians in the far north considered caribou reindeer to be their brothers. From the caribou, they made food, clothing, snowshoes, cooking vessels, and their houses. The Indians considered themselves to be rich, as they were warm, well fed, and had plenty of time for their arts and prayers.

Activity

Discover ways in which indigenous peoples have used resources by reading a story, visiting a museum or a library with an exhibit, or viewing a film. Invite members of the community who can share artifacts or crafts from your heritage.

Eleven to Fourteen Activity: You may wish to ask older students which indigenous cultures they are interested in exploring. Perhaps divide them into working groups to explore different aspects of one culture or several cultures.

You may wish to spend a couple of time periods on traditional wisdom.

Discuss the Reflection Points:
- Simplicity is learning from the earth.
- Simplicity teaches us economy — how to use our resources wisely, keeping future generations in mind.

Point out, or ask the students to explore, how the people of indigenous cultures were wise in doing this. Ask them which values are inherent in different practices.

Ask:
- Which aspects of their wisdom do you think it would be beneficial to practice in today's world?

Ask students to draw and write about the results of their investigation. They could do an art project, duplicating something from their heritage or the heritage of others. Younger students could make a clay model and tell their parents about it when they bring it home. In preparation for the at-home presentation, ask students to tell you their points about the object and its history. Tell them to write their points on the board and to practice with a peer partner before they take the object home.

Older students working in small groups could make posters or displays of their findings.

If possible, play music from the indigenous culture students are studying and ask them to use images from that culture to create a relaxation/focusing exercise.

SIMPLICITY AND CARING
FOR THE EARTH AND HER OCEANS LESSON 3
A Nature Walk

Begin with a song.

A nature walk easily offers the experience of the following Simplicity Reflection Points:

- ♦ Simplicity is natural.
- ♦ Simplicity is beautiful.
- ♦ Simplicity is relaxing.
- ♦ Simplicity is appreciating the small things in life.

Activity

Take a walk in a nearby park or go on a field trip to a botanical garden or the seashore. For 15 minutes of your time there, walk in silence. Observe the simple things: the light on the leaf, a tree, a small flower, a bird, or whatever element of nature you notice. Lie under a tree and watch the leaves. For a few minutes, simply be an observer, free from desires.

When you return, write a poem as though it were from part of nature. For example, a poem from the tree to you, a poem from the bird to the class, or . . .?

Homework: Give the students Simplicity-Is-Relaxing and Simplicity-Is-Not-Making-Things-Complicated homework. Ask them to spend five minutes every day for one week relaxing. They may wish to focus on a tree, a flower, or a light or lay on their back and enjoy observing the sky. Focus on the beauty of what is natural. Know that the natural you is beautiful.

Close with a relaxation/focusing exercise or play relaxing music and invite those who wish to do so to each share one word, phrase or sentence about nature.

SIMPLICITY AND CARING
FOR THE EARTH AND HER OCEANS LESSON 4
Simple Things in Life that Mean so Much

Begin with a song.

Discuss/Share

Talk about the simple things in life that mean so much. Invite the children to share the simple things in their life which they enjoy.

A Tiny Drop of Water Creative Visualization

Inform the children that you will be asking them to imagine that they are a tiny drop of water taking an imaginary journey inside a plant. This is to appreciate one of the simple things in life that we often take for granted.

Guide the children gently through the visualization as suggested below:

"Close your eyes. . . . You are a tiny drop of water. . . . You rain on the plant. . . . You drop onto a colorful rose — what does it feel like, smell like? . . . You go inside the rose and down the stem — what does it look like, feel like? . . . Can you see the sunlight coming through? What do you see? . . . You reach the root. It's dark! What do you feel and smell? . . . You go out of the root into the soil. It's dark! What do you feel and smell? . . . A bird pecks the ground and lifts you into its beak. As it flies up, it drops you on top of the same rose. You go to the favorite part of the rose. Where is it? . . . Wriggle your toes and fingers. . . . Open your eyes. . . . You are now back in the classroom."

Ask them to share about their journey. Their experiences will all be different. Accept all answers as correct.

Activity

Invite the children to create a storyboard with four to eight pictures, or a poem, or a creative story about the "Journey of a Drop of Water". Invite them to share the stories.

Reflection: Let's all appreciate the simple things in life that mean so much to us and we sometimes take for granted.

Other visualization stories could include:
> A walk through the park.
> What a bird sees through its eyes.
> What a dolphin sees through its eyes.
> The journey of water from liquid to ice to liquid to steam.

— Contributed by Peter Williams

SIMPLICITY AND CARING
FOR THE EARTH AND HER OCEANS LESSON 5
The Ocean

Educator Preparation: If there is internet capacity at your setting, you may wish to show the students a video of a humpback whale being saved from a fisherman's net. It is suggested that the video be shown after reading the following story.
http://www.youtube.com/watch?v=eG0cWYsfvKo

Begin with a song.

Share that simplicity is that value that helps us create sustainable development. Sustainable development means using the Earth's resources wisely, with the needs of future generations in mind. Tell them that you'll be doing some Living Green Values lessons together about the environment and taking care of our animal friends, ourselves and the Earth and her Oceans.

Please read the following story to the class. The Green Values Club has nine chapters.

Share a Story: Out in the Dinghy

Katie felt worried when she woke up, not at all like her usual cheerful self. The sky was gray through the window. She pulled on her robe and slipped down to the kitchen. She could smell the coffee her mother was brewing. She hugged her mother from behind and asked, "Is Papa home yet?"

Her mother's tired face answered her as she turned around. "I'm sure he's fine, Katie. They've been late getting in before."

"Not this late."

"I know." Mama gave her a quick hug.

George ran into the kitchen, yelling, "Is Papa home yet?"

Their silence answered.

"Oh." George slid into a chair, looking dejected.

"Come, let's have breakfast," said Mama, "and try not to worry. Your Dad is very smart and his partner is a good one."

"But it's not even stormy, it's just overcast," protested Katie. "So why is the boat so late?"

"Unusual things can happen at sea," said Mama. "Let's just trust that all is well, and keep praying."

They said a prayer for Papa and Hector before eating breakfast.

"I got a special feeling just now," said Katie, "that Papa is all right."

"You know, I did too," said Mama. Her smile was full of relief. "But, since we're all a little worried, let's stay together today. It's early. Let's do a few chores quickly and then I'll go out in the dinghy with you."

"You'll go out with us, Mama?" said George, shocked.

"I'm not as old as you think, George. I bet I can still swim faster than you and I'm sure I'm still good with an oar," laughed Mama.

"That I would like to see," laughed Katie. "Are you still a faster swimmer than me?"

"I don't know," smiled Mama, "you're growing up so fast, but I can still swim faster than a nine-year old," she said as she tousled George's hair.

It was fresh and bright by the time they got down to the dinghy. Katie and George were good rowers. Soon they were on their way out, enjoying the fresh air and the sparkle of the light on the blue of the water. The light shone like diamonds on the sea and an occasional splash from the oars shone through the air, landing on them to make them laugh.

Katie knew they were all watching for Papa's boat. As they rowed past the little island all of the sudden she saw it, "Look, look, it's Papa's boat!"

They waved and called and waved and called. Finally, they were close enough for Papa to hear them. Papa came to the side of the boat and gave them a huge smile.

"Welcome! Am I glad to see you!" he called. "Be careful. Come up closely and avoid the flukes!"

The flukes? And then they noticed! Next to Papa's boat was a whale! It was so low in the water they hadn't noticed it.

"Am I glad you're here," Papa repeated. He gave them all a special hug as they climbed on board.

Papa and his partner looked really tired. Papa began to tell them the story. He had noticed a whale in the water as they were coming in at sunset the night before. "Hector and I almost didn't notice it," he said. "When we did see it, we thought it was dead as it was so still and just floating. Then it finally took a breath. It's caught in a net. The net was so heavy that it was dragging the whale down. It's even wrapped around the flukes."

Katie and George looked in awe at the whale. It looked like a young one, an adolescent — it didn't have many barnacles on him. But it sure was big, maybe 12 meters long.

"So," Papa continued, "at sunset we rigged a line to lift some of the weight of the net off the whale and help him stay afloat, but we had to wait until daylight till it was safe to start cutting the net off."

Papa looked at Mama, "I'm so sorry, Lisa, not to have been able to tell you. I knew you would worry, but hoped you could tune in and know I was safe. I just couldn't let the whale die."

"And that's one of the reasons I love you," Mama smiled.

Papa and Hector had been taking turns since daylight getting in the water to cut the strings of the net. It was a commercial net with strong nylon. Papa was thankful that they were there with the dinghy. There was a lot of net to cut and they could use some help. It would be safer and faster to cut from the little boat.

So Katie and George and Mama all got a chance to help. One of them would keep the dinghy steady from the rear with an oar and the other two would cut at the net, string by string. Papa jumped back in the water to cut near the tail. Papa wouldn't let them go near the flukes.

The whale seemed to understand what they were doing. Katie noticed that his eye was watching them. She reached over to pat him. "You've going to be okay," she said as she rubbed his skin.

"We've worked so hard the last three years to get fisherman to stop using driftnets since it's been banned in this area," said Papa. "It looks like someone out there doesn't care about whales, dolphins or our ecosystem."

They worked hard for a couple of hours. Mama called, "The net is ready to fall away from the head now."

"Great," called Papa. "The middle section is already cut. I think I can ease the net off

Living Values Education Activities for Children Ages 8–14, Book 1

the flukes. Katie, he seems to like you patting him and looking at him. Keep doing that. We need him to stay still."

"Hector, are you ready to pull the net off?" Hector was poised near the pulley on the large boat.

Katie, George and Mama stayed at the whale's head and patted him, as Papa carefully eased the cut net off one side of the flukes.

"Okay," called Papa, "back away slowly. Stay peaceful."

George backed the dinghy away from the whale as Papa swam to the side of the boat. Hector began to use the pulley to haul away the cut net from the whale.

The whale started to move his head and tail, and the line holding part of the net from the boat eased the cut net off the middle part of the whale and the rest of the tail. All of the sudden the whale seemed to realize it was free and took off!

"Hooray," shouted George and Katie.

They all cheered as the whale swam away. When the whale was out about 200 meters it curved around toward them and began to rise in the air, right out of the water. It breached again and again as though it wanted to tell them something special.

George said softly, "I think he's very happy and saying thank you."

Katie, Mama, Papa and Hector laughed. "I think you're right," they chorused.

Discuss

- Have you ever heard a story before of a whale being caught in a net? (Say, "Yes, this is something that happens. Unfortunately, many dolphins and whales are caught in nets every year and die. Occasionally, people have found them in time and have been brave and caring enough to set them free. Driftnets are banned in some areas but not in others.")
- What values did Papa and Hector demonstrate?
- What values did Katie, George and Mama show?
- Would you want to help a whale or a dolphin if one was stranded? If "yes", why?
- What value do you have that makes you want to help?

➢ Show a video of a whale being freed, if possible.

Lesson Content — Information about the Ocean

Source: The following excerpts were taken from the website of One World One

Ocean. http://www.oneworldoneocean.org/pages/why-the-ocean

The ocean is Earth's life support.
- 50 to 70 percent of the oxygen we breathe comes from the ocean. That's more
  - than every one of the world's rainforests combined.
- The ocean is the #1 source of protein for more than a billion people. Sea life provides one-fifth of the average person's animal protein intake.
- The ocean regulates our climate, absorbs carbon dioxide, holds 97% of Earth's water, and supports the greatest abundance of life on our planet.
- More than 60% of the world's population lives on or near the coast. The ocean provides a livelihood, recreation, beauty, wonder, and untapped scientific discovery, leading to new medications, foods, and advanced technologies.
- Everyone, everywhere depends on a healthy sea.

Discuss/Explore

Reread the first section, "The ocean is Earth's life support", from the *One World One Ocean* information above. Then ask:
- Have all of you been to the ocean?
- What do you like about the ocean? (If they have not been to the ocean, ask what they think they would like about it.)
- Do you know how the ocean provides 50 to 70 percent of the earth's oxygen?

Share the following information:
Source: http://earthsky.org/water/how-much-do-oceans-add-to-worlds-oxygen
Scientists agree that there's oxygen from ocean plants in every breath we take. Most of this oxygen comes from tiny ocean plants — called phytoplankton — that live near the water's surface and drift with the currents. Like all plants, they photosynthesize — that is, they use sunlight and carbon dioxide to make food. A byproduct of photosynthesis is oxygen.

Say, "There are beautiful kelp forests in the ocean. They are phytoplankton and are essential for the health of the ocean, humans and animals as they provide much of the oxygen we breathe. They also provide food and shelter to thousands of species. Kelp forests also help to purify the ocean's water.

Living Values Education Activities for Children Ages 8–14, Book 1

The health and well-being of human beings depends on the well-being of the ocean, the marine life and the earth. The kelp forests' well-being depends on the actions of humans."

Activity Options

Choose one of the activities below, in accordance with the age of your students and what is available.

Eight to Fourteen Activity: Watch one of the One World One Ocean films, if possible, by MacGillivray Freeman Films to help students experience the amazing beauty of the ocean and the importance of protecting our ocean. There is a 3D film about the ocean, another on humpback whales. *To the Artic* is amazing. Or, watch another film about the beauty of the ocean. http://www.macgillivrayfreemanfilms.com)

Eight-year old Activity: Invite the students to draw a picture from the story, or draw a picture of what they like about the ocean.

Nine to Eleven Activity: If you have access to the internet, google Kelp Forests and enjoy the beautiful pictures and the information that is provided on many sites.

Twelve to Fourteen Activity: Invite students to study kelp forests with the aim of experiencing their visual beauty and understanding what helps them to thrive.

Close with a relaxation/focusing exercise.

SIMPLICITY AND CARING
FOR THE EARTH AND HER OCEANS LESSON 6
How Trash Effects Marine Animals

Begin with a song.
Ask how they are and if they have been thinking about the last lesson. Allow them time to share their thoughts. Listen and acknowledge.
Please read Chapter Two of the *Green Values Club* below.

Share a Story: Circling the Seagull

It was amazing to watch the whale they had just saved jump into the air again and again. He continued to breach, the sun glistening on sheets of water that came up into the air with him and splashed even wider as he landed. The whale seemed to be performing for them — communicating his joy at being free and alive.

Papa and Hector used the pulley to haul the huge net into their 15-meter boat. "Wow, this is heavy," said George as he helped.

"Many nets are more than a mile long," said Papa. "So many animals get caught in them, and they kill many kinds of fish that the fishermen are not trying to catch. The use of driftnets must stop, it's depleting the ocean, hurting the environment and actually ruining the fishermen's trade in the long run."

"I'm so glad you saw the whale in time," said Katie.

Papa gave her a wide grin, "Me, too."

When the net was on board so it couldn't do further harm, Mama said, "Katie and George, do you want to take the dinghy in and enjoy a swim? Or shall we tie it to the boat and haul it in? I think your Papa's going to want to rest when he gets home. Yes, Luke?"

"That would be great," said Papa. He did look worn out.

"George, I want to row in and go for a swim. How about you?" asked Katie.

"Sounds terrific!" yelled George. "I'll beat you to the dinghy! Bye, Papa," he called as he gave him a quick hug and started over the side of the big boat. "Bye, Mama, bye Hector!"

Katie gave Papa and Mama a hug. "Is a couple of hours, okay, Mama?"

"Yes, enjoy," said Mama.

"You two were a great help," called Papa over the side of the boat as Katie and George began to row away in the dinghy.

Papa's boat soon overtook them and in ten minutes they saw it dock.

"Shall we swim at Blue Cove?" asked George.

"Great," said Katie. "And am I glad we packed a lunch!"

"Double hooray," said George, "I'm famished."

The beach wasn't too crowded and soon George found a few friends to body surf with while Katie took a long swim.

"Gosh, there's a lot of trash around today," said George, kicking away a couple of cans and a pile of bottle tops and plastic bottles mixed with seaweed as they found a sandy spot under a tree.

"The beach looks ugly with all this trash. Maybe some of it came down the river with the rain a couple nights ago," Katie said as she unpacked their lunch.

"As Mama would say, people just don't realize how important it is to not trash our world," said George. "Papa would be upset if he saw how it looks today."

"Yeah, I've never seen it look so bad," said Katie.

238

As they began to devour their apples and sandwiches, a few gulls flew in, interested in their food.

"Look at that gull," said Katie, pointing. One was hopping awkwardly near the tree. His head would jerk down as he stepped on a tattered plastic bag wrapped around its head and a leg. One wing was lower than the other.

"Poor thing," said George. "Wow, looks like that bag has been around him for a long time."

"And look how skinny he looks," said Katie, "think we can catch him and take it off so he'll be free?"

"Hey," said George, "think I can creep up on him?"

As fast as George was, the bird kept managing to get away, half walking, half flying.

"Let's borrow a towel from someone," suggested Katie.

"Maybe my friends can help," said George.

Soon there were five of them. "Let's make a very big circle around him," suggested Katie, "and pretend not to notice him. They spread out and made a big circle around the gull.

"Stay peaceful," called George softly.

"Start to move in," called Katie softly. She was ready with the towel. As they circled in, Katie was soon close enough to throw the towel over the bird.

"Got it," yelled George, diving to secure one end of the towel as one of his friends secured the other end.

The boys watched as George and Tom held the protesting gull and Katie carefully took the tattered plastic bag off.

"Its wing is hurt," said Tom.

"Yes," said Katie, "looks like we'll have to take him home and see what Mama can do."

"You're lucky you got a Mom that knows how to do that," said Tom.

Katie gave him a smile. "She's great. Thanks for your help, guys."

It was tricky to row from Blue Cove to the dock with only one rower, but Katie and George took turns rowing and holding the gull.

"I think I'm as tired as Papa now," sighed George, "but what a day!" His smile was as wide as Katie's.

Discuss/Explore

- Have you ever helped a bird that was hurt? (Listen to and acknowledge

their stories.)
- What values did Katie and George demonstrate?
- The seagull in the story was hurt by trash, in this case a plastic bag. What other kinds of things discarded by humans can hurt animals?
- What was the whale hurt by?

Say, "Some people don't understand the harmful effect that trash created by humans has on marine life, animals and our world. Let's look at some information about animals in and near the ocean."

Lesson Content

Please read the following information.
Source: Dolphin Research Center's website,
http://www.dolphins.org/marineed_threatstodolphins.php

The Pollution Problem

Marine debris is anything from a discarded sandwich bag to a lost fishing net. Every ocean in the world is littered with some form of debris, which resembles food for marine life. Many animals accidentally **eat** marine debris causing internal injury, intestinal blockage, and starvation.

Getting tangled up in floating debris is another serious and growing problem for marine mammals.

(Note to Educator: Please read the following two sentences only to students that are 12- to 14-years old.) Entanglement is an especially serious threat to young marine mammals that tend to be curious and careless. Once a young animal becomes entangled, it dies a slow and painful death as its growing body is restricted by debris.

At least 43% of all marine mammal species and 44% of all seabird species become entangled in or ingest marine debris each year. Some of these include the most endangered marine species in U.S. waters: Hawaiian monk seals, hawksbill and green sea turtles, West Indian manatees, and right whales.

Almost everything we use has the potential to become marine debris, from the bottle of milk in the refrigerator to the refrigerator itself. The largest source of marine debris is runoff from land-based sources, such as storm sewers and parking lots. That means that the garbage we create each day is most likely what will end up in the oceans affecting dolphins, whales, and other marine life.

Activity

Say, "There are a lot of problems on our Earth caused by people that don't pick up their trash. In the two stories you heard about nets and plastic bags causing problems. Nets cause death to many whales and dolphins every year. Let's fill in the columns for the story we just heard and then name some other 'trash'."

Draw four vertical lines on the whiteboard, making four columns with the following headings.

1. TRASH	2. PROBLEM(S)	3. SOLUTION(S)	4. VALUES TO NOT CREATE TRASH
Plastic bags			

Ask:
- What kinds of trash do people leave on the shores of the ocean?
- What kinds of problems does that cause?

The educator will need to repeat the above two questions several times in order to have them create a list of some of the major kinds of trash and the problems it causes. This is also true for the questions below.

Ask:
- What kinds of trash do people leave in rivers and lakes?
- What kinds of problems does that cause?
- What kinds of trash do people leave on the land?
- What kinds of problems does that cause?
- What kinds of trash do you see around here?
- What would it look like without that?
- What would you like to see instead?

Divide students into small groups and allow them to fill in columns three and four for the different kinds of trash.

Ask each group to share:
- What solutions did you think of?

- What value or values would help create that solution? (For example, respect for the ocean, respect for animals, etc.)
- What would you like to see instead?

Close with a song about the beauty of nature or a relaxation/focusing exercise.

SIMPLICITY AND CARING
FOR THE EARTH AND HER OCEANS LESSON 7
Ocean Gyres

Begin with a song with lyrics about nature. Ask how they are and if they have been thinking about the last lesson. Allow them time to share their thoughts and any related actions. Listen and acknowledge.

Vocabulary word: You may need to define a gyre before the story if the students are not aware of this word. Our oceans are dynamic systems, made up of complex networks of currents that circulate water around the world. Large systems of these currents, coupled with wind and the earth's rotation, create "gyres", massive, slow rotating whirlpools. There are five major gyres in the oceans of the world in which plastic trash has accumulated. (Source: http://5gyres.org)

Please read Chapter Three of the *Green Values Club* below.

Share a Story: Toxic Plastic Soup

Katie and George took turns carrying the gull home after they tied the dinghy next to Papa's boat.

"He's heavier than he looks," panted George.

"I'll take him for a while," Katie replied, holding out her arms for the gull.

Papa and Mama were at the kitchen table when they got home. "Still hungry?" asked Papa. "You both did a lot this morning."

George and Katie told their story as they sat at the table while Papa poured some yummy smelling soup into two bowls.

Mama had taken the gull into her lap and was gently examining its wing. "He's had a rough time with that plastic bag, it looks like. Besides being underweight, it looks like he has a broken wing."

Mama soon had gauze tape wrapped around the gull to hold the broken wing still. "He should be almost as good as new in two or three weeks, unless he's been eating plastic," she said. "George, can you find a big box for him?"

"The beach was full of trash today," said Katie, "more than I've ever seen. Plastic caps and bottles, plastic cups, straws and bags, food wrappers, Styrofoam cups, soda cans — it was terrible."

Papa frowned. "People!" He said it like a swear word.

"Papa, you sound more upset than usual about the trash," said George, bringing in a big cardboard box.

"Yeah, I am," said Papa. "Here, let me give you a hand." He grabbed a knife and helped George cut the top of the cardboard box for the gull.

"I've known for years that sea birds, dolphins, whales, seals, sea turtles and many marine animals get caught in nets, fishing wire and human trash, but I just learned last week that *over 40 percent* of marine mammals and seabirds get entangled in human trash or eat marine debris. When they eat plastic trash it causes internal injury, intestinal blockage and starvation. I had no idea the percentage of animals being hurt was that high."

"And the gyres in the ocean are growing," said Mama softly. "There are now five huge gyres in different parts of the world where the plastic trash is accumulating. The plastic breaks down into small pieces over time and the animals are mistaking it for food and eating it."

Papa and George had finished cutting off the top of the box. The family went outside with the box, Katie cradling the gull. The gull seemed to know it was being cared for. It had stopped squawking when Mama immobilized his broken wing. It was bright and beautiful outside, with a soft breeze. The trees gave some needed shade to the patio.

"You're going to be just fine," said Katie as she and George petted the gull. Katie brought some food for the gull and George brought some water. They were happy to see the gull eating. They arranged the box so the gull was safe, putting a heavy grill over the box and anchoring it with four stones so a cat couldn't get him.

"What can we do about it?" Katie asked.

"About what?" said Mama.

"About the animals getting all entangled and the gyres."

Papa and Mama looked at her and then at each other.

"You know, Katie, you and George are terrific about not trashing our world, and your Papa and I shop carefully, but I think it's time to think more and do more and spread the word. Our Earth, our ocean, is in trouble."

"I want to help," said George.

"Great," Mama smiled. "I think not being a litterbug is important and our family never uses Styrofoam which is full of toxins, but it's time to do much more than that. We need to not buy things that harm the Earth. What's creating the gyres in the ocean is plastic. Some of them are thousands of miles by thousands of miles — it's like toxic plastic soup! The North Pacific Gyre is twice the size of the United States."

"How about we don't buy plastic?" asked George.

"Well, not buying any plastic is not practical," said Mama slowly. "A lot of things are made of hard plastic, like computer keyboards, games and certain car parts. We can recycle those things when they get old — and buy fewer things. It's mostly the one-use disposal plastic that is the problem. So not buying that is a great idea. If we really try we could probably cut buying one-use disposable plastic things by at least 90%."

"Do you mean like plastic cups, plastic straws, plastic bags and water in plastic bottles?" asked Katie.

"Exactly," said Mama.

"That's going to be a little hard," said George. "Does that mean no sodas in plastic bottles?"

"Yes. Can you do that?" asked Papa with a questioning look.

George winched. "Maybe for the gulls and the seals and the dolphins I could."

"And we could bring our own cloth shopping bags to the store," said Katie. "We could use a glass bottle or metal bottle when we want to bring water somewhere and we could use it over and over again."

"Terrific idea," said Mama. "And I could shop locally at Farmers Markets and try to not buy food wrapped in plastic. And we can wash our sandwich bags and reuse them, or use waxed paper or banana leaves."

"Your mother and I have been talking about this a lot the last few days," said Papa. "We're going to see if the city council will ban plastic bags and plastic straws. Would you like to come to the city council meeting with us?"

"Maybe some of our friends could come too," said Katie.

"Wow," said George, his face lighting up, "what if everyone did this? Maybe we could stop the gyres growing. Toxic plastic soup does not sound good for animals or the ocean. What do you think Mr. Gull?" he asked, looking at the seagull.

Did the seagull just nod in approval?

Discuss

- Why do you think the father was so upset in the story?

- What are some of his values?
- What ideas did the family come up with to help not create more toxic "plastic soup" in the gyres?
- How could you help to not create more "toxic plastic soup" in the gyres?

Lesson Content

Please share some or all of the following content with students, adapting it to their age and level of understanding.

Source: http://5gyres.org

Just two generation ago, we packaged our products in reusable or recyclable materials — glass, metals, and paper, and designed products that would last. Today, our landfills and beaches are awash in plastic packaging, and expendable products that have no value at the end of their short lifecycle.

The short-term convenience of using and throwing away plastic products carries a very inconvenient long-term truth. These plastic water bottles, cups, utensils, electronics, toys, and gadgets we dispose of daily are rarely recycled in a closed loop. We currently recover only 5% of the plastics we produce. What happens to the rest of it? Roughly 50% is buried in landfills, some is remade into durable goods, and much of it remains "unaccounted for", lost in the environment where it ultimately washes out to sea.

In the ocean, some of . . . plastics . . . and foamed plastics float on the oceans' surface. Sunlight and wave action cause these floating plastics to fragment, breaking into increasingly smaller particles, but never completely disappearing — at least on any documented time scale. This plastic pollution is becoming a hazard for marine wildlife, and ultimately for us.

The North Pacific Gyre, the most heavily researched for plastic pollution, spans an area roughly twice the size of the United States — though it is a fluid system, shifting seasonally in size and shape. Designed to last, plastic trash in the gyre will remain for decades or longer, being pushed gently in a slow, clockwise spiral towards the center. Most of the research on plastic trash circulating in oceanic gyres has focused on the North Pacific, but there are 5 major oceanic gyres worldwide, with several smaller gyres in Alaska and Antarctica.

We must demand zero tolerance for plastic pollution. Reducing our consumption and production of plastic waste, and choosing cost-effective alternatives will go a long way towards protecting our seas — and ultimately ourselves.

Activities

Eight to Eleven Activity: Show the students pictures of the gyres. There are many websites on this subject. Ask the students what messages the marine mammals and birds might wish to give to human beings. Divide them into small groups and have them create a poster with their message. They may wish to role play being the animal and giving the message.

Twelve to Fourteen Activity: Show the students pictures of the gyres. There are many websites on this subject. If there is time, allow the students to divide into small groups to further research this topic, such as the effects of Styrofoam and how plastic particles in the ocean "act as sponges for waterborne contaminants such as PCBs, DDT and other pesticides, PAHs and many hydrocarbons washed through our watersheds." (Same source as cited above.) Then allow the students to create posters with their message.

Sending Peace to the Earth Relaxation/Focusing Exercise

Say, "Please sit comfortably and let yourself be still inside. . . . Relax the body and breathe in the light of peace. . . . Let the light of peace surround you . . . . Breathe out any tension . . . and breathe in the light of peace. . . . Breathe out any tension . . . and breathe in the light of peace. . . . This peace is quiet and safe . . . it reminds me that I am peaceful inside. . . . Let yourself be very still and think . . . I am me . . . I am naturally full of peace and love. . . . Let your body relax even more . . . and now focus on feeling peaceful. . . . As you feel peaceful that peace will naturally go outward to nature . . . to the dolphins and the whales . . . to the birds . . . to the animals large and small. . . . I let myself be full of peace . . . and that peace naturally goes outward to the Earth . . . to the rivers and ocean . . . to the trees and the meadows . . . to the mountains and the sky. . . . I am full of peace. . . . I am one who is acting to help our Earth be healthy again. . . . This will happen in time. . . . Our planet will be well. . . . I picture the light of peace all around the Earth . . . and our beautiful oceans being healthy again . . . our beautiful Earth being healthy again. . . . Feeling relaxed and peaceful . . . now begin to be aware of where you are sitting and bring your attention back to this room."

**SIMPLICITY AND CARING
FOR THE EARTH AND HER OCEANS LESSON 8**

The Ocean's Dead Zones

Living Values Education Activities for Children Ages 8–14, Book 1

Begin with a song with lyrics about nature.

Please read Chapter Four of the *Green Values Club* below.

Share a Story: We Can Make a Difference

Katie talked to some of her friends at school on Monday. They were amazed to hear about the whale, felt sorry for the little gull, and totally didn't know about the gyres.

"Why don't you talk to the teacher?" asked Carol. "Let's see if she'll let you tell the class about the gyres and the poor animals that die because they eat plastic. Maybe we can all get involved in helping."

"You really think everyone will want to?" asked Katie.

"Well maybe not everyone," said Kinesha, "but kids our age have really good hearts. We care about our planet — and our animal friends."

The girls talked to their science teacher at break and she was delighted. "Great," Ms. Bennett said, "we're starting our unit on the environment today. Katie, it would be great to have you share your story, and then let's see what ideas everyone comes up with. Learning about things is good, but doing something for our Earth is proof that we care."

Katie shared her story about the whale, the seagull and learning about the gyres with the whole class. She was a little nervous, and kept clearing her throat. She shared the ideas she and her family had come up with about reducing their use of one-use disposal plastic by 90 percent. Katie was amazed at the interest and the willingness of most of the students to commit to using less plastic.

"No more plastic bottles for me," offered Dana.

"My aunt brings her own cup when she travels on planes," offered Ta.

"No more plastic cups or straws when I'm out," said Maria, "I can ask for a real cup or bring my own."

"Great ideas," said Todd. "If it's going to help, I'm willing to not buy plastic bottles of stuff. But, what if it's really, really hot and I really want a soda? What if I buy it in a can?"

"Well, using an aluminum can is taking something you don't need from the Earth," said Ms. Bennett, "but IF you recycle it's not so bad. It's much better than using plastic."

"Well, I don't know," said a girl named Pam in a doubting voice, "why should we even try? If just a few of us do this, it's not going to help. We can't affect thousands of square miles of toxic plastic soup."

"Think of the one whale and the one seagull," said Katie, all of the sudden feeling confident. "It was a small group of people that made a difference for them. Small groups of people can make a difference — and imagine what would happen if kids all over the world did this. Some adults are really into this already. What if all the kids got all their parents to help?"

Katie shared her parents' idea about going to city council to ask for a ban on using plastic bags and plastic straws in the city. "I asked if I could invite some friends to go with us. Would anyone like to help?"

"Me," "me," "me" was heard all around the room. Katie, Carol and Kinesha beamed at everyone and Ms. Bennett looked pleased.

Ms. Bennett divided them into three action groups on Friday. One group was going to make posters to support the ban on plastic bags and straws and another group was going to make up banners with slogans on respect for the ocean and the Earth by reducing the use of disposable plastic. The third group was going to create a petition to the superintendent to ban all Styrofoam and reduce the use of plastic.

Katie told Ms. Bennett that the city council meeting was going to be on Tuesday night and they were on the agenda. And Ms. Bennett told the whole class. "Everyone, if you want to go, you'll need to have an adult with you as it is not a school event."

"I'd love to go with you, Katie, to the city council meeting," said one of the girls shyly. Tanya rarely spoke to anyone and usually looked a little sad, "but I have to go home right after school and then I can't leave. My Mom is … sick."

Katie looked at Tanya carefully. Interesting, she had never noticed before but Tanya's eyes were the same as George's friend Tom and her hair was the same color and texture, a soft, thin brown. "Tanya, are you Tom's big sister?" she asked.

"Yes, I am," Tanya softly. "Do you know Tom? I hope he behaved himself around you," she said, looking worried.

"He's a good lad," said Katie. "He was one of the boys who helped George and me with the gull."

"I'm glad," said Tanya with a little smile. "He could use a good experience."

Katie had a feeling that Tanya could use a good experience, too.

George didn't talk to his teacher, but he did talk to Tom, Hank and Kevin, his friends that had helped capture the seagull. They were amazed about the huge areas of toxic plastic soup in the ocean and appalled that so many animals were getting hurt.

"I want to help," Tom said.

"Me, too," said Hank and Kevin.

"Terrific," said George. "I have an idea."

George and Katie talked on the way home. Katie told all him all about Ms. Bennett's science class on the environment.

"She told us," said Katie, "that there are dead zones in the ocean where there is little or no oxygen due to fertilizer-run-off and nitrogen pollution. She said that there are 405 reported dead zones and that they are doubling every ten years!"

"That's terrible," said George. "So what happens in these dead zones?" asked George. "There isn't enough oxygen for most fish to live?"

"Good thinking," said Katie. "Unfortunately, the fertilizer-run-off and nitrogen pollution and pesticides kill the kelp. She showed us some pictures of these really cool kelp forests. They are so beautiful. The kelp forests provide food and shelter to thousands of species — and 50 percent of the world's oxygen! Ms. Bennett said it's just as important to keep the kelp forests healthy as it is to keep the rain forests healthy!"

"So how do we stop the fertilizer-run-off and nitrogen pollution?" asked George.

"George, that's a really great question, and we didn't ask it," said Katie. "Let's ask Mama and Papa when we get home."

Katie's mind flashed back. What had Ms. Bennett said?

"The chemical fertilizers and pesticides pollute the rivers and ocean," Ms. Bennett had said. "Unfortunately, this can also impact the ground water and negatively affect the quality of the soil. Food grown with pesticides has been shown to have harmful effects on humans, contributing to many different kinds of disease."

Ms. Bennett had assigned different groups to research specific components of fertilizers and pesticides. Tanya was part of the group Katie was in. "Wow," Tanya had whispered to Katie, "no wonder we have dead zones in the ocean! Gyres and dead zones. We humans are not taking good care of our world."

Ms. Bennett had overheard, "You're right, Tanya," she smiled. "It's important to take care of our world." Tanya blushed at the positive attention.

Ms. Bennett continued, "I want each of you to really think over the weekend — and the next couple of months — about what one thing you can do that would have the most beneficial effect on the Earth and Ocean. What would happen if everyone on the planet did the same thing?"

Discuss

- Would anyone like to share their reaction to the story?
- What actions did the three groups take in the story?
- What do you think you can do to help solve this problem of plastic pollution that contributes to the gyres?

- Do you know any place that uses Styrofoam?
- Would you like to help encourage them to stop using it?
- How can you do that?

Lesson Content

Source: The following excerpts were taken from the website of One World One Ocean. http://www.oneworldoneocean.org/pages/why-the-ocean

The ocean is in trouble
90% of the big fish are gone. Tuna, swordfish, halibut, cod, and flounder populations have been devastated by overfishing. Many of the fish caught today never even have the chance to reproduce.

Discarded plastic bags and other trash have formed **a toxic "plastic soup"** that is gathering in five massive ocean gyres around the world. As the plastic breaks down, it is eaten by sea animals, birds, and fish, causing illness and death. It eventually enters our diets, too.

There are a reported 405 ocean **"dead zones"** — areas where there is little to no oxygen due to fertilizer run-off and nitrogen pollution. Dead zones are doubling every ten years.

Our oceans account for 71% of the planet, but **less than 2%** of our oceans are protected. We have protections in place for nearly 12% of all land (through areas like national parks).

The ocean is at a tipping point. Oceanographer Sylvia Earle says human actions over the next 10 years will determine the state of the ocean for the next 10,000 years.

Activities

As a whole group, ask the students to decide on two, three or four actions that they could implement locally that would help the environment. Help them decide on actions that are practical, sensible and appropriate to their age and skill level — so that they are likely to succeed in fulfilling those actions. A few of the actions could be implemented in the classroom. For example, ask them to think of ideas or ways to conserve in the classroom such as setting up a recycling bin, using paper on both sides, and saving magazines and little sticks to be used for art projects. At the school level, they could generate ideas about how to be careful about not wasting water, pick up litter or plant trees and bushes. They could research environmental concerns to do with the school. They could question whether we are polluting or wasting our water. For instance, if the grass is being watered in the afternoon, they could ask the school principal to change the watering schedule from the afternoon to the morning to conserve water.

Thirteen to Fourteen Activity: In addition to the above activity, you may wish them to further research their action. For example, if they decide to ask the school/school district or city to ban the use of Styrofoam, they may wish to know more about the negative effects on the environment and human health.

Close with a relaxation/focusing exercise.

SIMPLICITY AND CARING
FOR THE EARTH AND HER OCEANS LESSON 9
One Thing Effects Many Things — Systems Thinking

Begin with a song with lyrics about nature. Ask how they are and if they have been thinking about the last lesson. Allow them time to share their thoughts and any related actions. How is it going with your class conservation efforts? Listen and acknowledge.

Please read Chapter Five of the *Green Values Club* below.

Share a Story: To the City Council!

School was fun, but it was nice to get home. At dinner time, Katie shared what Ms. Bennett said about the dead zones in the ocean as they sat around the kitchen table. The sunlight was still softly lighting the trees and flowers outside. Birds were chirping their last calls of the day and flying through the skies as they did every night at dusk. Katie took another bite of corn bread.

Papa nodded. "Yes, Katie, all of this is connected. What we do as human beings ripples out with all kinds of consequences for the world. One thing affects something else and sometimes many things, and each one of those things affects other things and those things affect something else. The artificial fertilizers and pesticides affect the soil, the plants that grow and add pollutants to the water. Those are like small amounts of poison."

"If we just take the effect on the water, then we could look at the effect on health of humans, the need for water purification systems and the effect of the run-off that your teacher described when it goes down rivers and into the ocean. In some rivers the fish are dying off and mutating as a result of the pesticides. When rivers with a lot of artificial fertilizers and pesticides go into the ocean, it kills kelp, coral and fish. When the kelp dies off in those areas there is not enough food and oxygen for many fish to live. Added to that, the kelp is affected by overfishing as the kelp needs the waste products of fish to live. One thing affects another thing."

"As human beings in this age," said Mama, "we are just beginning to learn that we have to look and see the effects of something before we act. It is called systems thinking now. But native cultures understood it well hundreds of years ago. They would say, think ahead for seven generations."

"George thought of a question I wish I'd asked Ms. Bennett," said Katie. "George?"

"So how do we stop the fertilizer-run-off and nitrogen pollution?"

Mama smiled, "Stop using artificial fertilizers and pesticides."

"Go organic?" asked Katie.

"Yes," said Mama. "It takes work because the soil needs to be made healthy again, and crops need to be rotated, but it would sure help our Earth and its oceans immensely, and all of us humans and animals!"

"Wow," laughed Katie. "Maybe you just gave me my homework answer!" She told them about Ms. Bennett's homework assignment.

Papa laughed. "That's a great homework assignment. "Shall we all think about that one?"

"It's good we're having this discussion," said Mama. "I buy organic vegetables when it isn't so expensive because I know it's better for us, but I never thought about how it is much better for the earth and the ocean."

"Mama, Papa, could we have a little organic garden?" asked Katie.

Papa looked at Katie with a little frown. "It's a great idea, Katie, but it would take some work. You know your Mama and I both spend a lot of time working and your Mama already has enough to do."

"I could help," said George.

Katie flashed him a smile.

"Are you sure?" asked Papa with a little frown.

George nodded seriously.

"Consistently?"

Both George and Katie nodded.

"Okay," laughed Papa. "I'll help too. I'll help with the first deep dig."

"Yea!" chorused George and Katie.

"I had an idea," said George. "You know how our family and our friends at school are promising to cut our disposable plastic use by 90 percent? Well, that helps stop the gyres from growing, but what about all the plastic trash now? Shouldn't we be picking that up and recycling it so it doesn't go into the ocean?"

Katie gave George a tap on his shoulder. "You're totally cool for a nine-year old."

"Smart, I'd say," smiled Papa.

Papa said he wouldn't have time to dig for a couple of weeks. The gull was doing quite well in his new home and getting stronger. Mama said he would be ready for a test flight in a week. He was getting fatter and healthier looking, much to Katie's and George's relief. They had named him Captain.

On Tuesday night, the family went to the city council meeting. Katie and George were really pleased to see so many of their friends and classmates. Even Ms. Bennett came. They all gathered outside with their posters, greeting each other and introducing their parents.

There weren't enough seats for them all in the city council chamber, so some stood at the back, holding their posters so the council members could see them. When their turn to speak came, Mama stood at the microphone and asked the city council members to approve a ban on plastic bags being offered to customers at stores in their city and plastic straws in restaurants. She suggested paper bags be offered instead or that people bring their own bags to carry away their purchases. She suggested uncooked pasta noodles as a substitute for plastic straws if restaurants wanted to provide them. She spoke about gyres and how it was important for the health of marine animals, our ocean and humans to stop the toxic plastic waste.

When Mama finished, all the students and their parents applauded. The city council president looked around the room and said, "It looks like this suggestion has a lot of support — and it would certainly be good for our Earth. Would any of you young people like to speak?"

Carol and Kinesha looked at Katie, and Katie shook her head no. All of the sudden, Katie saw Tanya out of the corner of her eye with a woman who looked too old and frail to be her mother, and then there was Tom stepping up to the microphone.

"I think George's and Katie's mother is right," said Tom hesitantly. Then in one long breathe he said a bit louder, "There was a seagull the other day down at the beach that had an old plastic bag around it that must have been there for a long, long time and he was really hurt and we have to think about the ocean and the gyres or whatever they are called and the animals that get hurt and the Earth and stop being so selfish."

Everyone applauded. They clapped again when all the members of the city council voted for the ban on plastic bags and plastic straws.

Tanya gave a radiant smile to Katie before quietly slipping out with her mother and Tom.

Discuss/Explore

- What good ideas did the people in the story have?
- What do you learn from the story?
- What values do you think Tom used in the story?
- What other values did you see?
- What effect did those values have in the story?
- What effect would they have for us in our current environment?

Activity

Ask the students to make a flow chart of the effects described in one of the paragraphs of the story. (The paragraph from the story is below.) If needed, model how to do that, placing the word "water" at the highest point on the whiteboard, drawing three downward arrows, and then continuing to show how one thing affects other things.

"If we just take the effect on the water, then we could look at the effect on health of humans, the need for water purification systems and the effect of the run-off that your teacher described when it goes down rivers and into the ocean. In some rivers the fish are dying off and mutating as a result of the pesticides. When rivers with a lot of artificial fertilizers and pesticides go into the ocean, it kills kelp, coral and fish. When the kelp dies off in those areas there is not enough food and oxygen for many fish to live. Added to that, the kelp is affected by overfishing as the kelp needs the waste products of fish to live. One thing affects another thing."

Ask the students, and help them as necessary, to add other factors to the flow chart. For example, some fish dying off results in less fish for consumers and less recreational fishing; it may also result in poorer health for those who eat sick fish. Where does "dead zones" go in the flow chart?

Now do two more flow charts, one for "Using Pesticides" and another for "Organic Farming".

Eight to Eleven Activity: Ask the students to write a poem or a song about any one of the topics in the story. Invite those who wish to do so to share their poem or song with the class. Perhaps choose one to recite or sing together.

Twelve to Fourteen: Invite students to form small groups and investigate the effects of using pesticides versus organic farming and list all the factors that are affected. Then ask them to create a large mind map, with pesticides on one side and organic on the other of the central circle. Use the same topic branches on each side and detail out all the effects, using the flow chart effect on the branches and sub-branches to show how one change affects many things. Invite them to illustrate the mind map or create a song or poem contrasting the approaches.

Close with the Sending Peace to the Earth Relaxation/Focusing Exercise.

**SIMPLICITY AND CARING
FOR THE EARTH AND HER OCEANS LESSON 10**

The Exchange Between Trees and Humans

Begin with a song with lyrics about nature.
Please read Chapter Six of the *Green Values Club* below.

Share a Story: Trees, Oxygen and Hope

Katie felt wonderful the next morning when she awoke. It was gray and overcast with a bit of wetness in the air. She slipped outside to feed the gull. "Did you hear, Captain?" she said softly, "The city banned plastic bags and straws and we're all going to work together to try and make our oceans and beaches safe again so you and your friends can be healthy and free. We're going to have our first beach clean-up on Saturday."

The gull seemed to like her pats now. "And, you get to fly again on Saturday — in only four days! Mama said your wing is almost healed."

In science class they were now studying about the rain forest, deforestation, the interchange of oxygen and carbon dioxide between plants and humans.

"So, what can we do to help?" asked Todd.

"Well, if humans need the oxygen to breathe, and trees and plants produce that and process the carbon dioxide we exhale, what do you think would help compensate for the deforestation?" asked Ms. Bennett.

"Plant plants?" said Todd.

"Good thinking. And what are durable, long lasting plants?" asked Ms. Bennett.

"Trees!" said Todd, with a few echoes from around the room.

Living Values Education Activities for Children Ages 8–14, Book 1

"Great," smiled Ms. Bennett. "Actually, the United Nations Environmental Protection agency has a project asking people to plant one tree per person to help offset our carbon footprint. There was a one billion tree project in China and they achieved their goal of planting one billion trees. Green helps!"

"Speaking of green," she said, "Katie asked me if she could make an announcement just before the end of class."

Katie stood up in front of the class with Carol and Kinesha. "I've been talking with my family and Carol and Kinesha. My little brother wants to have a beach clean-up on Saturday. We could do it in the morning and play volleyball afterwards. Anyone interested?"

"Sounds great," "Sounds good." "Count me in," sprang from all corners of the room.

Katie, Carol and Kinesha beamed. "Terrific!"

"Ms. Bennett said maybe we could even do it as a school project," said Carol. "What do you think about calling it Seagulls?

"What about the river that comes down into the cove?" asked Pierce. "Don't we want to clean that up too?"

"Yeah, maybe we need a name that would mean more to more people," said Megan. "Clean water?"

"How about Green Values Club?" suggested a small voice from the back of the room. Katie was surprised to hear Tanya speak up in class. Everyone else must have been surprised too because they all turned to look. Tanya blushed.

"Great idea," said Todd, looking at Tanya.

"Yeah, terrific idea," said Dana.

Katie smiled, and Carol and Kinesha looked pleased. "Everyone in agreement?" asked Katie.

Even Pam nodded yes.

The day of the Green Values Club beach and river clean-up was sunny and bright. A few parents and whole families joined them. Half of the helpers picked up plastic and other things they could recycle, and the other half picked up trash that could not be recycled. The bags got a little heavy, but Papa and a few other parents would meet them, take the full bags and give them empty ones. Papa had arranged with the city to pick up all the trash bags later.

Some of the kids met at the beach and others who lived closer to the river walked down the river while picking up trash and met them for volleyball at 11:00. The older kids played volleyball and George and his friends went body surfing.

Katie was feeling hot and sweaty after an hour of picking up trash when she heard her name being called. She was surprised to see Tanya running toward her.

"Hi, Katie, hi Carol and Kinesha, I got to come! I haven't been to the beach in years!"

As Carol and Kinesha went ahead, Katie waited for Tanya to catch up.

"Why haven't you been to the beach in so long?" asked Katie.

"Well," said Tanya, reaching down to pick up some trash, and turning a little away from Katie as she spoke in one long sentence, "the short story is my Dad got into drugs about four years ago, and got really mean, and then got killed in a fight two years ago, and my Mom got really depressed and started taking drugs too and so I had to be at home all the time with her because she won't let me go anywhere and was crying all the time, only Tom could go anywhere cause she couldn't handle him and he would just leave, and now with what we are doing with green values it's like she has hope and I told her about your organic garden you want to make and she used to live on a farm when she was little and loved to garden and when she went to college she was a botanist and she said that if we kids could do something for the world then she had better start getting her own act together and so she stopped the drugs and is in rehab and said I could come this morning and said if you want her to help she would be honored to help you with your garden because she was going to be okay again."

Tanya was still looking down.

Katie reached out and squeezed Tanya's hand. "I'm so glad you told me. . . . I would like your Mom to help me with the organic garden. Would you and Tom like to help too?"

Tanya looked up. "Love to," was all she could say.

Tom, Hank and Kevin came home with George after the beach and river clean-up to watch Captain being released.

"Do you think he's ready, Mama?" asked George.

"Let's see," smiled Mama.

"We'll leave the box out with food and water for a couple days just in case he's not strong enough to go far," said Papa.

The boys lifted the stones and grill off the box. Katie lifted him out and put him on the railing of the patio and Mama carefully took off the gauze tape holding the one wing. "Okay, Captain," she said, "you're free."

Captain looked at her, flapped his wings a few times and took off.

Shouts of "Look at him go!" and "Go, Captain!" filled the air as the gull flew into the blue sky.

Discuss

- What feelings did you notice in the story?
- What values did you notice in the different people in the story?
- It sounded like Tanya's mother was very sad and had lost hope. Knowing that the young people were working to help do something positive for the environment gave her hope in the story. What is the feeling of hope? Do you think it increases our feelings of courage?
- Most of us have felt discouraged? What helps us feel encouraged again?
- Who remembers what we humans exhale?
- What do the trees and plants do with that carbon dioxide?
- Would you like our environment around here to be "greener"? (If the answer is "yes", ask, "How do you think we could make that happen?")

Activity

Explain more about the interchange of oxygen and carbon dioxide between plants and humans, how human beings breathe in oxygen and breathe out carbon dioxide and how plants take in the carbon dioxide and create oxygen. (For older students, allow them to research this if there is time and they do not yet have this knowledge.)

Then say, "The relationship between human beings and nature is very important. Our life depends on the creation of oxygen from nature and we also benefit so much from the beauty of nature."

Do something with nature today, perhaps planting a tree or planning to plant one, or taking a walk in a park and writing a poem to a tree or having a tree write you a poem. What would the trees of the world say? Allow those who wish to share a poem from a tree to do so.

Or, ask them to generate ideas for the home or the community. If litter or waste is affecting the clean water supply, address that issue. Perhaps plan to help clean up a local river. Some students may want to research local usage of pesticides and natural (and less expensive) alternatives which do not pollute the earth or its inhabitants. They could write to their local Mayor sharing their ideas. They could make up respect-for-the-earth slogans and post them at school and at sports-game locales in the community. Allow them time to plan and/or write the necessary letters/proposals.

Living Values Education Activities for Children Ages 8-14, Book 1

End with a relaxation/focusing exercise of their choice or a song or two about the beauty of the Earth or ocean.

SIMPLICITY AND CARING
FOR THE EARTH AND HER OCEANS LESSON 11

Growing Organic and Being Vegetarian Effects the Earth and Ocean

Begin with a song with lyrics about nature.
Please read Chapter Seven of the *Green Values Club* below.

Share a Story: An Organic Garden

"A perfect day to dig," joked Papa the next weekend as they sat and ate breakfast at the kitchen table. "You kids sure do have us working!"

"Papa, I wanted to ask if we could do a beach clean up every week," said George.

"And never relax another weekend in my life?" Papa joked. He looked at George's disappointed face.

"George, the clean-up is a great idea and I know you're enthusiastic," Papa said more seriously, "but I would suggest once a month. You and everyone else can always pick up trash whenever you see it — but there are other things to do in life so you might get more people if you do it once a month. That way you can keep the enthusiasm high."

George nodded.

"What do you think, Lisa?" Papa asked.

"Well said! It's nice to relax and rest occasionally, you two!" Mama smiled at both George and Katie. "But, I was thinking it would be nice to have a picnic on the beach the next time we do a clean-up."

George gave her a wide grin, "Could we?"

A few days earlier, Katie had asked if Tom, Tanya and Tanya's mother could come and help in the garden. The three of them came over after breakfast. They arrived a little shyly, quietly knocking on the front door and saying very little. Tom hung back, unlike his usual boisterous self. Katie noticed how pale their mother looked. But, she had a pretty smile and was soon digging with Papa and Katie, George, Tanya and Tom.

It was a beautiful morning outside. The sun was slanting down, creating pools of light on the greens, blues, yellows and pinks. The earth smelled good as they dug.

"I've been missing the earth," Tanya's mom said when she finally spoke. "We live in a little apartment so it's really nice to be here and feel the soil. This looks really healthy — and you have great worms."

She had brought some seeds and small vegetable plants with her and soon they were all chatting and planting the seeds and plants in the fresh new rows of earth. Tanya's mom told them in which direction to make the rows so the plants would get maximum sun, and showed them how deep to plant the seeds and plants.

It took a long time to dig and make the rows, so Mama invited them for lunch. The little family of three looked happy as they left.

When they were leaving, Tanya hung back to whisper to Katie, "Thank you, thank you, thank you."

Katie had told Mama and Papa what Tanya had told her about her mom.

"How sad," Mama said. Papa had nodded.

"Why would she take drugs when she didn't like her husband taking drugs?" asked Katie.

"Well, it sounds like things were really rough," said Mama. "Sometimes people take drugs because they have emotions they can't deal with, like hurt or fear. When so many bad things happen, life can feel overwhelming. I'm glad you welcomed them to come and help in the garden," said Mama. "People need to have hope and something valuable to do."

"Aristotle used to say that happiness is a result of virtue. Doing something good will help her be happy again," said Papa.

Later in the weekend, Katie announced at dinner, "I've decided on my answer to Ms. Bennett's homework question about one thing we can do that will most benefit the planet."

"What's that?" asked Mama.

"Be a vegetarian that eats organic food," said Katie.

"How would that help?" asked George looking puzzled.

"Well," said Katie enthusiastically, "if everyone was a vegetarian then people wouldn't fish and we wouldn't be overfishing and killing millions of fish, and if we all ate organic food then we wouldn't be poisoning the ocean and creating dead zones and the oceans would have healthy kelp forests and enough oxygen for a healthy ocean and enough fish again for the whales and the whales and dolphins wouldn't be getting trapped in nets because no one would be using nets!"

"You've really been thinking about this," said Papa, looking a little surprised.

"And," said Katie with a big smile, "that's not all. If everyone was a vegetarian, then we wouldn't be deforesting the Amazon because of the production of cattle and the demand for meat and the output of greenhouse gasses would be less so the whole planet would be healthier."

"Good reasoning," said Mama.

"But you're not really going to do it are you?" asked George.

"Do what?" asked Katie.

"Be a vegetarian."

"Well," said Katie, with a pause and a pleading look at her parents, "I was thinking that maybe I can't be a vegetarian that eats *only* organic food, but I could be a vegetarian that eats as much organic food as we can get." She took a deep breath as she looked at Mama and Papa. "I would really like to try it. Can I please? I really do think it would help our planet."

Mama looked at Katie, and then at Papa. "Luke?"

Papa looked at Mama. "It's okay with me. She has some great reasons. Is it okay with you?"

"Oh Katie," Mama said with a tiny worried look. "You would have to promise me that you would eat healthy."

"The World Health Organization says it's the healthiest diet for human beings," said Katie.

"*If* you eat healthy," said Mama firmly. "Promise?"

"Yes."

"Okay. Then it is okay with me," Mama said.

Katie sprang up and gave Mama and then Papa a big hug.

"I am proud that you've really thought about it and want to help our planet," said Mama.

"Is it okay if I'm a vegetarian with her for two months and see if it works for me?" Papa asked Mama with a quizzical look.

Mama just laughed as she looked at her husband. Then she looked at her son with a questioning look. "George?"

"Not me," cringed George. "It wasn't my homework!"

"Okay," laughed Mama. "Two veggies and two non-veggies. But if you two don't eat healthy, I'm changing my mind!"

Discuss

- What values did the people in the story show?

- Aristotle, a famous philosopher from the time of the ancient Greeks, said that happiness is a result of virtue. What does that mean?
- I want you all to remember a time when you were especially kind. How did you feel afterwards?
- If you had a little garden, what would you plant?

Activity

Eight to Twelve Activity: Work on the environmental project that the class has undertaken.

Thirteen to Fourteen Activity: Invite students to divide into three groups and study the following. Group One, the deforesting of the Amazon; Group Two, the impact of the production of cattle, chickens and other animals in response to the demand for meat and the relationship of this to the output of greenhouse gasses; and Group Three, the effect of greenhouse gases on the climate and global change. Allow each group to share their findings and understand the relationship of each to the information of the other two groups.

Close with the Sending Peace to the Earth Relaxation/Focusing exercise.

SIMPLICITY AND CARING
FOR THE EARTH AND HER OCEANS LESSON 12
Reducing Our Carbon Footprint

Begin with a song with lyrics about nature.

Vocabulary word: Please share with students the meaning of carbon footprint. To reduce your carbon footprint means that you are reducing your negative effect on the Earth.

> Your carbon footprint is the sum of all emissions of CO_2 (carbon dioxide), which were induced by your activities in a given time frame. Usually a carbon footprint is calculated for the time period of a year.
> (Source: http://timeforchange.org/what-is-a-carbon-footprint-definition)

Say, "To reduce your carbon footprint means that you are reducing your negative effect on the Earth."

Please read Chapter Eight of the *Green Values Club* below.

Share a Story: Carbon Footprints

"It's sort of like anything," laughed Papa, "it's easy *after* you figure it out!" It was early Monday morning and he and Katie and Mama were laughing as they ate breakfast and talked about what to pack for their Papa's and Katie's vegetarian lunch. They usually had fruit and oatmeal for breakfast, so breakfast was easy.

Katie and George went out after breakfast to water their organic vegetable garden before school.

"Look, these little plants over here must have grown a whole inch since Saturday!" said George. They were delighted with their garden.

But it was a bit of a rough day for Katie at school. She didn't have the usual lunch at school because it had meat in it and a couple of kids gave her a hard time when she told them she was going vegetarian.

"Oh, leave her alone," said Kinesha after one of the students said, "What are you going to eat when we have a barbeque, a carrot?"

"They act like there's nothing to eat if you're a vegetarian," said Katie, swallowing a lump in her throat.

"Just stay in self-respect," said Carol. "Some people get upset with others sometimes when someone does something they feel they should do but don't have the strength to do."

"It's not like I'm saying I'm better than them," said Katie forlornly. "I respect their choices. I don't make fun of them."

"And that's one of the reasons you're so wonderful, Katie," said Carol. "You really do respect everyone."

It was a relief to be in science class as all the students were part of the Green Values Club and supported whatever anyone was doing to help the environment, even Pam. When she heard from a friend that Katie was going to be a vegetarian, she smiled at Katie and said, "You have more determination than I do. Good for you."

Katie was surprised. "Thanks, Pam."

Ms. Bennett taught a class on greenhouse gases and the effect on global change. She explained more about the gases released by using cars, planes and buses as well as the raising and slaughtering of pigs, cows, sheep, turkeys and chickens.

"I saw a commercial when I went to Denmark," offered Megan. "It showed a man who was a vegetarian driving a large car and another man on a bicycle who was not a vegetarian and asked which one had a bigger carbon footprint. The surprise answer was the vegetarian driving the big car had less of a carbon footprint! I had no idea being

Living Values Education Activities for Children Ages 8–14, Book 1

vegetarian could help so much."

Kinesha and Carol looked at Katie and smiled.

At the end of class they spent time talking about how to reduce their use of electricity and gas. There were the usual things like turning down the heat and wearing a sweater when it's cool, turning up the thermostat and taking off the sweater when it's hot, and bicycling and walking more when possible. Ms. Bennett also introduced them to alternative green technology.

"Solar power is really advancing," she said, "and becoming more affordable. Some schools are converting to solar power for their electricity, and some of the electricity-recharging stations for the electric-powered cars are being powered by solar power — so there are no emissions at all."

The students had a great time researching the subject and were delighted to find a new technology that could convert disposable plastic back into petroleum. "The challenge of course," said Ms. Bennett, "is making that sort of thing widely available. It'll be wonderful to see all the things that are invented in the next decade to help."

One day they discussed reducing their consumption of "things" and the importance of considering what you are taking from the Earth when purchasing. "Not something most teenagers want to hear," smiled Ms. Bennett.

The next couple of months were great. Tanya, Tom and their mother, Nancy, were coming over once a week to help with the vegetable garden. Their mother was looking less pale and much stronger. She was teaching Katie and George about composting. And they had beach and river clean-ups every month, with volleyball and swimming afterwards — and picnics every other time. George was so pleased. More kids and their families were getting involved and picking up trash whenever they saw it and the beaches and rivers were much cleaner.

"Class," said Ms. Bennett one day, "three months ago I asked you to think about what one thing you could do that would have the most beneficial effect on the Earth and ocean — and what would happen if everyone on the planet did it? Your project will be due next week. On Wednesday, one-third of you will be able to present your proposal, with another one-third of you on Thursday and the last third on Friday. You can mind-map your ideas or present your ideas on poster board. Those of you who wish to give a PowerPoint presentation for your three to five-minute talk may do so, but you will also need to create a poster. The following week I will ask those with similar ideas to get together in groups and create songs, poems or skits/dramas. We will end the semester with those. So, ladies and gentlemen, begin creating!"

Living Values Education Activities for Children Ages 8–14, Book 1

Discuss

- How do you think Katie felt when someone made fun of her being a vegetarian?
- How do you feel when others make fun of you or a friend of yours?
- What anti-value are they using?
- What value could they use instead?
- Does anyone have any questions about the story?
- Have you thought about the homework that Ms. Bennett gave to Katie's class? What is one thing you can do that will help our Earth and the ocean — and what would the effects be if everyone in the world did that? (Accept as many answers as they wish to give and list them on a piece of flipchart paper and save the list for the next Living Green Values lesson.)

Lesson Content

Please share the following as it explains more about what a carbon footprint means and what kinds of human activities cause the release of carbon dioxide — in addition to breathing! Please simplify the language for young students.

Source: http://timeforchange.org/what-is-a-carbon-footprint-definition

The total amount of greenhouse gases produced to directly and indirectly support human activities, usually expressed in equivalent tons of carbon dioxide (CO_2).

In other words: When you drive a car, the engine burns fuel which creates a certain amount of CO_2, depending on its fuel consumption and the driving distance. (CO_2 is the chemical symbol for carbon dioxide.) When you heat your house with oil, gas or coal, then you also generate CO_2. Even if you heat your house with electricity, the generation of the electrical power may also have emitted a certain amount of CO_2. When you buy food and goods, the production of the food and goods also emitted some quantities of CO_2.

Human-Related source of Carbon Dioxide

Source: http://www.epa.gov/climatechange/emissions/co2_human.html

A variety of human activities lead to the emission and removal of carbon dioxide (CO_2):

- The largest source of CO_2 emissions globally is the <u>combustion of fossil fuels</u> such as coal, oil and gas in power plants, automobiles, industrial facilities and other sources.

- A number of specialized <u>industrial production processes and product uses</u> such as mineral production, metal production and the use of petroleum-based products can also lead to CO2 emissions.
- <u>Carbon sequestration</u> is the process by which growing trees and plants absorb or remove CO2 from the atmosphere and turn it into biomass (e.g., wood, leaves, etc.). Deforestation, conversely, can lead to significant levels of CO2 emissions in some countries.

On the One World One Ocean website they suggested that people do four things to help the Earth and ocean.
- Use less electricity
- Use less gas
- Offset your carbon footprint
- Lower your food miles

Discuss

Say, "Please tell me what reducing your carbon footprint means." (Help them understand if they are still not clear about the concept.)

Ask:
- How can you use less electricity?
- What if the electricity is solar powered — would that be better for the planet than using electricity made from coal or oil? Why?
- How can we use less gasoline?
- Would walking and bicycling more help reduce your carbon footprint?
- What if you had a car powered by electricity? Why would that be better for the planet?
- What if the electricity in the car was recharged by a station that used solar power? Would that reduce the negative effect on the planet even more?

Offsetting your carbon footprint means doing something "green" to help the planet to negate the effect of the carbon dioxide emissions. So, planting trees would help if you drove a lot and used a lot of gas.

Ask:
- We can all plant trees, and that would "offset" your carbon footprint, but we need to work both ways, doing something beneficial for the Earth and reducing our

carbon footprint. So, how can you reduce your carbon footprint?
- How can you lower your food miles? What do you think that means? (Buy locally-grown food.)
- What else do you think you can do?
- Do you think we can do anything differently in this class that would help?

Activity

Ask the students to draw a large footprint on a piece of paper. Inside the footprint they are to write all the things that contribute to their carbon footprint. Ask them what things they think they can do to reduce their carbon footprint. For example, they can walk or bicycle more or not buy so many material things. They can repair or recycle their toys and other material things. They can also reduce their footprint by planting a tree or ____? Ask them to make another picture with another footprint that is smaller, writing all the things they can do to make that happen.

Close with the Sending Peace to the Earth Relaxation/Focusing exercise.

SIMPLICITY AND CARING
FOR THE EARTH AND HER OCEANS LESSON 13
What's one thing I can do to help the Earth?

Begin with a song with lyrics about nature.
Please read Chapter Nine of the *Green Values Club* below.

Share a Story: Living Green Values

You could feel the excitement of the students in science class on Wednesday. Ms. Bennett had posted a sign-up sheet for the presentations on Monday. Some of the kids wanted to be first and some wanted to be last, so those spots were taken first. Empty spaces were awaiting their posters on the wall.

"I just want to get it over with," Carol had muttered.

Todd had already signed up for the first spot. He gave a very good presentation on the beneficial effects of solar and wind power on the climate. He thought switching from carbon-based energy production to renewable sources would stop the rising temperature of the planet and consequent slow melting of the ice caps and rising sea levels. He showed the system changes it would make, including cleaner air, the savings of not moving entire island-based communities, and the many health benefits, such as less children being affected by lead poisoning near freeways. He ended to applause from the class — and gave his classmates a smile of relief. "Glad it's over!" he said.

Carol was second. She was also a little nervous. "I will start with a song," she said to everyone's surprise. Her clear voice was pretty as she sang . . . and comical as she slowed down dramatically on the last line of each stanza.

> Be friends with each other,
> Be respectful and kind,
> To children and adults and all of humankind,
> Don't forgot the animals on the earth and in the sea,
> Be friends to them all, like you are to me.
> Friends … pick up … their … trash ….
>
> Don't pollute the water,
> Don't waste things please,
> Don't poison the ground,
> the water, sky or trees.
> Pick … up … your trash!
>
> If we can do this,
> Imagine what will occur,
> Kelp forests will blossom,
> And land mines disappear!
> Pick … up … your trash!
>
> Humans are smart,
> But learn to be kind,
> Then we'll all live safely,
> And have a wonderful time.
> Pick … up … your trash!

Everyone laughed and sang the last line with her. Picking up trash was the center circle of Carol's mind map poster. She had cleverly defined trash as anything that was harmful to humans or animals, so land mines were included. Each branch radiating from the middle was filled with factual details showing the many effects of picking up trash. Under clearing land mines was the increase in agricultural land and food production, reduced deaths and amputees, lower medical costs, greater well-being of families and increased production for society.

Each and every presentation was filled with good reasoning and enthusiasm. Some students were more nervous than others, but their work and determination showed through. Some were creative, some funny and some artistic. A lot of good ideas came out.

Katie was a little nervous about presenting her mind map. She'd worked hard on the facts and had taken pictures of the organic garden. She had many branches coming from the center circle that noted the benefits, included a reduction in greenhouse gasses, pollution of rivers and dead zones in the ocean, and an increase in the nutritional value of food and healthy kelp forests. Katie gave the class a big smile when the clapping finished.

The presentations continued Thursday and Friday. The last name on the sign-up list was Tanya's. Tanya came up slowly to the front of the class with a big roll of paper. It was much bigger than the other posters that had been presented.

Tanya stood up and smiled at everyone. Katie noticed that Tanya was less pale and looked more confident than she'd ever seen her look before. "Would someone please help me by holding this?" she asked.

Todd and Pam were there before Katie was halfway out of her seat. When the very large poster was unrolled all the students gasped and Ms. Bennett started to laugh. The poster was gorgeous. The circle in the middle was a picture of the Earth from space and there was a green circle around that with white letters. There were an amazing number of branches and sub-branches on the mind map and each and every inch of the poster was covered with fine writing and hand-drawn pictures. Around the picture of the Earth the words written were, *Living Green Values, Respect and Care for Earth, and its Humans and Animals*.

Everyone started clapping. They clapped so long Katie could see Tanya's eyes swimming in happy tears.

"I thought that if we really respected the Earth and all humans and animals we would do all the things we've been talking about," said Tanya. "So, I just wrote them down."

The next week was fun. Ms. Bennett had them get together in small groups to create skits/dramas on the environment and songs and poems. Pam asked if they could do a show for the other students at their school and at the primary school. Pam sure was smiling a lot more now. "Hmm," thought Katie, "I think she has more hope."

269

Ms. Bennett accepted Papa's offer to take the whole class out on his work boat for a picnic on the little island near the place where Papa had found the whale. George and his friends, Mama, and Tanya's mom, were coming too.

"But," said Katie to the class with a somewhat worried look, "everything's going to be organic and vegetarian. Is that okay?'

Shouts of "Yes!", "Hooray!" and "Let's hear it for veggie burgers!" filled the air.

Discuss

- In addition to learning about the environment, what else do you think Katie's class learned?
- What do you think helped Tanya and her mother?
- What are other values besides respect and care that you think benefit the Earth?

Bring out the list that the students created during the last lesson to Ms. Bennett's homework question.

Ask:

- Is there anything else that you would like to add to this list?
- Is there anything that you would like to take away?

Activity

Help them in forming groups to mind map their ideas, showing how that one thing, if everyone did it, would affect many other things in the world.

If there is time, allow each group to share their results, they may need more time to make their mind map complete. Older groups may wish to research some of the results so they can do a thorough job

Close with the relaxation/focusing exercise, Sending Peace to the Earth.

SIMPLICITY AND CARING

FOR THE EARTH AND HER OCEANS LESSON 14

Advertisements Try to Get You to Believe . . .

Begin with a song.

Share the following concept with students: Appreciating the beauty of nature and the earth sometimes allows us to appreciate the natural beauty of the self more. The more we appreciate natural beauty, the less we are fooled into thinking we have to own certain things or look a certain way to feel good about ourselves or be accepted by others.

In order to sell things, businesses hire advertising firms to create impressive advertisements so people buy their products. Often they imply that you will be more attractive if you use their product or feel better about yourself if you own what they are selling.

These advertisements can fool people into thinking they need these things to be okay and for other people to consider them okay. When people hear many messages like this, they often forget about the importance of inner beauty. These messages do not encourage people to respect the earth or the inner self. The self knows there is natural beauty inside. When we have that awareness in our own mind, we can be content about our own value, enjoy others for who they are, and give happiness. Simplicity is being natural. Simplicity is beautiful.

Activity

Ask:
- What ads are aimed at young people your age?

List the ads they mention on the board. Take one ad at a time and ask them to discuss them. You may wish to ask the questions below about several different ads.
- What message is this ad giving?
- Tell us about specific advertisements. What is their message? What is the implication or the hidden message?
- What do they want you to do? Why?
- Is their message beneficial for you?
- Is their message beneficial for our planet? Why or why not?

➢ Then make another list, and ask them to create thoughts they think are closer to nature and natural beauty. Take another example and repeat. Keep a list of their examples.

Reflection Point for Ages 12 to 14: Discuss the following point.
- Simplicity asks whether we are being induced to purchase unnecessary products. Psychological enticements create artificial needs. Desires stimulated by wanting unnecessary things result in value clashes complicated by greed, fear, peer

pressure, and a false sense of identity. Once fulfillment of basic necessities allows for a comfortable lifestyles, extremes and excesses invite overindulgence and waste.

Homework for all ages: For one week, ask everyone to experiment with simplicity by wearing simple clothes to school or when out with friends. Say you would like them to remember to keep in mind the following simplicity points: *Simplicity is being natural. Simplicity is beautiful.*

End the lesson, by playing a simple game or cultural activity that does not require purchasing anything. This could be a circle game with physical movement and song, a native cultural dance or song, a camp game or line dancing with a chant. Enjoy simplicity!

Follow-up Activity: At the end of the week, ask for their feelings and reactions about the homework. Ask them to write a short essay on their experience.

SIMPLICITY AND CARING FOR THE EARTH LESSON AND HER OCEANS 15
Freedom from Desires

Begin with a song.

Ask students how they are feeling about their experiment of wearing simple clothes.

Activity

List the Reflection Points below on the board. Ask the students to form small groups and discuss the points.

The following points were offered by students at West Kidlington School:

- Simplicity is freedom from material desires and emotional desires — permission to simply "be."
- Simplicity avoids waste, teaches economy, avoids value clashes complicated by greed, fear, peer pressure, and a false sense of identity.
- From simplicity grows generosity and sharing.
- Simplicity is putting others first with kindness, openness, pure intentions — without expectations and conditions.

Include the following Reflection Point in your discussion:

♦ Simplicity is giving patience, friendship, and encouragement.

Ask them to make up a slogan on simplicity that they would like to communicate to others. Allow them different options to decorate it.

Close with a creative visualization or a relaxation/focusing exercise.

SIMPLICITY AND CARING
FOR THE EARTH AND HER OCEANS LESSON 16
Enjoying Simple Things

Begin with a song.

Discuss/Share

Say, "Think for a moment of a time when you enjoyed something that you could not buy in a shop."

Ask:
- What are the simple things you enjoy?
- How often have you said you were bored?
- Was it you that were bored or the things around you that were boring?
- How did our grandparents entertain themselves before TV?

Activities

Sentence Completion: Verbally or in written form, as you think most beneficial for your particular group, ask them to complete the following sentences.

    I find life too complicated when . . .

    I can calm myself down by . . .

Small group sharing: Form groups of four to five to discuss a simple pleasure you both enjoy, and what you think about in quiet moments. Report to the class.

– Contributed by Linda Heppenstall

Dance: Put on some music and ask the students to dance simplicity.

Close with a relaxation/focusing exercise.

SIMPLICITY AND CARING
FOR THE EARTH AND HER OCEANS LESSON 17
A Play

Begin with a song.

Activity

Write a class play about rediscovering the simple things in life/nature. Perhaps perform it for an assembly.

— Contributed by Linda Heppenstall

Additional Simplicity
and Caring for our Earth and Her Oceans Lessons and Activities

SIMPLICITY LESSON 17
The Precious Present

Begin with a song.

A story that ties in well with the theme of simplicity is "The Precious Present" by Spencer Johnson. It is a simple story about someone who knows when we stay in the present moment, we are free to enjoy it and be nourished by it. We are free from guilt from the past and worry for the future. The story relates well to the following Simplicity Reflection Points:

♦ Simplicity is staying in the present and not making things complicated.
♦ Simplicity is enjoying a plain mind and intellect.

Activity

After the students read it, ask them to write about what they learned and to draw a picture about their story (for younger students) or create a poem. For students ages eight to ten, attach the stories to the pictures and form a big book of lessons learned.

Close with the Drop of Water Creative Visualization.

Simplicity Challenge — Declutter

Natasha Panzer, an 8th grade teacher at Mizzentop School, likes to offer the following Simplicity Challenge to her students.

She shares: "During this month, your simplicity challenge is to declutter your bedroom and your work space in your home. There is no specific time frame for this assignment. You will need to pick a time that works for you. Clutter is one of the biggest causes of stress in our lives. When we clutter our lives physically and mentally, it drains our energy. When we declutter our homes, we create more space for peaceful living."

Discuss with the students the above idea and the Reflection Points:
- My mind settles more quickly and I feel clearer when my living space is not cluttered.
- I do not need so many things in my life to live richly.

She gives students the following information in written form:

Your goal is to only have objects out in your bedroom and your work space that are useful and/or bring you joy. Try to minimize the decorative items for the sake of this challenge and see how having only a few of your most prized possessions out changes the way your living space feels. After you declutter, try to keep your bedroom and your work space uncluttered for as long as possible. Happy decluttering!

P.S. Playing your favorite music while you declutter will help the process along.

After you go through this process, please answer the following questions and return to me.

1. What possessions did you choose to leave out in plain view?
   _____
   _____

2. Did you find belongings to donate?
   _____
   _____

3. Was the process of decluttering difficult, liberating, fun, or torturous? Explain how you felt during the process and how you feel now that your space is uncluttered.
   _____
   _____

APPENDIX

Item 1: All Values

Mind Mapping

A Mind Map is a powerful graphic technique that engages both sides of the brain. It can be used in many different ways — to outline stories, plan talks, organize details for functions, or to create and develop thoughts about a topic. It is simple to use. Using the values words is an excellent way to begin to learn "mind mapping" and understand the effects of values and anti-values.

How to Mind Map

1. Take a blank piece of paper this size or larger and place it horizontally, or use a whiteboard with a large group.
2. Start in the center with a Central Image that personally represents the topic about which you are writing/thinking. You can put the value of focus inside one side of a circle, and the name of the anti-value on the other side. Images can be added to the circle later, representing the overall outcome of the group's input.
3. The Main Themes around the Central Image are like the chapter headings of a book. Print the words and place them on lines of the same length. The central lines can be curved and organic, i.e., like branches of a tree to the trunk. For example, when exploring values you might always want to use Self, Family and Our organization/school, but feel free to explore many other aspects such as Society, Business, Health, Environment and World.
4. Start to add a Second level of thought for one of the branches. Allow the students to supply all the answers and acknowledge them as you write their responses. These words are linked to the main branch that triggered them. The lines connect and are thinner.

5. Add a Third or Fourth level of data, as response continue. Use images as much as you wish. If students are doing a mind map individually, they may "hop about" the Mind Map as the links and associations occur to them.

6. Add Dimension to your Mind Maps if you wish. Box and add depth around the word or image, use different colors and styles, and if you like, add arrows to show connections.

7. Have fun making each Mind Map beautiful, artistic, colorful, and imaginative.

Item 2: Peace

Conflict Resolution Steps

Ask both students: Do you want help?
If they both answer "yes", proceed. If one says "no", tell them to go to the office.

To Student One: What is your name?   To Student Two: What is your name?

To Student One:
Please tell us what happened.

To Student Two:
Please repeat what he or she said.

To Student Two:
Please tell us what happened.

To Student One:
Please repeat what s/he said.

To Student One:
How did you feel when that happened?

To Student Two:
Please repeat what s/he said.

To Student Two:
How did you feel when that happened?

To Student One:
Please repeat what s/he said.

To Student One:
What would you like to stop?

To Student Two:
Please repeat what s/he said.

To Student Two:
What would you like to stop?

To Student One:
Please repeat what s/he said.

To Student One:
What would you like him/her to do instead?

To Student Two:
Please repeat what s/he said.

To Student Two:
What would you like him/her to do instead?

To Student One:
Please repeat what s/he said.

To Student One: Can you do that?   To Student Two: Can you do that?

To both: Can you make a firm commitment to try to behave in the way you both have agreed? If they both say "yes", compliment their good listening and working on a solution.

If one of them says "no," ask each student to think of something he or she would like the two to do that would solve the problem. Ask them to think of ideas until they both agree they have a good solution and can commit to trying to carry it through.

Item 3: Respect

Lily the Leopard
By John McConnel

Lily the Leopard thought there was something gravely wrong with her. Unlike all the other leopards she knew, her spots were not black but pink. It would not have been so terrible if the other leopards had accepted her. But the other leopards would not accept her. In fact, even her own family shunned her. Her mother had cried upon seeing her baby daughter covered in pink spots, and her father and two brothers, Julian and Ricky, were deeply ashamed to have such a strange looking leopard in the family. The other leopards in the neighborhood ignored her, laughed at her, and even attacked her at times, just because her spots were a different color from their spots. Much of the time she felt afraid and sad, which at times made her very angry. She spent a great deal of time alone. She spent her days lying in a bush, watching the other leopards frolic about. Even when they would occasionally call Lily to come play, she would remember their past insults and would growl low in response to their invitation.

It was not her fault. She was different and could not help that. She often wondered why the other leopards did not understand. She had done her best to rid herself of her pink spots. Lily tried scrubbing and washing them away. She tried bleaching them. Once, she even painted them black, but the pink soon shone through the paint. It was no good. Nothing worked. After a while, she realized that she was stuck with them. What else could she do?

One day, after four young cubs tried to scratch her, Lily decided to run away from home. She had had enough. She ran off into the jungle as fast as she could. Lily ran for hours and hours, just stopping to rest now and then and to wipe the tears from her eyes. Eventually she came to rest in a clearing and fell asleep. She was awakened by the soft touch of a tongue on her nose. As she looked up, she saw the most amazing sight. Before her stood a great big leopard with bright green spots! Lily was so surprised by what she saw that she blinked twice just to make sure she wasn't dreaming. She had often had dreams of other leopards with different colored spots, but she never imagined that there actually were such leopards. The great leopard with bright green spots told her his name was Lenny and asked her what she was doing so far from home. As he spoke, he seemed to glow with confidence and happiness. His eyes were filled with kindness, and so Lily felt safe and soon found herself telling her story.

Lenny quietly listened to her story. When she finished, he gave her a warm hug and helped her dry her eyes. He then smiled at her and said, "What you need is some self-respect."

"I do?" asked Lily. "What's that?"

"Self-respect means liking yourself, even when others do not. It means appreciating all the special things about yourself."

"There's nothing special about me, except these pink spots and I hate them" she cried. "I am so strange and ugly. I wish I was never born!"

"Don't be silly" said Lenny. "You're very special. There is no one like you in the whole world, and I can see that you have many good qualities." Lenny paused for a moment. He seemed to be thinking. "I have an idea," he said. "Let's make a list of all the things you like about yourself."

"Okay" said Lily, brightening a little. She sat for a few moments thinking, and then said: "Well, I'm kind and caring and I try to be friendly. I help my mom and dad, and I'm very loving . . ." Lily paused for a moment, her voice trailing off. Lenny nodded his head eagerly in order to encourage her. Lily felt safe again, and so she continued, "I have beautiful gold eyes, and I'm a real fast runner. I'm brave and strong and . . ."

Just then Lucy the Leopard appeared with Laura the Leopard. Lucy was covered with blue spots and Laura in purple spots. As soon as they saw Lily, they were delighted. They smiled grandly and leapt into the air. "What a lovely leopard you are, and what a beautiful coat you have."

"Thank you" Lily replied, smiling as she remembered that there was much more to her than met the eye. Suddenly, she felt much better.

"It's okay to be different," she thought. "In fact, I think my spots are rather pretty! If other leopards do not like me because of my pink spots, that's because they don't know better. I'm okay. I'm glad I'm unique."

Lily spent a few more hours playing with her new-found and brightly colored friends. But as the sun began to set, Lily began to think about her family. They might be worried about her, she thought. Lily waved goodbye to Lenny and Lucy and Laura. She promised them, however, that she would visit them again soon and off she went. As she walked home, she watched the sun set. For the first time, she noticed the many brilliant colors in the sky. The sky was pink, blue, green, purple, and orange. "How beautiful," she thought. "I wonder why I never noticed all those colors before."

When Lily finally arrived home, her mom and dad and two brothers ran to meet her. As they came closer to Lily, they noticed that there was something different about her. She seemed to shimmer and glow. She held her head high as she trotted forward and smiled at them warmly. "She is really quite beautiful," they thought. And they wondered why they had never noticed before.

Item 4: Respect

Pillars of the Earth
Adapted from a story by Pedro Pablo Sacristan

There was once a boy who always treated his mother horribly, shouting at her and insulting her. It didn't matter to him how sad he made her. One day, without knowing how, Max woke up in an immense place all alone. He was sitting on a gigantic rock. There was a huge pillar near him and three other pillars of similar size in the distance. They rose up into space and appeared to be supporting the entire world.

He sat, still and scared. It was lonely on this rock. In the distance, an enormous flock of birds appeared and flew closer. As they drew nearer he saw they were crows. They seemed to have beaks of steel. They landed noisily on the rock near him and set about violently chipping at it.

After a few minutes, a small door in one of the huge pillars opened and a pretty girl ran out. She ran at the crows, shouting and shooing them away. She kept running and shooing until they took flight. She collapsed in a heap next to Max.

"I'm so glad you're here," she said, a bit out of breath. "Have you come to help?" She gave him a big smile. "That's great!"

Max was puzzled. Spotting his confusion, the little girl explained, "So you don't know where you are? This is the center of the Earth. These pillars support the whole planet, and this rock keeps the pillars in place."

"And how do you think I can help?" asked Max, feeling confused.

"Well, to help look after the rock, of course. Anyone can see by your face that you're a good person for the job," answered Leela. "The birds you saw are increasing in number and if we don't look after this rock it will eventually crumble and everything will come crashing down."

"And what do you see in my face?" exclaimed the boy, surprised. "I've never looked after a rock in my whole life!"

"You still have love inside," said the little girl. "All young people still have love inside, sometimes they just forget about it," she explained. "Love lets you give respect. You'll learn how to protect the rock, even if you've never done it. I'll show you."

The little girl's expression then changed as she looked at Max. "Oh, no!" she exclaimed, horrified. "Quick, look in this mirror," said Leela, holding one in front of the boy's face.

Max looked in the mirror and saw that his human face was beginning to change. His forehead and cheeks were starting to narrow and his nose was becoming sharp and pointy and turning slightly silver gray, the color of steel. He stood, shocked and worried, not a word passing his lips.

"Quick," she cried, speaking quickly. "You're already starting to change. Say something positive to yourself like 'I believe in goodness. I believe in respect. I am good.'"

The little girl spoke very quickly, in one breath, "All those crows used to be people like you and I, but they came here when they were older than us and their hearts had already hardened. They're mean birds and just destroy. Up to now, I'm the only one who has looked after the rock. You haven't done much to look after things on our earth, but if you tune into your goodness and your respect for everyone you will stop turning into a crow and you can help me preserve earth." She stopped, out of breath, a strong but slightly pleading look in her eyes. "Will you help?"

Max didn't quite understand, but he was saying to himself over and over again, 'I believe in goodness. I believe in respect. I am good. I believe in goodness. I believe in respect. I am good.'" Was his face getting a little wider? To the little girl he said, "I don't understand."

The little girl pointed at one of the pillars. "Come, look closely."

Max looked closely at the pillar she was pointing to and then came even closer. He saw that the pillar was made of thousands and thousands of small figurines. On each figurine words of virtues were written: sincerity, peace, effort, love, honesty, generosity…. His eyes widened and he could feel his face really was starting to become wider.

The little girl gave him an encouraging smile. "You'd forgotten your goodness and respect for others, didn't you?"

Max nodded. As he looked down at the ground beneath him, he noticed that what he thought was granite seemed to be moving. The closer he looked, the more he saw tiny patterns of movement, like little videos. He realized with a start of shock that the enormous rock was made up of moving images of children showing respect to their mothers, fathers, grandparents, brothers, sisters, classmates and old people. And there were even videos of adults showing respect to children and other adults.

"Are the crows trying to …?" he looked at the girl.

"Yes, the crows come to cover over scenes of respect and caring by carving scenes of shouting and insults with their becks."

He looked down. Next to his feet, he could see a carving of himself, the last time he had shouted at his mother.

"You mean respect is what makes the pillars stand and support the earth?"

The girl nodded, "Yes, respect sustains the world." She looked at him seriously. "The world needs our help."

Max nodded slowly. Filled with regret, he stayed there and looked after the rock for many days with Leela. Max grew happier every day even though he was working hard. After a few days, Leela ran up to him and whispered, "More children are coming to help!"

When there were just two of them, he and Leela often had to go without sleep to repel each crow attack. When Leela came with several young people his age, without steel becks, they all smiled and laughed together. He then fell asleep, exhausted from his efforts.

When Max woke, he could feel softness beneath him. He was not on rock. He looked around and slowly realized he was back in his bed at home. To this day, he doesn't know if it had all been a dream. However, what he is sure of is that no crow would ever again get the chance to carve a picture of him shouting at his mother.

Item 5: Respect

Crazy Like a Fox

Note to Educator: Part of LVE's Street Children Family Stories, this story is part of the Bully No More lessons for students 11 to 14 years of age. In this story, Mohammed is 17 years old, Fred is 14 and Marion is 12. They are a street-children family. Tony and Keemen are two other street children who are their friends.

Mohammed, Fred and Marion decided to visit Tony and Keemen after their workshop at the street-children school. As they walked down the alley, they heard Tony's voice shouting, "You want to steal something? You thieves. I'll give you something!"

"Let's go," said Fred. Fred, Marion and Mohammed started running toward the sound of the yelling and fighting. Tony and Keemen were on the ground fighting three other boys as they rounded the corner. Fred, Marion and Mohammed stopped running as soon as they saw the boys.

"Hello, Tony. Hello Keemen," said Marion brightly.

"Hey guys, I got some tangerines. Want one?" asked Fred.

"You guys all look pretty good at what you're doing, maybe you can help us with our next play. We're doing it in the park on Saturday. How about it?" asked Mohammed.

"Yeah, it's a great play," said Marion. "Have you seen it, Tony? How about you, Keemen?

"I think they would fit in really well in the second act, don't you Mo?" asked Fred. "You know, right after that terrific song."

Tony and Keemen had paused. The three boys they were fighting looked up, surprise and puzzlement on their faces.

"Well," said Mohammed, "do you think you could do this in one of our plays? It's a great scene."

"Are you putting me on?" asked one of the three strangers.

"Are you crazy?" asked one of the other boys.

Fred pulled out the tangerines, "Anyone want a tangerine?"

Tony started laughing. He reached his hand up for a tangerine.

Mohammed looked down at one of the three boys who were strangers. He offered him a tangerine and sat down beside him. He started to peel another for himself. "Being a street kid is hard enough without us fighting each other."

"These are the guys that stole our guitar!" said Keemen, anger rising in his voice.

"Okay," said Mohammed. "Let's be human beings for a minute and listen. These are our brothers. They probably had a real good reason for doing what they did. Do you know their story?" He looked at the boy who had accepted the tangerine. "My name is Mohammed. I bet you had a real good reason for taking the guitar. Would you like to share your story?"

The boy looked at Mohammed and shook his head. Another said, "Let's get out of here." The three jumped up and ran, but one paused before he rounded the corner and gave Mohammed a little nod, still holding the tangerine he had accepted in his hand.

"What's the matter with you?" Keemen asked Mohammed. "With you two we could have beat them up. It would have been four against three instead of two."

Mohammed looked at him in silence. He slowly ate his tangerine.

Fred said, "Great tangerine, Mo."

"Yeah, Mo, thanks," said Marion.

"I don't get you guys," said Tony. "You come and help and then don't help us beat them up."

"But we stopped the fight, didn't we?" smiled Marion. "Distraction as an art of nonviolence."

Tony started to eat his tangerine and Keemen sat and just looked at them. His eyes looked like he was trying to understand something new.

"Do you want to be like them?" asked Mohammed quietly.

"I don't know what you're taking about," said Keemen.

Mohammed was silent.

"I don't want to be like them," said Tony.

"What happens when you fight?" asked Fred. "They beat you up, you beat them up. They knife you, you knife them. They shoot you, you shoot them. It only gets worse. Gangs are like that. They kill each other."

"What comes around goes around," said Mohammed.

"But how do you stay alive if you don't fight?" asked Keemen.

"You use your head," said Fred. "You got to be smart to survive on the streets. But to do better than survive is possible. You can create beauty. You can help others to see their beauty."

"Are you crazy?" asked Keemen.

"Crazy like a fox," smiled Marion.

Translator Note: A fox is considered clever in English. Please put in the name of an animal or mythical character which is considered clever in the culture of the children.

Item 6: Respect
Samosas and Peace in the Face of Danger

Note to Educator: Part of LVE's Street Children Family Stories, this story is part of Respect II Lesson 10C, Keeping Your Head in the Face of Danger for students 11 to 14 years of age. In this story, Mohammed is 17 years old, Fred is 14 and Marion is 12. They are a street-children family.

Nelson, Marion, Joe, Fred and Mohammed enjoyed putting on the AIDS skits at the park on Friday nights and at the community center on Saturday nights. The teacher thought that it was making a difference. Joe had a part in the play and was happy that he was part of helping. After the play, they walked home — a bit tired but happy. "Do we have enough money for something from the vendor tonight?" asked Joe. "I'm hungry."

Marion whispered to her younger brother so only he could hear, "That was a nice way of asking, Joe. You have learned to ask without whining. Wow!"

Nelson said, "I think this is your lucky night, Joe. Fred and I had lots of customers today."

Their favorite vendor stall was just up the street from the big tree. They had just reached the big tree and were just beginning to eat the hot corn on the cob and the samosas (Translator Note: Please substitute a common local hot food that is not expensive.) when the feeling of danger intruded. Two youths came up out of the dark shadows with knives in their hands.

"Give us all your money," one said in a menacing tone.

"Quick," added the other. "Or you'll be sorry."

Marion took in a sharp breath. She tried to stay calm. What if they hurt Joe? She didn't move. Just stay peaceful she told herself. Be still. Be peace. Give peace. Be still, she repeated to herself. Be peace. Give peace.

The others must have been doing the same. Mohammed and Fred had trained them well.

Mohammed said quietly, "We just got some hot food from the vendor. We have enough to share. Would you like some?"

"Just give us your money," said the first youth in a threatening tone of voice.

"You look a little hungry," said Fred softly. "Please, do sit down and join us."

Joe surprised Marion, "You can have mine," he said. "My sister always shares with me."

"I'm not taking no food from a little kid," said the first youth angrily.

"It's a little cold out and the food is hot," said Fred. "Where are you from? Have you been living on the streets long?" Fred lifted up a samosa. The second youth grabbed it and stuffed part of it in his mouth. He wolfed down the samosa hungrily.

"It's tough living on the street. It's good you have each other as friends," said Mohammed.

"You guys are really strange," said the first youth and he sat down. He put his knife on the ground. "I'll have one too."

"Great," said Nelson. To the other youth he said, "Here, have another."

Marion smiled to herself as the boys started to chat. She had seen this happen many a time. But it worked. It always worked. Their street-children family must have more friends than anybody, she thought. When they treated others how they wanted to be treated — it seemed they were protected.

After the two youths left, fed by the warmth of the food and the company, Marion asked, "Mo, does that always work? It always seems to work out when you're around."

"Well," said Mohammed, "I guess I'm lucky. I avoid trouble if I can. I think if you can truly stay peaceful and give them real respect almost all people come around. I think people get all nervous inside when they are about to rob you and are threatening you. So, if you get nervous or scared or angry it makes them feel more nervous. That's when they can get violent. If you don't get all scared — but stay peaceful and steady . . . and they don't feel threatened . . . then they usually calm down."

"That's the hard part," said Nelson, "staying all peaceful inside — and not losing your head."

"Yes. If you can stay peaceful then your head works better. Then you can watch them. Be steady inside. You got to use your head and watch them — make sure they aren't wound up too tight," Mohammed said thoughtfully. "If they are too high on drugs and crazed — and have a knife or gun in that state — sometimes the best thing to do is to run. See how they are first. But if they get crazy or are mean all the way through the best thing to do is run. Most people miss when they shoot when you're running."

"Another reason to eat well and not take drugs," laughed Marion, "so you can run fast."

"Great samosas and corn," said Fred with a little light in his eyes. "I think I'll run up and get some more. Imagine, we still have our money!"

"Great," said Joe with a happy laugh.

Item 7: Happiness

The Heart School

By Diana Hsu

Marc lived in a small town not far away from here. He lived with his mother in a small apartment (flat). The house was surrounded by grassy fields and huge trees, and the school he went to was within walking distance. Marc sometimes thought how lucky he was not to have to live in one of those large cities where there were hardly any parks in which he could play with his friends.

Besides playing outside a lot, Marc liked to spend time in his room. He was always busy. He liked to collect stamps from all over the world, play with his cars and buses,

Legos and airplanes. But one thing he did not like very much was going to school.

One Monday morning, as he started to walk to school, he somehow felt this would be a very special day. It was a bright day, the sun was shining, the birds were singing, beautiful butterflies were flying by, and the air was filled with the sweet fragrance of colorful flowers. He felt as if this would really be the most special day in his whole life. Marc stopped walking. He lay down on the grass and closed his eyes. As he started to enjoy this, he relaxed. Then suddenly, with his eyes still closed, he saw himself walking ahead and reaching a heart-shaped house. As he came nearer to this house, he could feel that this was a very special place. Now he could read the letters above the door:

The School for Loving Children

As if by a magnet, Marc was drawn to look through the window and . . . "Ooohh!" he exclaimed, ". . . what a wonderful world!" He saw a classroom decorated with light-colored paintings of butterflies, rainbows, flowers, and happy children playing. He saw mobiles of angels, stars, and hearts. The curtains and furniture were brightly-colored, and in the windows were transparent pictures and collages through which the light was shining like a rainbow.

Marc saw the teacher and her children sitting in a circle on a carpet. He looked at the faces of the children. They were sparkling with happiness. And then his eyes were drawn to one particular child. "It's me! It's really me!" he thought. "I am one of these happy, loving children, shining with so much joy!" Marc was surprised that suddenly he felt so light — it was as if his heart was saying, "I am a happy, loving child!" And then suddenly the school disappeared. Marc got up from the grass and with light steps continued onward to school, wishing his own school was like the one he had just seen.

The next morning, Marc could hardly wait to reach that same spot on the grass again. He wanted to see that heart school again. He searched and searched, but the school was nowhere to be found. Was it all a dream? Somehow, he knew it was not. He felt a sudden disappointment. "I feel . . . I feel . . . I want to cry!" thought Marc.

"Marc, Marc," he heard someone whisper. He looked up, and floating down from the sky, seated on a giant rainbow-balloon, was a smiling Golden Bear. As the balloon landed, the heart-shaped school appeared behind him.

"Hello," said the Golden Bear. Taking Marc's hand, he whispered gently, "Come and see yourself, Marc." And as he looked through the window, he could see himself standing with the others, holding hands in a circle and listening to the teacher.

"Maria, can you please play the flute?" the teacher asked.

When Maria started to play her flute, they all formed a circle. What fun they were having! And Marc noticed that no one was pushing, breaking the circle, kicking, or being nasty to the others as they danced around the room — and no one was left out. The room was filled with magical sounds.

As Marc continued to watch, the children and the teacher were moving from one activity to another without any unkind words being spoken. A little while later, Marc saw himself drawing and sharing his pencils with the others. The teacher, with a smiling face and kind eyes, was going from child to child, listening quietly, while each child was telling her about his or her drawings. After all the drawings were finished, Marc saw the children packing away their things and then decorating the walls. Each child was admiring the work of the others. What harmony there was!

The children then sat in groups at their tables and took out their arithmetic books. Everyone quietly listened to the teacher who spoke in a clear, soft voice, explaining what needed to be done.

Marc watched as the teacher looked over the shoulder of the boy who looked like him and said, "Well done, Marc! All your sums are correct, and your work is neat."

Marc looked up at the Golden Bear. "How can that be me? I am not good at arithmetic. My work is not neat and the teacher is seldom pleased with me!"

The Golden Bear just smiled and held Marc's hand tightly. "Just watch, just watch!"

When Marc looked up through the window again, he saw himself confidently reading aloud to the class. Much to his surprise, everyone was listening eagerly. "Look at that, I can do it, I can do it!" he said to the Golden Bear. "I can read without feeling scared and stumbling over the words!"

"Of course you can!" said the Golden Bear. He seemed to know Marc well. What a wonder!

Then the children sat down in a circle to have their lunch. As the food was passed around, Marc could see himself waiting patiently. No one was pushing and no one was calling out, "Me first! That's mine! Give that to me! I am not your friend anymore." And no one snatched the food away from anyone else.

Marc saw himself asking his friend, "Would you like a piece of cake?"

"Thank you" replied his friend, and he offered Marc some fruit and nuts.

After lunch, Marc noticed that the children seemed happy helping one another. No one laughed at another's mistakes. Everyone seemed to be friends — and happy to see one another succeed!

When it was time to go home, the teacher said, "It was fun being with you all! I look forward to seeing you again tomorrow. Every single one of you is very special to me!"

As Marc saw himself leaving, the teacher turned and said, "Goodbye, Marc. Tomorrow we will have another happy day together!"

Marc turned to the Golden Bear, "How can I be like that?"

The Golden Bear just smiled and said, "If, from your heart, you really want to change . . . just wait and see . . . just wait and see! Goodbye, Marc." And off the Golden Bear floated.

When it was bedtime, Marc thought about how wonderful it would be to dream of the heart-school again. Marc closed his eyes and waited. But, no heart-school appeared. He waited some more and nothing happened. "Oh well," he thought. "It was nice while it lasted." But then, right in front of him, slowly and gently, the Golden Bear floated down to the foot of his bed, holding onto his rainbow-balloon. Marc smiled and said, "It's you! I was wondering whether I would ever see you again!"

"Hello!" said the Golden Bear, "I was listening to the thoughts of your heart. You want to be the happy you, the real you. Everyone likes to be loved by all."

"Yes" said Marc slowly, "it's like magic how you seem to know everything!"

"Well," said the Golden Bear, "it is not as difficult as you think! Shall I help you a little? I am going to show you a secret. Look, here are two boxes. Read what is written on them."

HAPPY   UNHAPPY

The Golden Bear took the UNHAPPY box and asked, "What do you think is in this box?"

"I don't know" replied Marc, "but it can't be anything good!"

The Golden Bear opened the UNHAPPY box and took out four cards.

"What's written on them?" Marc impatiently asked the Golden Bear.

"Guess first!" said the Golden Bear.

"Mm, mm . . . I don't know!" responded Marc.

The Golden Bear looked amazed. "But you do know what makes you unhappy, don't you?"

"Well, yes," Marc started slowly, "when I push or hurt others, or if they push or hurt me, that makes me unhappy!"

"That's right!" said the Golden Bear. "Now I will read what is written on the cards: "Pushing and kicking others, speaking harsh and hurtful words, thinking 'I can't do it' and being impatient."

"Is that what makes me really unhappy? asked Marc. "When I hurt others or when I am impatient?"

"Yes, that's right." said the Golden Bear, "and then everyone is unhappy with you as well!"

"Please take the cards from the HAPPY box now," Marc asked the Golden Bear.

The Golden Bear took four cards from the HAPPY box and read them to Marc. "Be patient, say only kind words, help others, and always have good thoughts about yourself and others."

"Is that the secret of being happy?" Marc asked?

"Yes," explained the Golden Bear, "and when you are happy, that is when you are the real you! That is why it is so easy to change. "I'll help you!" he added, seeing the look on Marc's face.

"Listen very carefully now," said the Golden Bear. "Tomorrow, when you pack your school bag, open the HAPPY box and take out one card. Read the message carefully, and when you're in school, just do what the card says. If you follow it, it will work! I'll see you tomorrow evening to hear how your day went."

And swiftly the Golden Bear lifted off and floated away with his rainbow-balloon, waving and smiling as Marc waved back and smiled.

The next morning, Marc got out of bed early and got ready quickly. This was going to be the first day of happiness at school. When everything was ready, Marc took a card out of his HAPPY box. As he was taking the card, he thought he heard the voice of the Golden Bear saying, "What have you picked Marc? Tell me."

Astonished, Marc looked around but could not see the Golden Bear. "Strange" he thought, but he really had heard his voice. "Tell me what you have picked," Marc heard again."

"Okay, I took a card and it says, 'Do everything with a smile,'" Marc said out loud.

"Oh, that is wonderful," Marc could hear the Golden Bear saying. "It is easy! Tell me, what are you going to do?"

Marc started slowly, "I will . . . I will . . . I will say good morning to everyone with a smile. If someone is unfriendly, I will smile instead of hitting him or saying something mean. If my teacher tells me to write neater, I will smile at her instead of getting upset, and . . ." he finished in a rush, "anyway, I will do everything with a smile today."

"Okay," smiled the Golden Bear, "see you this evening!"

When Marc came home from school that day, he could hardly wait to see the Golden Bear to share all the news with him. Marc looked around and soon the little Bear appeared, floating down on his rainbow-balloon.

"I could see your happy face from afar," the Golden Bear said with a smile.

"Yes, Bear, oh, it was a wonderful day! I did everything exactly as I told you this morning and guess what? Not only did I smile," Marc said proudly, "but others started to smile too and seemed to get on better with each other."

"Well done!" said the Golden Bear.

"Yes," added Marc. "And, Hugo wanted to kick me. But I just stood there fearlessly and smiled . . . and you know what happened then? He forgot about kicking me! He sort of looked at me in a funny way and turned around and walked away. I think he forgot about kicking altogether today. It is amazing!" exclaimed Marc. "Oh, I am looking forward to taking another card from the HAPPY box tomorrow. Will you come tomorrow to hear about my happy day?"

"Yes, I will come! Good luck for tomorrow, and be strong!" said the Bear. As the Golden Bear was flying off with his balloon, Marc ended the day happily. Oh, how exciting life can be when you discover something new!

The next morning, Marc got up early again and picked his card for the day from the HAPPY box. "Little Bear, can you hear me? Today I've picked, *Be patient*. I've thought about what I will do. Shall I tell you?"

I will let others go first.

I will not rush to finish my work too quickly (I always want to finish first, so that I get praised.

I will help others patiently and will wait happily when others are speaking.

I will listen carefully to what my teacher is telling me.

"Oh, I can hardly wait to go to school today!" said Marc.

Marc had a long day at school. His face was not so happy when he got home. He finished his dinner slowly and went to bed early.

"Oh, I almost forgot, the little Golden Bear wanted to come," thought Marc. It was as if the Bear heard his thoughts, for he was suddenly standing right in front of him.

"It wasn't so easy today, was it?" gently asked the Bear, looking at Marc's face.

"Well, do you know what happened? I did everything as I said this morning, but I forgot one thing, and that was to be patient with myself," said Marc. "I rushed to finish quickly, and because of that, I dropped some paint and it splashed all over the floor! And only then did I remember that I wanted to be patient with myself. Bear, it wasn't pleasant at all! You know why? Not only did I drop the paint, but when one of my classmates started to laugh at me and made fun of me, I said some hurtful words to him. And then I felt awful afterwards."

"Cheer up, Marc! You've only just started to become the happier you! That needs a little time, and these things happen sometimes. Just try not to make the same mistake

Living Values Education Activities for Children Ages 8-14, Book 1

again," the Golden Bear said in his most encouraging manner.

"I'm glad to hear that, Bear. It makes me feel a lot better!" said Marc.

With a big smile the Bear opened the UNHAPPY box and turned to Marc saying, "Write down your unhappiness about the spilled paint and about being angry with your classmate, and slip it into the UNHAPPY box. Then close the box, and it is over and done with! As easy as that! What's past is past. There's no need to worry or to be upset about it! Try to understand what went wrong, tell yourself that you won't make the same mistake again, and then forget it completely. Remember only what went right today and what made you happy, and think about what you are going to do tomorrow to be happy!" The Golden

Bear paused a moment and then added, "Tomorrow you will try again, and you will succeed, and that's a promise! You are loving and very special, Marc!"

Marc suddenly felt so light and full of confidence. "Yes, tomorrow I will try again and succeed! Oh, I can hardly wait until tomorrow to take the next card!" Marc laughed happily as the Golden Bear grabbed the string of his rainbow-balloon and got ready to float away. The Bear looked at him. His eyes where full of love and hope. Suddenly, Marc felt that his heart too was filling with love and hope. He could feel the great confidence the Bear had in him. "He believes in me and I know it will work! With the help of the little Bear I will be victorious and become the real me, happy and loving!"

Dear children, now that you have just listened to this story, how do you think it will end? Share your ideas with others in your class or with your family.

Okay, listen now to what happened. Day by day, Marc would take a card from his HAPPY box and think about how to use it at school. Most of the time he was good and successful, but sometimes he would make a mistake. When he made a mistake, he would not get upset or worry. Instead, he would try to understand what went wrong, write it on a piece of paper, and tell himself he will not let the same mistake happen again. Then he would slip the paper into the UNHAPPY box and close the lid and forget about it!

And so, day by day, Marc grew stronger and stronger and happier and happier. The amazing thing was that after a while, the other children in the class changed too, because he was such a good example to them and his growing happiness worked like magic! Do you want to know what happened in the end?

Gradually all the children in the class discovered the secret about the HAPPY box and asked every day, "Marc, what are you doing today to become happier?"

Marc would share with them what was written on the card. Do you know what happened next? They joined in. In a short time, all the children were becoming happier and happier until in the end all the children in the class were treating each other like friends and being loving and caring toward each other.

Oh, it was such a joy to see this happen!

IT WAS JUST LIKE MAGIC!

Item 8: Responsibility

TC Wants a Dog
By Ruth Liddle

When TC Briggs told his mother he wanted a dog, she looked up from the breakfast table, fixed her big brown eyes on him, and simply shook her head.

"But why not?" he asked. "Please Mum, please."

"Because I don't want another animal to look after."

"But I would look after it," TC stated emphatically.

"Like you do your goldfish, your hamster, and your cat, I suppose," Mrs. Briggs said wearily. "No, I don't think you are ready for the responsibility of owning a dog."

TC looked down at the table. He was feeling guilty. It was true what Mum said. He had enjoyed caring for his other pets when he first got them. But now Mum fed the cat, and he never seemed to remember to feed the fish or the hamster. And nowadays he was always too busy at the weekend to clean them out. TC glanced at the goldfish bowl. The water was so cloudy he could hardly see the fish.

"I'll clean that out tonight," he promised himself. "From now on I'm going to do all my pet chores without being reminded. And I'll do my homework, too. That will show Mum I am more responsible now."

TC didn't mention the subject of the dog again for a few weeks, until one Sunday afternoon. His baby sister was sleeping and his mother was relaxing on the couch.

"It's not that I don't want you to have a dog," Mrs. Briggs explained. "I just don't want to be the one to have to feed it, clean up after it, and take it for walks. Owning a dog is a responsibility for the whole of its life — not just a job for a week or two until you get tired of doing it."

"But this would be different, Mum," TC pleaded.

"Maybe," said his mother with a smile. "But I need convincing. You need to show me you are ready for that sort of responsibility. I'll tell you what, you find out what type of dog would make a good family pet, how to train and care for it, and I'll seriously consider getting you one. But you must be very sure you want to take on the responsibility. Remember it's a life-long commitment."

Leaning over, Mrs. Briggs ruffled TC's hair and gave him a big hug. "I already know you are showing more responsibility at school," she added. "Your teacher called me and said you are the first to hand in your homework these days. Well done. Now, off you go — you've got work to do. Love you!"

"Love you too, Mum!" TC called out as he raced out the door.

"And thanks for cleaning out the fish and remembering to feed the hamster," Mrs. Briggs called after him. But TC was already halfway down the street. His best friend, Mohammed, had just what he needed, a book titled *Caring for Your Pet Dog*.

Mohammed and TC worked together for the rest of the afternoon gathering the facts on dog care, training, and different breeds of dogs. TC arranged their findings on note cards and prepared to present them to his mother. Mohammed's mother listened to his presentation. She said it would be okay with her if Mohammed looked after the dog if ever TC and his family were away. "Thanks!" said TC. Now he was sure he had everything he needed.

Mrs. Briggs listened carefully as TC shared his information on dog care and training and told her which dogs would make good pets for a family with a baby and a busy mother.

"Well, TC," his mother responded, "I'm impressed. You certainly know your stuff, and it's a great help to know Mohammed and his mother can help out when we're away."

"There's one more thing, Mum," TC said, passing her a carefully rolled up piece of paper. "Read this."

Mrs. Brigs unrolled the paper and read the promise that had been carefully written in TC's best handwriting:

I, THOMAS CHARLTON BRIGGS, HEREBY PLEDGE TO CARE FOR MY DOG IN A RESPONSIBLE WAY FOR AS LONG AS IT LIVES. Signed, *TC Briggs*

His mother looked up at him and smiled.

"Well, TC, it looks like we're going to have a dog in the house after all. I can see that you are ready for the responsibility. I'm proud of you."

A few days later, TC became the proud owner of a friendly little dog called Ticka.

Living Values Education Activities for Children Ages 8–14, Book 1

Item 9: All Values

Relaxation/Focusing Exercises

Physical Relaxation Exercise

Sit comfortably . . . and relax. . . . As you relax, let your body feel heavy and focus your attention on your feet. . . . Tighten all your muscles for a moment . . . and then relax them . . . let them stay relaxed. . . . Now become aware of your legs, letting them be heavy . . . tightening the muscles . . . and then relaxing them. . . . Now the stomach . . . tighten the muscles for a moment . . . and then relax. . . . Be aware of your breathing, and take in a deep breath. . . . As you breathe out, let go of any tension. . . . Be in the present moment. . . . Breathe in deeply again . . . let the air out slowly . . . and let go of any tension. . . . Now tighten the muscles in the back and the shoulders . . . and then relax them. . . . Tighten the muscles in your hands and arms . . . and then relax them. . . . Gently move your neck . . . first to one side, then to other . . . relax the muscles . . . now tighten the muscles of the face . . . the jaw . . . and then relax the face and the jaw. . . . Let the feeling of wellbeing flow through the body. . . . Focus again on your breathing, breathing in deeply . . . and then letting go of any tension. . . . I am relaxed . . . I am peace . . . I am ready to be at my best.

Peace Relaxation/Focusing Exercise

Let the body be relaxed and still. Let go of thoughts about the day, and slow down within. . . . Be in the present, focusing on this moment in time. . . . Breathe in deeply . . . and let go of any tension through the bottoms of your feet. . . . Breathe in deeply . . . and let go of any tension through the bottoms of your feet. . . . Breathe in deeply . . . and let the mind be still. Slowly absorb waves of peace. . . . Imagine being outdoors. . . . You might imagine sitting under a tree, looking at the sky . . . or being by the ocean . . . or in a meadow. . . . (Pause for a full minute.) As you picture the beauty of nature in front of you, absorb waves of peace. . . . Let the self feel totally safe and relaxed. . . . Enjoy being still inside and absorbing peace. . . . You are naturally peaceful . . . still. . . . Now surround the self with love . . . surround the self with peace. . . . You are important . . . you are part of creating a peaceful world. . . . Now bring your attention back to the room. . . . You are peaceful . . . focused . . . alert.

Living Values Education Activities for Children Ages 8–14, Book 1

Peaceful Star Relaxation/Focusing Exercise

Note to Educator: Please speak slow and allow there to be soft music or silence so the students have at least eight minutes to relax and be.

One way to be peaceful is to be silent inside. For a few moments, think of the stars and imagine yourselves to be just like them. They are so beautiful in the sky, and they sparkle and shine. They are so quiet and peaceful. Let the body be still. . . . Relax your toes and legs. . . . Relax your stomach . . . and your shoulders. . . . Relax your arms . . . and your face. . . . Be still . . . be in the present. . . . Let the feeling of being safe emerge . . . and a soft light of peace surround you. . . . You, the tiny star, are full of peaceful light. . . . Relax into the light of peace. . . . Let the self be still and peaceful inside . . . You are focused . . . still . . . concentrated. . . . You are peace . . . a star of peace.

Flowers of Respect Relaxation/Focusing Exercise

Sit comfortably and let your body relax. . . . As you breathe slowly, let your mind be still and calm. . . . Starting at your feet, let yourself relax. . . . Relax the legs . . . the shoulders . . . the neck . . . the face. . . . Let your mind become still . . . calm. . . . Breathe deeply. . . . Concentrate on stillness. . . In your mind, picture a flower. . . . Imagine the smell. . . . Enjoy its fragrance . . . . Observe its shape and color. . . . Enjoy its beauty. . . . Each person is like a flower. . . . Each one of us is unique . . . yet we have many things in common. . . . We are all naturally good inside. . . . Picture a garden around you with many varieties of flowers . . . all of them beautiful. . . . Each flower with its color . . . each flower with its fragrance . . . giving the best of itself. . . . Some are tall with pointed petals, some with rounded petals, some are big and others little. . . . Some have soft colors and others have bright colors. . . . Some attract the eye because of their simplicity. . . . Each one of us is like a beautiful flower. . . . Enjoy the beauty of each one. . . . Each adds beauty to the garden. . . . All are important. . . . Together they form the garden. . . . Each flower has respect for itself. . . . When one respects the self, it is then easy to respect others. . . . Each one is valuable and unique. . . . With respect, the qualities of others are seen. . . . Perceive what is good in each one. . . . Each has a unique role. . . . Each is important. . . . Let this image fade in your mind, and turn your attention to this room again.

— Contributed by Amadeo Dieste Castejon

Living Values Education Activities for Children Ages 8–14, Book 1

Star of Respect Relaxation/Focusing Exercise

Let's think of the stars and imagine ourselves to be just like them. . . . They are so beautiful in the sky, they sparkle and shine. . . . They are so quiet and peaceful. . . . Be very still. . . . Breathe in peace. . . . Breathe out any tension. . . . Relax your toes and legs. . . . Relax your stomach . . . and your shoulders. . . . Relax your arms . . . and your face. . . . Feel safe . . . and allow a soft light of peace to surround you. . . . Inside you are like a beautiful little star. . . . You are a star of respect. . . . You are lovable and capable. . . . You are who you are. . . . Each person brings special qualities to the world. . . . You are valuable. . . . Enjoy the feeling of respect inside. . . . You are a star of respect. . . . Be still . . . peaceful. . . . Focus . . . . You are concentrated . . . full of respect . . . content. . . . Now, slowly bring your attention back to the room.

Sending Love Relaxation/Focusing Exercise

Let's be peace stars for a few minutes and send love to people all over the world. . . . Think of the stars and imagine yourself to be like them. . . . They are so beautiful in the sky, and they sparkle and shine . . . quietly and peacefully. . . . Relax your toes and legs . . . relax your back . . . and your shoulders. . . . Relax your arms . . . and your face. . . . We are safe . . . a soft light of peace surrounds you. . . . Inside you are like a beautiful star . . . full of peaceful light . . . full of love. . . . We can all send love and peace any time we want. . . . Let the self be still . . . filled with the light of caring and kindness. . . . Allow that love to automatically flow to people all over the world. . . . Let the body relax. . . . Take in more love. . . . You are focused . . . still . . . contributing to a kinder world. . . . Let the mind be still. . . . Begin to bring your attention back to this room. . . . Wiggle your toes, move your legs and let your self be content . . . powerful . . . and alert.

I Am Lovable and Capable Relaxation/Focusing Exercise

Let the body be relaxed and still. Let go of thoughts about the world outside, and slow down within. . . . Allow yourself to be in the present, focusing on this moment in time. . . . Let the mind be still, and slowly absorb waves of peace. . . . Imagine being outdoors in a world where everyone is kind and caring. . . . Imagine a garden or a meadow . . . or an ocean or river . . . whatever you wish. . . . And in the picture of your mind imagine a world where everyone understands that they are lovable and capable. . . . Breathe in slowly and relax. . . . Know you are lovable and capable. . . . All children are naturally lovable and capable. . . . Sometimes they forget this as sometimes the adults in the world forget that they are lovable and capable . . . . The truth is that you are lovable and capable. . . . Allow yourself to breathe in love. . . . Allow yourself to know that you are capable. . . . Sometimes we don't always act loving to the self or others. . . . Allow yourself to think of a time you were not caring or loving . . . and what you would like to do instead. . . . Think of the quality you would like to have . . . or the value you would like to live. . . . Imagine yourself holding that quality or living your value in a similar situation in the future. . . . Breathe in that quality or value. . . . Enjoy feeling that quality or value. . . . If you can think of that quality or value it is yours. . . . Each child comes into the world to bring a special gift of his or her qualities . . . and his or her talents. . . . Be still . . . quiet within . . . focused . . . and enjoy feeling full of love and peace. . . . As you begin to bring your attention back to this place . . . know that you are capable and allow yourself to be alert and focused, concentrated . . . ready to do well. . . . Please wiggle your toes and move your legs . . . and bring your attention fully back to this place.

Taking Care of Me When I Feel Sad Relaxation/Focusing Exercise

Let the body be relaxed and still. Slow down within. . . . Breathe in deeply . . . and as you exhale, begin to relax. . . . Be aware of how you are feeling. . . . Breathe in deeply . . . and relax as you exhale. . . . Are your arms tight or your chest? . . . . Is there a feeling of sadness or hurt inside? . . . Allow yourself to feel where you are holding emotion in your body . . . perhaps in your throat . . . perhaps in your chest . . . perhaps in your stomach . . . perhaps in your gut. . . . Breathe in deeply . . . and exhale slowly. . . . Lovingly accept your emotions. . . . Be in the present . . . and lovingly accept how you feel. . . . Pay attention to that feeling . . . accept it with love . . . and it will quiet down a little. . . . Surround your sadness or hurt with the light of love. . . . Visualize the light of love surrounding that pain . . . and feel that love. . . . Breathe in . . . and relax as you breathe out. . . . Let the mind be still . . . and absorb the light of love. . . . Perhaps that area of pain is getting smaller as you absorb the light of love. . . . Feel that light of love. . . . You are lovable and capable. . . . Breathe in slowly and relax. . . . Know you are lovable and capable. . . . Allow yourself to breathe in love. . . . Think for a moment of what quality or value would help you now. . . . Imagine that quality or value taking the form of a jewel and let that jewel appear in front of you. . . . It may be a jewel of love . . . or courage . . . compassion for yourself . . . or others . . . patience . . . or fearlessness. . . . You are a beautiful jewel. . . . You have the courage to be kind to yourself . . . and to live your truth. . . . Be still . . . quiet within . . . focused . . . absorb the light of love and peace. . . . Gradually begin to bring your attention back to this place . . . Wiggle your toes and move your legs . . . and bring your attention fully back to this place.

Sending Peace to the Earth Relaxation/Focusing Exercise

Sit comfortably and let yourself be still inside. . . . Relax the body and breathe in the light of peace. . . . Let the light of peace surround you . . . . Breathe out any tension . . . and breathe in the light of peace. . . . Breathe out any tension . . . and breathe in the light of peace. . . . This peace is quiet and safe . . . it reminds me that I am peaceful inside. . . . Let yourself be very still and think . . . I am me . . . I am naturally full of peace and love. . . . Let your body relax even more . . . and now focus on feeling peaceful. . . . As you feel peaceful that peace will naturally go outward to nature . . . to the dolphins and the whales . . . to the birds . . . to the animals large and small. . . . I let myself be full of peace . . . and that peace naturally goes outward to the Earth . . . to the rivers and ocean . . . to the trees and the meadows . . . to the mountains and the sky. . . . I am full of peace. . . . I am one who is acting to help our Earth be healthy again. . . . This will happen in time. . . . Our planet will be well. . . . I picture the light of peace all around the Earth . . . and our beautiful oceans being healthy again . . . our beautiful Earth being healthy again. . . . Feeling relaxed and peaceful . . . now begin to be aware of where you are sitting and bring your attention back to this room.

CITED BOOKS, STORIES, WEBSITES AND SONGS

Books, Stories and Websites

Belloc, Kilaire. *Matilda.* New York: Knopf, 1992. Distributed by Random House.

Cohen, Barbara. *Molly's Pilgrim.* New York: Lothrop, Lee and Shepard Books, 1983.

Free the Slaves. *Slavery in History.* https://www.freetheslaves.net/about-slavery/slavery-in-history/?gclid=EAIaIQ Accessed September 2018.

Gill-Kozul, Carol, Naraine, Gayatri and Strano, Anthony. *Living Values: A Guidebook.* London: Brahma Kumaris, 1995.

Gordon, Thomas. *Parent Effectiveness Training.* New York: Van Rees Press. 1970.

Hawkes, Neil. *How to inspire and develop Positive Values in your classroom.* Cambs, U.K.: LDA, 2003.

International Day of Tolerance. http://www.un.org/en/events/toleranceday Accessed May 2018.

Johnson, Spencer. *The Precious Present.* New York: Doubleday, 1984.

Lovat, Terry and Toomey, Ron. (Ed.) *Values Education and Quality Teaching, The Double Helix Effect.* Riverwood, NSW, Australia: David Barlow Publishing, 2007.

Lumsden, L.S. *Student motivation to learn.* ERIC Digest, Number 92. Eugene, OR: ERIC Clearinghouse on Educational Management, 1994.

North, Vanda with Buzan, Tony. *Get Ahead: Mind Map your Way to Success.* Limited Edition Publishing: Buzan Centre Books, Bournemouth, U.K, 1996.

Otero, H. "The Two Birds." *Parabolas en son de paz.* Madrid: Editorial CCS, 1993.

Ramsay, Barbara. *Finding the Magic.* Sydney: Eternity Ink, 1995. ISBN 064624003.

Satir, Virginia. *Peoplemaking.* Palo Alto, CA: Science and Behavior Books, Inc, 1972.

Sacristan, Pedro Pablo. "Pillars of the Earth." Adapted with permission by Diane Tillman. http://cuentosparadormir.com. Accessed April 2018.

Senge, Peter. (Ed.) *Schools that Learn: A Fifth Discipline Fieldbook for Educators, Parents, and Everyone Who Cares About Education.* NY: Doubleday, 2000.

Stopbullying.gov. A website of the U.S. Department of Health and Human Services. *Bullying Definition.* http://www.stopbullying.gov/what-is-bullying/definition. Accessed April 2014.

The Boy Who Cried Wolf is sometimes found as a separate illustrated picture book. A facsimile of the 1912 edition is "The Shepherd's Boy and the Wolf." Aesop's Fables. New trans. Jones, V.S. Vernon. New York: Avenel Books. Distributed by Crown Publishers. ISBN 0-517-17198-8.

Tillman, Diane. (2012). *Living Green Values for Children and Young Adults.* Available for free-download at www.livingvalues.net

Tillman, Diane. (2000). *Living Values Activities for Children Ages 3–7.* Deerfield, FL: HCI.

Tillman, Diane. (2000). *Living Values Activities for Children Ages 8–14.* Deerfield, FL: HCI.

Tillman, Diane. *Living Values Activities for Drug Rehabilitation.* 2005. *(Restricted-access work:* special LVE Educator Training required prior to obtaining materials.)

Tillman, Diane. *Living Values Activities for At-Risk Youth.* 2012. *(Restricted-access work:* Special LVE Educator Training required prior to obtaining materials.)

Tillman, Diane. (2003). *Living Values Activities for Street Children Ages 7–10. (Restricted-access work:* special LVE Educator Training required prior to obtaining materials.)

Tillman, Diane. (2003). *Living Values Activities for Street Children Ages 11–14. (Restricted-access work:* special LVE Educator Training required prior to obtaining materials.)

Tillman, Diane G. (2014) *Nurturing with Love and Wisdom, Disciplining with Peace and Respect: A mindful guide to parenting.* NC: CSIP.

The Joy of Reading Project. (2014–2018). Gave permission for their stories to be used by LVE and posted for free download at www.livingvalues.net site. Under For Schools /Children Ages 8–14 / Download Free Stories. The stories in LVEAC 8–14, Book 1 are:

> Bunting, Eve. "One Green Apple."
> Centre for Addiction and Mental Health. "Can I catch it like a cold? coping with a parent's depression."
> DeMers Hummel, Linda. "A Christmas I'll Never Forget."
> Jahanforuz, Rita. "The girl with a brave heart: A Tale from Tehran."
> Lipp, Frederick. "Running Shoes."
> Munson, Derek. "Enemy Pie."
> Park, Frances and Ginger and Zhong-Yuan Zhang, Christopher. "The Royal Bee."
> Perkins, Mitali. "Rickshaw Girl."

Polacco, Patrica. "Chicken Sunday."

Williams, Mary. "Brothers in Hope — The story of the lost boys of Sudan."

Wojtowicz, Jen. "The Boy Who Grew Flowers."

United Nations Human Rights, Office of the High Commissioner. (1989) *Convention on the Rights of the Child* https://www.ohchr.org/en/professionalinterest/pages/crc/aspx Accessed August 2018.

UNESCO. *1995 United Nations Year for Tolerance.* Paris: Office of Public Information, UNESCO, 1995. Available at the U.N. Bookstore.

Songs

Grammer, Red and Kathy. *Teaching Peace.* New York: Smilin' Atcha Music, 1986.

Jackson, Michael. "Heal The World." Epic Record Company.

Lennon, John. "Imagine." Parlophone Record Company. 1971.

Loggins, Kenny. "Conviction of the Heart." *Outside: From the Redwoods.* Columbia, 1993.

Nass, Marcia and Max. Songs for Peacemakers. Educational Activities, Inc., 1993. P.O. Box 392, Freeport, NY 11520 USA.

Pebblespash694. "A Song of Peace." www.youtube.com/watch?v=mxidrVmwznU

USA for Africa. "We Are The World." Qwest Record Company.

ACKNOWLEDGMENTS

Educators around the world have contributed activities to Living Values Education since its inception in 1996. Special appreciation to Peter Williams, Batool Arjomand, Ioanna Vasileiadou and the wonderful team of educators at the Kuwait American School in Kuwait for their activities and inspiring work in recent years, and to Linda Heppenstall and the team at West Kidlington School in England for their activities and excellent work in the first few years of LVE. Marcia Maria Lins de Medeiros wrote values activities in Brazil when LVE began; she and Paulo Barros have continued to contribute activities and inspire and provide LVE professional development workshops to hundreds of educators.

Many thanks to Pilar Quera Colomina, Sabine Levy, Encarnación Royo Costa, Teresa Garcia Ramos, Carlos Izquierdo Gonzlez, Guillermo Simó Kadletz, Tom Bingham, Janardhan Chodagam and Amadeo Dieste Castejón for their values activities, and to Samantha Fraser, Dominique Ache, Trish Summerfield, Ruth Liddle, Natalie Ncube, Ann Stirzaker and Diana Beaver for hearing the call to create. Educators who contributed more than one activity are listed on the cover page of this book.

Vanda North has been doing Mind Mapping activities with children. Thank you so much, Vanda, for coming to meet me and inspiring me to use this wonderful method.

Many appreciative regards to John McConnel, Lamia El-Dajani, and Wendy Marshall who heard the request for stories and applied their talents. Thanks to Pedro Pablo Sacristan who generously offered his "Pillars of the Earth" story. He has an entire website of values stories in English and Spanish. Immense thanks to The Joy of Reading Project whose creators have given permission to ALIVE to post their wonderful stories on the LVE international website so that educators and parents around the world can avail them free of charge.

Thank you, Marcia and Max Nass, for lovingly offering your songs.

Many thanks to I Wayan Agus Aristana, with Media Productions of the Karuna Bali Foundation in Ubud, Bali for your artwork depicting each value. You and the LVE team in Indonesia are amazing.

Loving appreciation to Diane Holden for your consistent and happy willingness to proofread the LVE books, and to David Warrick Jones for always being ready to help with graphic design and technical support.

As I have been updating this book, I have remembered Diana Hsu and Wajeeha Al-Habib many times — for their outstanding work with children through LVE, their laughter, and wonderful times together before they passed. Your love and life's work lives on in the beauty and happiness you created in the lives of others.

Living Values Education continues to thrive because of the dedication, contributions and support of the Association for Living Values Education International Board of Directors, the ALIVE Associates and Focal Points for LVE, and tens of thousands of LVE educators around the world. Thank you all immensely for your work to create a values-based atmosphere for young people so they can grow toward their potential, for living your values, and for helping create a better world.

I appreciate our LVE family around the globe. Special thanks to Peter Williams, Trish Summerfield, Chris Drake, Raj Miles, Gudrun Howard, Paulo Barros, Taka Gani and Wayan Rustiasa for your continuing commitment and your invaluable cooperation.

Creating LVE is a cooperative event!

*

Thank you to those reading this,
for your love for children, and your interest in helping create a better world for all.

About the Author

Diane G. Tillman is the primary author of the award-winning Living Values Education Series of five books, and ten additional educational resources, including Living Values Education Activities books for street children, children affected by war, young offenders, at-risk youth and young people in need of drug rehabilitation. A Licensed Educational Psychologist and Marriage and Family Therapist, Ms. Tillman worked in a California public school system for 23 years as a School Psychologist. She has worked with Living Values Education since its inception in August of 1996, and continues to develop content and training materials. Additionally, she has authored a children's book and a parenting guide, "Nurturing with Love and Wisdom, Disciplining with Peace and Respect". In the latter, she illustrates how to bring values into parenting by sharing not only theory but stories about her life, her work with children and parents, and experiences with LVE around the world. Tillman has traveled to more than 30 countries in all regions of the world to conduct professional development workshops and LVE seminars at conferences, retreat centers and refugee camps, for educators, UNESCO, street-children agencies and Ministries of Education. She is on the Association for Living Values Education International (ALIVE) Board of Directors and is the President of LVEP, Inc, the non-profit ALIVE Associate in the U.S.A.

Made in the USA
Middletown, DE
30 June 2023